# Emeril's
## POTLUCK

*WM*

WILLIAM MORROW

*An Imprint of HarperCollinsPublishers*

# Emeril's POTLUCK

## COMFORT FOOD WITH A KICKED-UP ATTITUDE

### EMERIL LAGASSE

HarperCollins books may be purchased for educational, business, or sales promotional use. For information please write: Special Markets Department, HarperCollins Publishers Inc., 10 East 53rd Street, New York, NY 10022.

FIRST EDITION

DESIGNED BY WILLIAM RUOTO

PHOTOGRAPHS BY QUENTIN BACON

PRINTED ON ACID-FREE PAPER

LIBRARY OF CONGRESS CATALOGING-IN-PUBLICATION DATA

Lagasse, Emeril.
Emeril's potluck / Emeril Lagasse. — 1st ed.
p.    cm.
Includes index.
ISBN 978-0-06-200645-5
1. Buffets (Cookery)    I. Title.

TX738.5.L34    2004
642'.4 — dc22
2003067580

10 11 12 WRB/WCF 10 9 8 7 6 5 4 3 2 1

Here's to all the people in my life who have shared their cooking with Alden and me. Your cooking has led to inspired eating and has also inspired our lives. I hope that you enjoy these recipes as much as we have enjoyed the foods you have shared with us. Pot Luck to all of you — and thank you!

# CONTENTS

# ACKNOWLEDGMENTS

Just like a real potluck dinner, the book *Emeril's Potluck* is the result of many wonderful people working together toward the common good. My heartfelt thanks go out to every one of you:

- My immediate family—my always supportive parents, Miss Hilda and Mr. John, my amazing wife, Alden, and my darling children, Jessie, Jillie, and E.J.—all who give special meaning to my potluck dinners
- Charlotte Armstrong Martory, who is just a little gem with incredible vision and also an amazing cook. I thank you for your hard work and dedication and am proud to have you as a great friend.
- The Emeril's culinary team—Chef David McCelvey, Chef Bernard Carmouche, Marcelle Bienvenu, Charlotte Armstrong Martory, Trevor Wisdom, Alain Joseph, and Sarah O. Etheridge, who never tired of trying just one more casserole!
- Marti Dalton, whose creativity invigorates every project
- Mara Warner, who always keeps me on track
- My comrades—Eric Linquest, Tony Cruz, Mauricio Andrade, and Scott Farber—some of my favorite people to gather around the dinner table
- Jim McGrew, for his expert legal counsel in all matters
- Our Web guys, Damion Michaels and Ivan Bryant, for their expert in-house photo documentation of all stages of *Emeril's Potluck*
- Everyone at my headquarters, Homebase—the amazing people behind the scenes who work wonders
- The hardworking staffs at all my restaurants: Emeril's Restaurant, NOLA, and Emeril's Delmonico Restaurant in New Orleans; Emeril's New Orleans Fish House and Delmonico Steakhouse in Las Vegas; Emeril's Restaurant Orlando and Emeril's Tchoup Chop in Orlando; Emeril's Restaurant Atlanta; and Emeril's Restaurant Miami
- Photographer Quentin Bacon, whose eye always knows best, and his assistant on this project, Mandy Ward

- All the folks at William Morrow/HarperCollins who worked so hard to make this book a reality:

Jane Friedman, chief executive officer
Michael Morrison, publisher
Harriet Bell, my friend and editor with a vision
Lucy Baker, editorial assistant
Karen Lumley, production manager
Leah Carlson-Stanisic, design director, and William Ruoto, designer
Ann Cahn, production editor
Roberto de Vicq de Cumptich, creative director
Carrie Bachman, director of publicity
Gypsy Lovett, senior publicist

# *Emeril's* POTLUCK

# INTRODUCTION

I hate to play favorites, but I have to tell you that I am crazy about this book. *Emeril's Potluck* brings together everything that I love about cooking and eating. The food is straightforward, delicious, and meant to be shared—it brings family and friends together. I cannot imagine a better time! Seriously, some of my best memories are of potluck parties. I always enjoy such gatherings, whether it's Classic Seafood Gumbo on a lazy Christmas afternoon at home with Alden and my kids, enjoying Gigi's Carrot Cake at Thanksgiving with my good friends the Gunthers, or diving into a creamy dish of Kicked-Up Spinach and Artichoke Dip at a Super Bowl party with my comrades Eric, Tony, Mauricio, and Scott. These are the times we remember, and these are the foods that make these times shine.

I look back at all these good times, and I am struck by the warmth. No, I'm not talking about that Louisiana heat! I am talking about the warmth that comes when you share with those you love. That is the very essence of the potluck tradition—sharing—and that is what I want to pass along to everyone, whether young or old, novice cook or seasoned veteran. I tried to create recipes that would cross all lines and really live up to potluck's past, but also anticipate its future.

I am talking about dishes ranging from potluck classics—like deviled eggs and tuna casserole—to nouveau potluck—like endive salad and risotto casserole. These are dishes that fit a variety of occasions. How about sharing Lasagna Bolognese at your book club? Or hosting a jambalaya party on the next family birthday? Or taking Blue Cheese Coins to a wine-tasting dinner? I would welcome any of these dishes anytime, anywhere!

Of course, a big part of potluck is transportation, so I have included storage tips and easy ways to make sure your dishes travel well. I even devised an easy way to carry fried chicken! And for your further ease, many of these dishes can be made in advance. So don't stress out if you are short on time—just pull a homemade casserole from the freezer!

I really want your potluck experience to be a joy that becomes part of your everyday life. The key ingredient is sharing. Potluck doesn't demand a special occasion—just good friends enjoying good food together. I don't think there is any real documentation of potluck's beginnings, but if I had to guess I would imagine that it was spontaneous. That's what I encourage in you—just come together and cook!

# BASICS

Hey, don't forget your basics. Sure, you can go to the store for a lot of these things—like chicken stock, mayonnaise, even piecrust—but if you have the time, why not give the dish that extra bit of love that can come only from your own kitchen. Making stock requires only a little extra time for a huge amount of taste. The same goes for piecrust and salsa. And if you never have had homemade mayonnaise, then you ain't really living!

# CHICKEN STOCK

• MAKES 3 QUARTS •

This basic chicken stock adds richness to any of the soups or sauces in this book. If you've never made stock before, I urge you to try it. It is a simple process, the flavor is unequaled, and it beats that store-bought stuff any day of the week.

4 pounds chicken bones

2 cups coarsely chopped yellow onions

1 cup coarsely chopped carrots

1 cup coarsely chopped celery

3 garlic cloves, smashed

4 bay leaves

1 teaspoon black peppercorns

2 teaspoons salt

1 teaspoon dried thyme

½ teaspoon dried rosemary

½ teaspoon dried oregano

1.  Put all of the ingredients in a heavy 2-gallon stockpot. Add 1 gallon of water, which should cover the ingredients by 1 inch, and bring to a boil over high heat. Reduce the heat to medium-low and simmer, uncovered, for 2 hours, skimming the surface occasionally with a slotted spoon to remove any foam that rises to the surface.

2.  Remove the pot from the heat and strain the stock through a fine-mesh sieve into a clean container. Let cool, then cover the stock and refrigerate in an airtight container for up to 3 days or freeze for up to 2 months.

# — CHICKEN STOCK —

Be sure to keep all stocks at a simmer as you cook them.
This way the impurities will rise to the surface, allowing
you to skim them off. If the stock is boiled, the impurities
will reemulsify with the stock, resulting in a cloudy
broth.

# MAYONNAISE

· MAKES ABOUT 2 CUPS ·

Though store-bought mayonnaise works just fine, there is nothing like the silky texture and fresh flavor of homemade. This recipe can be made up to one day in advance and stored in an airtight nonreactive container in the refrigerator.

1 large egg
1 large egg yolk
2 teaspoons fresh lemon juice
1 teaspoon Dijon mustard
½ teaspoon salt, or more to taste

1¼ cups vegetable oil
¼ cup olive oil
⅛ teaspoon cayenne pepper
(optional)

1. Place the egg, egg yolk, lemon juice, mustard, 1 tablespoon of water, and the salt in the bowl of a food processor or blender and process on high speed for 20 seconds. With the motor running, slowly pour in ¾ cup of the vegetable oil and process until the mixture begins to thicken. When the oil has been incorporated, add 1 more tablespoon of water. With the motor running, add the remaining vegetable oil and the olive oil in thin streams and process on high until all the oil is incorporated. Adjust the seasoning to taste with salt and cayenne, if desired.

2. Chill the mayonnaise and use as needed. (The mayonnaise will keep, stored in an airtight nonreactive container in the refrigerator, for up to 24 hours.)

EMERIL'S POTLUCK

6

# — MAYONNAISE —

Always be extra careful with mayonnaise because it spoils
rapidly. A lot of picnic foods use mayonnaise and then
are left to sit in the sun—this can lead to food poisoning!

# Simply Salsa

• MAKES 3 CUPS •

*S*alsa is the Mexican word for "sauce." With all of the different brands of salsa on the market, perhaps you've had trouble deciding which one is best. Why buy it when it's so easy to make my version. Of course, you can be creative and add some chopped jalapeño peppers for a little heat or a few dashes of your favorite hot sauce to kick it up. Dip your chips into it. I like to spoon it over poached or fried eggs, or spread it on just about any kind of sandwich. Add a little zip to a plain old ham and cheese. Hey, you'll find a lot of uses for it.

½ cup chopped red or yellow
onions
1 teaspoon minced garlic
¼ cup packed fresh cilantro leaves
¾ teaspoon salt

2 tablespoons fresh lime juice
1½ pounds ripe plum tomatoes,
cored and coarsely chopped, or
one 28-ounce can whole
tomatoes, drained

Put all the ingredients in a food processor and pulse about 12 times. The mixture should be slightly chunky. Transfer the salsa to a bowl, cover, and set aside until ready to use. Can be stored in an airtight container in the refrigerator for several days.

# SAVORY PIECRUST

Lots of folks are scared easily when it comes to making piecrust. Trust me—it's not difficult. The trick is not to overwork the dough. And I'll tell it like it is—with a little practice, as with everything else, you'll become a pro in no time.

- 1½ cups plus 2 tablespoons all-purpose flour
- ½ teaspoon salt
- 8 tablespoons (1 stick) cold unsalted butter, cut into ¼-inch pieces
- 2 tablespoons solid vegetable shortening
- 3 tablespoons ice water

Sift the flour and salt into a large bowl. Using your fingertips, work the butter and shortening into the flour until the mixture resembles small peas. Work the ice water into the mixture with your fingers until the dough just comes together; be careful not to overmix. Form the dough into a disk, wrap tightly in plastic wrap, and refrigerate for at least 30 minutes before rolling out.

# SHRIMP STOCK

• MAKES 3 QUARTS •

Once you make this stock from shrimp shells, I'll bet you never throw them away again! Do as I do: every time you use fresh shrimp, save the shells in a plastic container in the freezer until you have accumulated enough to make a batch of stock. You can freeze the stock in small containers for up to 2 months, and use as needed. This way there's no waste and you have shrimp stock anytime you need it.

1 pound (about 8 cups) shrimp shells and heads

1 cup coarsely chopped yellow onions

½ cup coarsely chopped celery

½ cup coarsely chopped carrots

3 smashed garlic cloves

3 bay leaves

1 teaspoon black peppercorns

1 teaspoon dried thyme

2 teaspoons salt

1. Place the shrimp shells and heads in a large colander and rinse under cold running water.

2. Place all the ingredients in a heavy 6-quart stockpot, add 4 quarts water, and bring to a boil over high heat, skimming to remove any foam that rises to the surface. Reduce the heat to medium-low and simmer, uncovered, for 45 minutes, skimming occasionally.

3. Remove the stock from the heat and strain through a fine-mesh sieve into a clean container; let cool completely. Refrigerate the stock for up to 3 days or freeze in airtight containers for up to 2 months.

# SIMPLE SYRUP

• MAKES 2¼ CUPS •

Simple Syrup is—as you might suspect—a simple sugar syrup that can be used in many ways for adding sweetness to recipes when a granular texture is not desired. Often used in making cocktails, simple syrup may also be used to glaze baked goods, add moisture to cakes, or as a poaching liquid for fruits, just to name a few of its most common uses. Simple syrup is also great for sweetening iced tea and lemonade.

1½ cups sugar                    1½ cups water

1.   Combine the sugar and water in a medium saucepan over medium-high heat and cook, stirring, until the sugar dissolves.

2.   Bring the mixture just to a boil, then remove from the heat.

3.   Let the mixture come to room temperature, then refrigerate in an airtight container until ready to use. Simple Syrup can be made up to two months in advance.

# DRINKS

Hey, there is absolutely nothing wrong with coffee, tea, soft drinks, wine, or cold beer, but sometimes the occasion calls for a little something special. At potluck parties I love to have a big batch of something that just puts you in the mood. Think Champagne Punch, Frozen Mint Juleps, or Milk Shakes for Grown-ups! On hot summer nights pass around a couple of pitchers of Emeril's Fresh and Fierce Margaritas or Green Vodka Coolers! During the holidays impress everyone with homemade eggnog and Hot Apple Cider. Or kick up your brunch with my very own Orange Emeril.

# MILK SHAKES FOR GROWN-UPS

If you're looking for an outrageously delicious drink, then look no further. This is an adult milk shake, and let me stress the adult part! Who knew that a milk shake could make you feel so good! I make my version with Nocello—one of my favorite liqueurs—but try your favorite nutty liqueur to make it your own. Just be sure to use high-quality ice cream, because that's what makes this kicked-up milk shake come to life!

2 pints vanilla ice cream

6 cups ice cubes

⅔ cup vodka

⅔ cup Kahlúa

⅔ cup Nocello

Cocoa powder, for garnish

Combine 1 pint ice cream, 3 cups ice, ⅓ cup vodka, ⅓ cup Kahlúa, and ⅓ cup Nocello in a blender. Process on high until smooth, about 2 minutes. Pour into tall glasses and garnish each one with a sprinkle of cocoa powder. Repeat with the remaining ingredients.

# — MILK SHAKES FOR GROWN-UPS —

Frozen drinks can be a bit tricky as far as figuring out the best ratio of liquor to ice. After lots of experimentation, I've finally discovered the perfect combination. For my 5-cup blender I use 1 cup of liquor to 3 to 4 cups of ice and then fill the blender with whatever other juices or flavorings I might be using. Use this as a guide for all your frozen drink making!

# GREEN VODKA COOLERS

• MAKES 8 SERVINGS •

I came up with this recipe with my good friend Marcelle Bienvenu. She lives down here in southern Louisiana and enjoys nothing more than entertaining friends on her patio overlooking the bayou. This drink is perfect for such an occasion in the springtime or summer. Chill your vodka in the freezer ahead of time to make the drinks extra cool!

2 cups fresh lime juice

¾ cup sugar

2 cups vodka

8 cups crushed ice

Lime slices, for garnish

Combine the lime juice and sugar in a bowl and whisk to dissolve the sugar. Pour half of this mixture into an electric blender, add 1 cup vodka and 4 cups ice and blend until smooth. Divide among 4 glasses, such as margarita glasses or other wide-mouthed, stemmed glasses. Repeat with the remaining ingredients. Serve immediately with lime slices for garnish.

# Emeril's Fresh and Fierce Margaritas

• MAKES 2 QUARTS, 8 TO 10 SERVINGS •

You might wonder what makes these margaritas so fresh and fierce. Well, let me tell you—one taste and you will see what I mean! Fresh lime and lemon juice and zest steeped in a simple syrup form the base, which is positively magical. With just the right balance of sweet and sour, these margaritas are rockin'! Oh, baby!

1½ cups fresh lime juice

½ cup fresh lemon juice

½ cup water

½ cup sugar

2 tablespoons lime zest

2 tablespoons lemon zest

2 cups premium tequila

1½ cups triple sec

Lime slices, for garnish

¼ cup coarse salt

1. Combine the lime juice, lemon juice, water, sugar, lime zest, and lemon zest in a small saucepan over medium heat. Bring to a boil, stirring, and cook until the sugar dissolves. Remove from the heat. Cool to room temperature.

2. Combine the cooled citrus syrup with the tequila and triple sec and chill thoroughly.

3. Meanwhile, chill margarita glasses and then wet the rim of each with a lime slice. Put the salt in a saucer and dip the rims into the salt.

4. Serve the chilled margarita mixture in salted glasses, over ice if desired, garnished with lime slices.

# WATERMELON DAIQUIRIS

• MAKES ABOUT 2 QUARTS, 8 SERVINGS •

No food says summer more than watermelon. So I say marry it with the perfect warm-weather cocktail—the daiquiri—and you have a match made in heaven! I boost the flavor of watermelon with some fresh pineapple and a ginger syrup. Oh yeah, baby! Just freeze your fruit and rum ahead of time, and you are in business. This is the perfect treat on the Fourth of July, when watermelons are really in their prime. Add the leftover ginger syrup to lemonade or fruit salads, or chill it for more daiquiris!

4 cups peeled, seeded, and chopped
   watermelon
¾ cup chopped cored fresh
   pineapple
2 cups light rum
1 cup Ginger Syrup (recipe follows)

½ cup fresh lemon juice
4 cups ice cubes
Small, thin watermelon wedges,
   about 2 inches, for garnish

1.   Put the watermelon and pineapple in plastic containers and place in the freezer until completely frozen, at least 4 hours. Also, place the rum in the freezer for at least 4 hours.

2.   Combine 2 cups of the watermelon, ¼ cup plus 2 tablespoons of the pineapple, 1 cup rum, ½ cup Ginger Syrup, and ¼ cup lemon juice in a blender. Blend on high speed until well combined. Add 2 cups ice and blend until smooth. Pour into a pitcher. Repeat with the remaining ingredients. Serve in margarita glasses or other wide-mouthed, stemmed glasses. Garnish with watermelon wedges.

## Ginger Syrup

MAKES ABOUT 1 QUART

5 cups sugar
2½ cups water
2 cups thinly sliced peeled fresh ginger

Combine the ingredients in a large saucepan over low heat. Simmer for 10 minutes, remove from the heat, and allow to cool. Once cool, strain out the ginger.

## — WATERMELON DAIQUIRIS —

You will notice that in this drink frozen fruit takes the place of some of the ice. This is a great trick to use when making frozen drinks. Freeze peaches, strawberries, bananas—you name it!

# FROZEN MINT JULEPS

• MAKES ABOUT 2 QUARTS, 8 SERVINGS •

Try this recipe for a super minty, frozen version of the quintessential Southern cocktail—the mint julep! By making a mint syrup, you intensify that great mint flavor. And by throwing it all in the blender with some ice, you create a super-refreshing crowd-pleaser. I serve these during the Kentucky Derby or on a lazy day by the pool.

1½ cups sugar, plus more for garnish

1 cup water

2 cups packed fresh mint leaves, coarsely chopped

8 cups ice cubes

2 cups bourbon

Orange slices, for garnish

Mint sprigs, for garnish

1. Combine the sugar and water in a small saucepan and simmer until the sugar dissolves. Remove from the heat and add the mint leaves. Allow to steep until cool. Once cool, strain out the leaves.

2. Combine half of the mint syrup, 4 cups ice, and 1 cup bourbon in a blender. Blend until smooth. Pour into a pitcher. Repeat with the remaining ingredients. Rub the rims of julep cups, if available, or wide-mouthed, long-stemmed glasses with orange slices and dip the rims in sugar, then fill with the frozen mint juleps. Garnish each with an orange slice and mint sprig and serve immediately.

# DARK AND STORMY

Liven up a summer get-together with this Jamaican drink. The key is to use Jamaican ginger beer. If you can not find this, substitute a high-quality ginger ale. This spicy soda delivers a whole lot of zing, making it the perfect foil for the rum and lime juice. Most specialty food stores carry ginger beer in their beverage section.

4 cups Jamaican ginger beer or
   high-quality ginger ale
2 cups dark rum
½ cup fresh lime juice

4 tablespoons Simple Syrup
   (page 11)
Crushed ice, for serving
Lime slices, for garnish

Combine the ginger beer, rum, lime juice, and Simple Syrup in a decorative bowl or pitcher. Stir to combine. Serve in old-fashioned, highball, or tall glasses over crushed ice. Garnish each drink with a lime slice.

# ORANGE EMERIL

• MAKES 2½ QUARTS, 10 TO 12 SERVINGS •

I know you remember that mall favorite—the Orange Julius. So how about kicking it up with some fresh ingredients and a little extra love to create an Orange Emeril! This is the perfect breakfast drink for all ages. Of course, you could kick it up a bit more with some chilled vodka for the adults, making it a wonderful cocktail for brunch. Either way, you are sure to enjoy!

4 cups fresh orange juice

4 cups ice cubes

¾ cup honey

⅔ cup heavy cream

2 tablespoons orange zest

1 teaspoon pure vanilla extract

Orange slices, for garnish

Combine 2 cups orange juice, 2 cups ice, ¼ cup plus 2 tablespoons honey, ⅓ cup cream, 1 tablespoon orange zest, and ½ teaspoon vanilla in a blender and process on high speed until smooth and frothy. Pour into a pitcher. Repeat with the remaining ingredients. Pour into tall glasses, garnish each with an orange slice, and serve immediately.

# Mango Lassi

• MAKES ABOUT 2 QUARTS, 8 SERVINGS •

A lassi is a chilled yogurt drink that is popular in India and is very similar to the American smoothie. It's the perfect drink for a spring or summer brunch, especially outdoors. The only unusual ingredient is rose water, which can be found at most specialty food stores, or you can do without it for a less exotic drink.

3 cups diced fresh mango or
   frozen diced mango

1 cup fresh orange juice

1 cup ice cubes

¼ cup honey

2½ teaspoons rose water

3 cups plain yogurt

Combine 1½ cups mango, ½ cup orange juice, ½ cup ice, 2 tablespoons honey, and 1¼ teaspoons rose water in a blender. Process on high speed until well combined, about 30 seconds. Add 1½ cups yogurt and process until frothy, about 45 seconds. Pour into a pitcher. Repeat with the remaining ingredients. Serve immediately in tall, chilled glasses.

# SANGRIA

• MAKES ABOUT 2 QUARTS, 8 SERVINGS •

Sangria is great for parties because it is best made in large batches and goes with a wide variety of foods. Traditionally, sangria is a Spanish cocktail made with red wine, soda water, and fruit. Sangria can be made with white wine, too, but I prefer mine made with red wine. Whichever one you choose, use a dry wine because the syrup and fruit make this drink sweet enough.

½ cup sugar
¼ cup water
1 large lemon
1 large orange
1 small apple, cored and thinly
    sliced

One 750 ml bottle dry red wine,
    such as Rioja
½ cup Grand Marnier
16 ounces club soda, chilled

1.    Combine the sugar and water in a small saucepan over medium heat and cook, stirring, until the sugar dissolves. Remove from the heat and allow to cool.

2.    Thinly slice half the lemon and half the orange. Combine in a large pitcher or decorative bowl. Juice the other halves of the lemon and orange and add the juice and rinds to the pitcher. Add the apple, wine, Grand Marnier, and chilled syrup to the pitcher and stir to combine. Refrigerate until thoroughly chilled, about 2 hours.

3.    Just before serving, pour in the chilled club soda and stir to combine. Serve straight up or on the rocks in wineglasses or old-fashioned glasses.

# CHAMPAGNE PUNCH

• MAKES ABOUT 3 QUARTS, 12 TO 16 SERVINGS •

Next time you have a crowd coming over and you'd like to serve a festive drink, whip up a batch of this super-refreshing Champagne punch. It's deceptively light and goes down easy—but beware, it packs a punch. If you plan to make this just before your guests arrive, make sure that all the ingredients are well chilled.

1⅓ cups fresh lemon juice
1 cup superfine sugar
½ cup Grand Marnier
½ cup triple sec
½ cup Cognac

½ cup fresh orange juice
Two 750 ml bottles chilled dry
    Champagne or sparkling wine
Orange or lemon slices
Fresh strawberries (optional)

1.    Combine the lemon juice, sugar, Grand Marnier, triple sec, Cognac, and orange juice in a large nonreactive bowl and stir until the sugar is completely dissolved. Add the Champagne and stir to combine. Cover and refrigerate until chilled, about 1 hour.

2.    Pour into a decorative bowl or pitcher. Garnish with orange or lemon slices and fresh strawberries, if desired. Serve in Champagne flutes, wineglasses, or punch cups.

## — CHAMPAGNE PUNCH —

Serve this in a punch bowl and keep it cool—make a decorative ice ring by freezing your favorite fruit juices together with sliced fruit or whole berries in a cake pan. Think color!

# EMERIL'S EGGNOG

• MAKES ABOUT 1½ QUARTS, 6 TO 8 SERVINGS •

Eggnog is my favorite holiday drink, and I'm not talking about the canned variety! Homemade eggnog is a breeze to make and a real treat for your friends and family. Since we're using eggs here, just play it safe and cook the base before spiking it with your favorite dark liquor. I prefer a combination of bourbon and brandy to really kick it up, but some prefer rum. Whatever you decide, make plenty—this classic is always a hit. Omit the alcohol for the kids!

8 large eggs, 2 separated
¾ cup sugar
⅛ teaspoon salt
2½ cups heavy cream
2 cups whole milk

1 tablespoon pure vanilla extract
½ teaspoon freshly grated nutmeg, plus more for garnish
¾ cup bourbon
¼ cup brandy

1. Combine the 6 whole eggs, 2 egg yolks, sugar, and salt in a medium mixing bowl and whisk together. Heat 2 cups heavy cream with the milk in a large saucepan over medium-low heat. When the cream and milk are hot, ladle about 1 cup into the egg mixture and whisk to incorporate. Pour the egg-milk mixture into the hot cream mixture, and continue to cook, stirring continuously, until the mixture thickens enough to coat the back of a spoon, 3 to 5 minutes. Remove the pan from the stove and strain the custard immediately through a fine-mesh sieve. Allow the custard to cool for 10 minutes before proceeding.

2. Add the vanilla, nutmeg, bourbon, and brandy to the eggnog and stir well to incorporate. Beat the 2 egg whites to soft peaks in a clean mixing bowl and fold them into the custard base. In a separate bowl, beat the remaining ½ cup cream to soft peaks, and fold into the eggnog as well. Cover and refrigerate until chilled, about 1 hour.

3. Pour into a decorative bowl or pitcher and garnish with nutmeg. Serve in small punch cups or old-fashioned glasses.

# Hot Apple Cider

• MAKES ABOUT 2¼ QUARTS, 8 TO 10 SERVINGS •

Everyone needs a little "warm-up" during those cold winter months. This super-simple cider is perfect for a last-minute gathering. Studding the apple with whole cloves enhances the cider's flavor. And if you leave out the rum, this is perfect for the kids' holiday party!

1 apple
2 teaspoons whole cloves
1 orange, thinly sliced
2 quarts apple cider
½ cup light brown sugar

1 teaspoon allspice
Pinch of freshly grated nutmeg
1 cup dark rum
Cinnamon sticks, for garnish

Stud the apple with the cloves. Combine the studded apple with the remaining ingredients except the rum and cinnamon in a medium pot. Bring to a simmer over low heat. Simmer until the flavors come together, about 10 minutes. Remove from the heat and add the rum. Discard the apple. Ladle into mugs and garnish each serving with a cinnamon stick.

# STARTERS

I'm such a fan of starters that I could make a whole meal of them. Hey, that may be an idea—have a potluck starter party! Seriously, starters, appetizers, munchies—whatever you want to call them—are a great way to lead into the meal. In fact, I would say that starters are a key part of any potluck party because they are the essence of the potluck mentality—fun food. While nibbling on the starters, you get to kick back, relax, and enjoy the company. And starters can be very, very simple. For example, take some mushrooms and marinate them. Simple? Yep! And good! Or take those mushrooms and stuff them with a sausage mixture. And what about good old deviled eggs? Man, I have a couple of variations that will take you back to the days when your mama made them to take along on picnics! Of course, I have a couple of dips (one made with blue cheese and another with crabmeat) that are ideal to pack up and tote to parties! Don't forget the crackers and chips!

# CLASSIC BLUE CHEESE DIP

• MAKES ABOUT 3 CUPS •

This is my take on that old-fashioned favorite—rich, creamy blue cheese dip. Of course, I had to add a little more gaaaahlic, but have a try and you'll find that the intense flavors of garlic and blue cheese make friends well. Now, if you ask me, this dip is just begging to be dipped into with an assortment of fresh vegetables. Choose the vegetables you like best to create your own signature crudité platter next time you're planning a get-together. Or do as I do and spoon some of this dip over a wedge of crisp iceberg lettuce next time you're having a steak dinner. Oh, baby, talk about taking me back!

1 cup sour cream
½ cup heavy cream
4 ounces cream cheese, at room temperature
¼ cup finely chopped onions
1 tablespoon minced garlic
1 teaspoon hot sauce

1 teaspoon salt
⅛ teaspoon cayenne pepper
¼ cup finely chopped fresh parsley
8 ounces blue cheese, crumbled
Fresh vegetables, such as celery and carrots cut into sticks, and cherry tomatoes

Combine all the ingredients except the blue cheese and the fresh vegetables in the bowl of a food processor and process until smooth. Transfer to a large bowl and stir in the crumbled blue cheese. Transfer the mixture to a serving bowl, cover, and chill for at least 1 hour or for up to 3 days before serving. Serve with a platter of fresh vegetables.

# Baba Ghanoush

• MAKES ABOUT 2¼ CUPS •

Baba what? I know, I know. The name is a bit of a tongue twister, but this is one of my favorite Middle Eastern appetizers. It's an eggplant dip; I kicked mine up a bit by roasting the eggplant and caramelizing the onions to give it a wonderful sweet flavor. The only unusual ingredient is tahini, a sesame seed paste that you can find at specialty food stores and many supermarkets. This can be made a day in advance and refrigerated until ready to serve.

4½ pounds eggplant (about 4 large globe eggplants)
1 tablespoon olive oil
1½ cups chopped onions
¼ cup plus ½ teaspoon fresh lemon juice
1 tablespoon extra virgin olive oil
2 teaspoons minced garlic

¼ cup plus 2 tablespoons tahini
1 tablespoon plus 1 teaspoon salt
2 teaspoons freshly ground black pepper
½ teaspoon cayenne pepper
2 teaspoons chopped fresh parsley, for garnish
Pita Chips (recipe follows)

1. Preheat the oven to 500°F. Line a rimmed baking sheet with aluminum foil.

2. Poke the eggplants randomly all over with the tines of a fork and place on the prepared baking sheet. Roast, turning once, until the eggplants are soft, about 30 minutes. Remove from the oven and let cool.

3. Meanwhile, heat the olive oil in a medium skillet over medium-low heat. Add the onions and cook, stirring, until lightly golden, about 10 minutes. Remove from the heat and set aside.

4. Peel the eggplants and put the flesh into the bowl of a food processor. Add ¼ cup of the lemon juice, 2 teaspoons extra virgin olive oil, the garlic, tahini, salt, black pepper,

and cayenne. Process until smooth. Transfer the mixture to a serving bowl and fold in the onions. With the back of a spoon, make a shallow indentation in the middle of the dip. Drizzle in the remaining teaspoon extra virgin olive oil and ½ teaspoon lemon juice, sprinkle with the parsley, and serve with Pita Chips.

## PITA CHIPS

MAKES 32 CHIPS

½ cup extra virgin olive oil
1 tablespoon minced garlic
1 teaspoon Emeril's Original Essence
4 pita breads, each split in half

1. Preheat the oven to 300°F.

2. Combine the olive oil, garlic, and Essence in a small bowl and whisk to mix. Brush the mixture evenly over each pita bread half. Stack the pita breads and cut into quarters. Arrange the pita pieces evenly on a baking sheet and bake until golden brown and crispy, about 20 minutes. Remove from the oven and let cool before serving.

# KICKED-UP SPINACH AND ARTICHOKE DIP

. MAKES 6 TO 8 SERVINGS .

Everyone loves spinach dip! Seriously, have you ever seen leftovers? My friends go crazy over this version. With three cheeses, how can you go wrong! The cubes of Brie partially melt, and you bite into a piece of heaven. Just watch your friends come back for more and more and more . . .

Two 10-ounce packages fresh spinach, well rinsed and stems trimmed

4 tablespoons unsalted butter

1 cup finely chopped onions

1 tablespoon minced garlic

1 teaspoon salt

½ teaspoon freshly ground black pepper

¼ teaspoon cayenne pepper

¼ cup all-purpose flour

1 cup milk

1 cup heavy cream

2 teaspoons fresh lemon juice

1 cup (6½ ounces) ½-inch cubes Brie cheese, rind removed

1 cup grated Monterey Jack cheese

One 6½-ounce jar marinated artichoke hearts, drained and chopped

4 strips crisp fried bacon, chopped

¼ cup freshly grated Parmesan cheese

Assorted chips, such as pita chips, tortilla chips, and bagel chips, for dipping

1. Preheat the oven to 350°F. Lightly grease a 9-inch round ovenproof chafing dish and set aside.

2. Bring a medium pot of water to a boil. Add the spinach in batches and cook until wilted, 2 to 3 minutes. Drain and refresh under cold running water. Squeeze the spinach to remove excess water and chop. Set aside.

3. Melt the butter in a medium pot over medium-high heat. Add the onions and cook, stirring, for 3 minutes. Add the garlic, salt, black pepper, and cayenne and cook,

stirring, for 1 minute. Add the flour and cook, stirring constantly, to make a light roux, about 2 minutes. Add the milk and cream in a steady stream, and cook, stirring constantly, until thick and creamy, 2 to 3 minutes. Add the cooked spinach and lemon juice and stir to incorporate. Add the cubed Brie and grated Monterey Jack cheeses, artichoke hearts, and bacon and stir well. Remove from the heat and pour into the prepared dish. Top with the Parmesan cheese and bake until bubbly, about 10 minutes. Remove from the oven and serve hot with chips.

# HOT CRAB DIP

• MAKES ABOUT 2 QUARTS, 12 TO 16 SERVINGS •

Nothing is more elegant than crabmeat. Unfortunately, it has a price tag to match. But here, a little goes a long way when combined with cream cheese and mayonnaise to create a sinfully rich dip. This is perfect for a fall or winter dinner when you crave that creamy comfort!

1 tablespoon olive oil

1 cup chopped onions

1 cup chopped green bell peppers

1 tablespoon minced garlic

2 teaspoons salt

1 tablespoon plus 1 teaspoon Emeril's Original Essence

1 pound cream cheese, at room temperature

1 cup mayonnaise

¼ cup chopped fresh parsley

1 tablespoon minced green onions

1 tablespoon fresh lemon juice

1 pound lump crabmeat, picked over for shells and cartilage

½ cup cracker crumbs (saltine or butter crackers)

2 tablespoons unsalted butter, melted

Toast points, croutons, or assorted party crackers, for serving

1. Preheat the oven to 350°F.

2. Heat the olive oil in a large skillet over medium heat. Add the onions, bell peppers, garlic, 1 teaspoon of the salt, and 1 teaspoon of the Essence. Cook, stirring, until the vegetables are soft, 2 to 3 minutes. Remove from the heat and set aside.

3. Combine the cream cheese, mayonnaise, parsley, green onions, lemon juice, and the remaining teaspoon salt and tablespoon Essence in a food processor. Process until smooth. Transfer the mixture to a mixing bowl and fold in the vegetables and crabmeat.

4. Transfer the mixture to a 2-quart casserole. Combine the cracker crumbs with the melted butter and stir to blend. Spread the crumb mixture over the crabmeat mixture and bake until hot and bubbly, about 30 minutes.

5. Serve warm or chilled with toast points, croutons, or assorted party crackers.

## — CRAB DIP —

Make sure you are careful when cooking with crab. This delicate seafood spoils very easily if not used immediately. So make this dip no more than one day in advance. Also, promptly refrigerate any leftovers and eat them within a day.

# SPICED NUTS

• MAKES 4 CUPS •

I make a big batch of these spiced nuts to keep on hand during the holiday season just in case . . . Seriously, that time of year lends itself to impromptu gatherings, and it's nice to have something to pull out when the doorbell rings. Spiced nuts go well with cocktails or can be tossed with some greens for a quick salad. And they will keep in an airtight container for up to two weeks. What more can you ask for?

½ teaspoon ground cumin
½ teaspoon cayenne pepper
½ teaspoon ground cinnamon
4 cups unsalted mixed nuts, such as walnuts, pecans, hazelnuts, and almonds

4 tablespoons unsalted butter
6 tablespoons brown sugar
1 teaspoon salt

1. Mix spices and reserve.

2. Heat the nuts in a dry skillet and cook, stirring frequently, until they begin to toast, about 4 minutes. Add the butter and cook, stirring, until the nuts begin to darken, about 1 minute. Add the spices, the sugar, 1 tablespoon water, and the salt and cook, stirring, until the sauce thickens and the nuts are glazed, about 5 minutes.

3. Remove the nuts from the heat and transfer to a baking sheet lined with aluminum foil, separating them with a fork. Let the nuts stand until cooled and the sugar has hardened, about 10 minutes. Store in an airtight container.

# — SPICED NUTS —

These nuts make excellent gifts. Just place them in a festive tin, and you are set. And remember, the assortment of nuts and type of seasoning is up to you—customize the recipe for your favorite person!

# MARINATED OLIVES

Have you noticed that almost every grocery store has giant bins of olives? Well, did you ever imagine that an impressive hors d'oeuvre could be as close as those bins? Those grocery store olives (even the jarred variety) are just right on their own, but if you jazz them up a bit . . . now we're talkin'! All they need is a little love in the form of your favorite herbs and vinegar, some time to rest (preferably at least overnight), and voilà—a little finger food for your picnic, drinks, or dinner! But wait—don't throw out the marinade. You can dip some French bread into it or use it as a sauce for pasta. You know, share the love!

- 1 pound assorted olives, such as Kalamata, Niçoise, oil-cured, and pimiento-stuffed green olives
- 1 cup extra virgin olive oil
- 4 garlic cloves, peeled and crushed
- 4 bay leaves
- 4 sprigs fresh thyme
- 1 teaspoon red wine vinegar
- 1 teaspoon freshly ground black pepper
- ½ teaspoon crushed red pepper
- ½ teaspoon lemon zest

Combine all of the ingredients in a large bowl and stir to mix. Cover and refrigerate for at least 24 hours. Remove from the refrigerator and allow to come to room temperature before serving. (Leftovers can be stored in an airtight container in the refrigerator for up to 2 weeks.)

# MARINATED MUSHROOMS

● MAKES 1 QUART, 6 TO 8 SERVINGS ●

Marinated mushrooms are a classic, delicious starter that, sadly, is seldom seen these days. I love them so much, I've brought them back! These mushrooms are simple and delicious. I like mine in a classic Italian vinaigrette, but you could play around until your taste buds are happy. (Sometimes I like to put some small pieces of Parmesan cheese in with mine.) Make sure that you let these babies rest overnight so they soak up all those good flavors.

¼ cup fresh lemon juice

2 teaspoons salt

2 teaspoons minced garlic

1 teaspoon freshly ground black pepper

1 teaspoon dried basil

1 teaspoon dried oregano

¾ cup extra virgin olive oil

2 pounds white button mushrooms, wiped clean, stemmed, and quartered

Whisk together the lemon juice, salt, garlic, pepper, basil, and oregano in a small mixing bowl. Gradually add the olive oil, whisking constantly. Put the mushrooms in a large bowl and add the marinade. Toss to coat evenly. Cover and refrigerate for at least 24 hours. Let come to room temperature before serving.

# — MARINATED MUSHROOMS —

Marinated foods like these mushrooms and the Marinated Olives (page 39) are always great for picnics because they only become better with time. You can even use this technique on other vegetables, like tomatoes and cucumbers. So for your next outside gathering—marinate!

# EMERIL'S DEVILED EGGS

• MAKES 2 DOZEN •

Everyone loves deviled eggs. And they are ideal for so many occasions—picnics, luncheons, even cocktail parties. There are many variations, but here are my favorites—a classic version plus two alternatives, one casual and one dressy.

1 dozen hard-boiled large eggs, peeled

½ cup Mayonnaise (page 6)

1 tablespoon plus 2 teaspoons Creole or other whole-grain mustard

2 teaspoons Emeril's Original Essence

¼ teaspoon cayenne pepper

Pinch of salt

¼ teaspoon paprika

Slice the eggs in half lengthwise and carefully remove the yolks. Press the yolks through a fine-mesh sieve into a mixing bowl. Add the mayonnaise, mustard, Essence, cayenne, and salt. Stir to blend well. Spoon (or pipe with a pastry bag) the mixture into the egg whites. Cover and chill for at least 1 hour. Sprinkle with the paprika just before serving. (If the paprika is added too early it will stain the eggs.)

## Devilish Eggs

MAKES 2 DOZEN

1 dozen hard-boiled large eggs, peeled

½ cup Mayonnaise (page 6)

1 tablespoon plus 2 teaspoons Creole or other whole-grain mustard

1 tablespoon plus 1 teaspoon minced pickled jalapeños

2 teaspoons Emeril's Original Essence

½ teaspoon cayenne pepper

½ teaspoon Emeril's Kick It Up! Red Pepper Sauce, or other hot sauce

¼ teaspoon paprika

Slice the eggs in half lengthwise and carefully remove the yolks. Press the yolks through a fine-mesh sieve into a mixing bowl. Add the mayonnaise, mustard, jalapeños, Essence, cayenne, and hot sauce. Stir to blend. Spoon (or pipe with a pastry bag) the mixture into the egg whites. Cover and chill for at least 1 hour. Sprinkle with the paprika just before serving. (If the paprika is added too early it will stain the eggs.)

## — DEVILED EGGS —

Unless you are lucky enough to own one of those nifty retro egg carriers, deviled eggs can be a bit tricky to relocate. Do as my friend Marcelle does and nestle the eggs in a "bed" of wax paper inside a covered container.

# SALMON-DILL EGGS

MAKES 2 DOZEN

1 dozen hard-boiled large eggs, peeled
¼ cup mayonnaise
¼ cup sour cream
2 ounces smoked salmon, finely chopped
2 teaspoons chopped fresh dill, plus more for garnish
1 teaspoon fresh lemon juice
1 teaspoon freshly ground black pepper
½ teaspoon salt

Slice the eggs in half lengthwise and carefully remove the yolks. Press the yolks through a fine-mesh sieve into a mixing bowl. Add the mayonnaise, sour cream, salmon, dill, lemon juice, pepper, and salt. Stir to blend. Spoon the mixture into the egg whites. Cover and chill for at least 1 hour before serving. Sprinkle with chopped dill before serving.

# ALAIN'S SWEET AND SPICY ASIAN WINGS

• MAKES 8 TO 12 SERVINGS •

I borrowed this recipe from my good friend Alain Joseph, who has been with our company for years. Alain first started toying with the idea of Asian wings when he was a cook at Emeril's in New Orleans. He fine-tuned the recipe in the test kitchen at Homebase, and voilà! These wings are positively addictive. The only ingredient you might not have is mirin, a sweet rice wine, which is available at many supermarkets or at specialty food stores.

2 cups fresh orange juice

1 cup canned pineapple juice

2 tablespoons orange zest

2 tablespoons minced garlic

2 tablespoons minced fresh ginger

2 tablespoons minced green onions

1 tablespoon sesame oil

½ cup soy sauce

½ cup mirin

1 cup sugar

1½ teaspoons crushed red pepper

3 quarts peanut oil, for frying

10 pounds chicken wings, separated at the joints, wing tips reserved for another use

2 cups cornstarch

4 tablespoons Emeril's Original Essence

Salt

¼ cup chopped fresh cilantro

¼ cup toasted sesame seeds

1. Combine the orange juice, pineapple juice, orange zest, garlic, ginger, green onions, sesame oil, soy sauce, mirin, sugar, and crushed red pepper in a large skillet set over medium-high heat. Bring to a boil, stirring occasionally, until the sugar is dissolved and the liquid has reduced to a thick syrup, 18 to 20 minutes.

2. Meanwhile, place the peanut oil in a 6-quart pot and heat to 375°F. Place the chicken wings in a large bowl. In a small bowl, season the cornstarch with the Essence. Place the seasoned cornstarch in a 1-gallon heavy-duty plastic food storage bag and add

the chicken pieces in batches. Shake the bag to coat the chicken, then remove and place 8 to 10 pieces in the hot oil. Fry the chicken, stirring occasionally, for 6 to 8 minutes, or until the chicken is cooked through. Remove and place in a clean large bowl; season lightly with salt to taste. Continue until all the chicken has been fried.

3.    Preheat the oven to 275°F. Spoon the sauce over the chicken and toss to evenly coat. Sprinkle the chicken with the cilantro and sesame seeds and place in a large ovenproof dish. Keep warm in the oven until the guests arrive.

# Asian Boiled Shrimp

Rest assured that these are not the same old boiled shrimp that you see at party after party. These shrimp are kickin'! The boil itself turns out shrimp so tasty that they hardly need a sauce. So if you are in a hurry, simply serve them warm without the Asian Mayonnaise, but try it the next time—you won't be sorry!

One 2-inch piece peeled fresh ginger, thinly sliced

3 lemons, halved and juiced, shells reserved

½ cup soy sauce

¾ cup sugar

4 bay leaves

2 tablespoons chopped green onions (green and white parts)

2 teaspoons chopped garlic

1 tablespoon salt

1 teaspoon freshly ground black pepper

2 teaspoons crushed red pepper

2 pounds large shrimp, peeled and deveined

2 teaspoons Emeril's Original Essence

1 recipe Asian Mayonnaise (recipe follows)

1. Combine 6 cups water with the ginger, lemon shells, lemon juice, soy sauce, sugar, bay leaves, green onions, garlic, salt, black pepper, and crushed red pepper in a large heavy saucepan and bring to a boil over high heat.

2. Season the shrimp with the Essence and add to the boiling mixture. Cook for 2 minutes, remove from the heat, and steep for 2 minutes. Remove the shrimp with tongs or a slotted spoon and transfer to a large platter to cool. When cool enough to handle, serve, either warm, at room temperature, or chilled, with the Asian Mayonnaise.

## Asian Mayonnaise

MAKES ABOUT 1 CUP

1 large egg yolk
2 teaspoons fresh lemon juice
1 teaspoon minced fresh ginger
½ teaspoon minced garlic
½ teaspoon minced green onions
1 cup vegetable oil
1 tablespoon soy sauce
1 tablespoon chopped fresh cilantro leaves
½ teaspoon freshly ground white pepper
½ teaspoon sesame oil
¼ teaspoon salt

Combine the egg yolk, lemon juice, ginger, garlic, and green onions in a food processor and process for 15 seconds. With the motor running, slowly add the vegetable oil through the feed tube. The mixture will thicken. Add the soy sauce, cilantro, pepper, sesame oil, and salt. Pulse once or twice to blend. Serve immediately or store in an airtight container for no more than 24 hours before using.

# COCKTAIL CRAWFISH TURNOVERS

• MAKES 40 COCKTAIL TURNOVERS, 8 TO 10 APPETIZER SERVINGS •

These bite-size crawfish turnovers are perfect for parties—why not bring a taste of the bayou to your next get-together by including these on your menu? If you happen to live in an area where crawfish are hard to come by, don't worry—chopped cooked shrimp or lobster would be equally at home in these flavorful turnovers.

3 tablespoons unsalted butter

¼ cup chopped onions

2 tablespoons chopped green bell peppers

2 tablespoons chopped celery

1½ teaspoons Emeril's Original Essence

¼ teaspoon salt

⅛ teaspoon cayenne pepper

½ teaspoon chopped garlic

2 tablespoons all-purpose flour

¾ cup whole milk

½ pound peeled crawfish tails

¼ cup grated Pepper Jack cheese

2 tablespoons chopped green onions

2 teaspoons chopped fresh parsley

One 17.3-ounce package frozen puff pastry (2 sheets), thawed in the refrigerator

2 egg yolks, beaten with 2 teaspoons water

1. Heat the butter in a medium skillet over medium-high heat. Add the onions, bell peppers, and celery. Season with the Essence, salt, and cayenne and cook, stirring, until the onion is slightly soft, about 2 minutes. Add the garlic and cook, stirring, until fragrant, about 30 seconds. Add the flour and cook, stirring until the mixture is lightly golden, about 3 minutes. Add the milk, and continue stirring until the mixture is smooth and thick, about 3 minutes. Remove from the heat. Add the crawfish tails, cheese, green onions, and parsley. Stir to mix well. Remove from the heat and let cool to room temperature.

2. Preheat the oven to 425°F.

3. Roll out each pastry sheet to 12 × 15 inches on a lightly floured surface. Trim the edges to make them even. With a sharp knife, cut each sheet into twenty 3-inch squares. Mound about 2 teaspoons of the crawfish mixture in the center of each square, brush 2 edges of the squares with the egg wash, fold over diagonally, and seal. Crimp the edges with a fork. Lightly brush the tops of the turnovers with some of the egg wash. Using the tip of a paring knife, make a tiny slit in the top of each turnover so that steam can escape during baking.

4. Line a baking sheet with aluminum foil or parchment paper. Place the turnovers about an inch apart on the sheet and bake until golden, 12 to 15 minutes. Remove from the oven and let cool for 5 minutes before serving.

## — CRAWFISH TURNOVERS —

These turnovers are the perfect party food because they can be assembled ahead of time and frozen unbaked until the day of your get-together. Simply defrost them and bake just before serving.

# Sausage-Stuffed Mushrooms

• MAKES 2 DOZEN, 8 SERVINGS •

Stuffed mushrooms are the perfect hors d'oeuvre—easy to make and easy to eat! I stuff mine with a combination of sweet and hot Italian sausages to really kick things up! Hey, when you're talking about sausage, how can you go wrong? And if you really want to use your time wisely, then make the stuffing a day in advance so you can stuff and bake the mushrooms just before the festivities begin!

¼ cup plus 1 teaspoon extra virgin olive oil

1½ pounds large button mushrooms, wiped clean and stemmed (reserve 1 cup minced stems)

6 ounces hot Italian sausage, removed from casings

6 ounces sweet Italian sausage, removed from casings

¼ cup finely chopped onions

2 tablespoons finely chopped green bell peppers

2 tablespoons finely chopped celery

1 teaspoon minced garlic

¼ cup plain bread crumbs

¼ cup freshly grated Parmesan cheese

2 tablespoons plus 2 teaspoons minced fresh parsley

1 teaspoon Emeril's Original Essence

1. Preheat the oven to 400°F.

2. Pour ¼ cup olive oil into a large mixing bowl. Add the mushroom caps and toss to coat.

3. Cook the sausages in a medium skillet over medium-high heat until browned, about 2 minutes. Add the onions, bell peppers, celery, and reserved minced mushroom stems and cook until softened, about 3 minutes. Add the garlic and cook until fragrant, about 30 seconds. Remove from the heat. Transfer the sausage-vegetable mixture to the

bowl of a food processor. Add 2 tablespoons bread crumbs, 2 tablespoons Parmesan, 2 tablespoons parsley, the Essence, and the remaining teaspoon olive oil. Pulse until the stuffing comes together, about 30 seconds.

4. Fill each mushroom cap with a heaping teaspoon of stuffing. Place the mushrooms on a baking sheet. Combine the remaining 2 tablespoons bread crumbs and 2 tablespoons Parmesan in a small mixing bowl. Sprinkle over the mushroom caps. Bake the mushrooms until browned and tender, 15 to 18 minutes. Remove from the oven and let cool slightly. Garnish with the remaining 2 teaspoons parsley and serve warm or at room temperature.

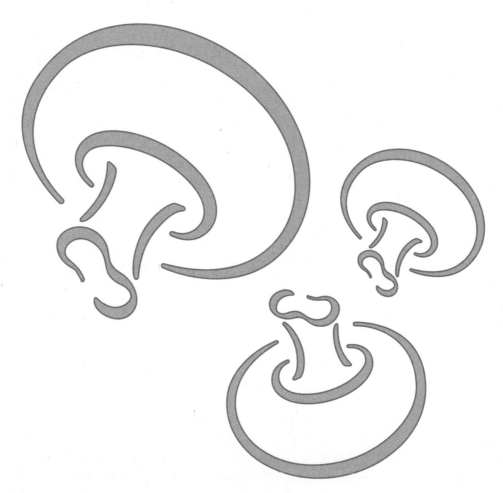

# Blue Cheese Coins

Cheese straws are a cocktail party staple in the South. They are essentially Cheddar cheese crackers and, boy, are they addictive! Well, I decided to create my own variation with one of my favorite cheeses—blue—and I added some walnuts for good measure. These are great to serve with wine before dinner.

2 cups all-purpose flour

1 teaspoon freshly ground black pepper

½ teaspoon salt

½ pound (2 sticks) unsalted butter, at room temperature

½ pound blue cheese, at room temperature

1 cup finely chopped walnuts

1. Preheat the oven to 350°F.

2. Sift the dry ingredients. Cream the butter and cheese with an electric mixer. Add the dry ingredients and mix to combine. (Alternatively, cream the butter and cheese with a rubber spatula and stir in the dry ingredients with a wooden spoon.) Fold in the nuts with the wooden spoon. Drop the batter by heaping teaspoons onto an ungreased baking sheet. Bake 15 to 18 minutes, until golden. (Store the baked cheese coins in an airtight container for up to 2 weeks.)

These make great gifts for the holidays—or anytime! Just be sure to package them carefully in layers of wax paper because they are a bit fragile.

# HELEN'S SAUSAGE-STUFFED FRENCH BREAD

● MAKES 12 TO 16 SERVINGS ●

This deliciously cheesy stuffed French bread is a hit at all of my friend Helen's parties. Some folks like to scoop the filling out of the bread with corn chips, while others prefer to eat slices! I've given instructions for both methods of serving. Helen suggests preparing the filling a day or two in advance. Store it in the refrigerator and then add it to the hollowed-out French bread just before baking.

Two 15-inch-long French baguettes
1 pound bulk breakfast sausage
2 tablespoons chopped jalapeños
1 cup chopped green bell peppers
¼ cup chopped green onions (green and white parts)
8 ounces cream cheese, at room temperature

8 ounces sour cream
8 ounces grated sharp Cheddar cheese
1 teaspoon Emeril's Original Essence
Chopped fresh parsley, for garnish
Corn or tortilla chips, for dipping (optional)

1. Preheat the oven to 350°F.

2. Using a serrated knife, trim the upper quarter off the length of the top of each loaf. Hollow out the center of the loaves, leaving a ½-inch-thick shell. Set aside.

3. Brown the sausage in a large skillet over medium-high heat for about 5 minutes, stirring to break up any clumps. Add the jalapeños, bell peppers, and green onions. Cook, stirring, until the vegetables are soft, 3 to 4 minutes. Add the cream cheese, sour cream, and Cheddar and stir until completely melted, about 2 minutes. Add the Essence and remove from the heat.

4.   Fill the hollowed-out bread loaves with equal amounts of the sausage-cheese mixture and wrap each loaf in aluminum foil. Place the loaves on a baking sheet and bake for 1 hour. Remove from the oven, unwrap, and sprinkle with parsley.

5.   Serve warm with chips for dipping, if desired, or cut the bread crosswise into 2-inch slices.

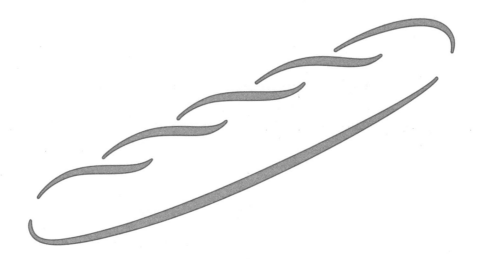

# Roasted Vegetable and Goat Cheese Terrine

Hey, don't be intimidated by the word *terrine*. It sounds fancy, but in this case it refers more to the fact that this is prepared in a mold, and can be turned out and served while retaining its shape. Though pâtés and terrines are often made of ground meats and seasonings, this one is a vegetable lover's dream come true! Made from layers of colorful roasted vegetables and herbed goat cheese and topped with a tangy Sun-Dried Tomato Sauce, it is an attractive, delicious addition to a buffet. And, hey—it can be made several days in advance and easily transported to a potluck party.

One 1-pound globe eggplant, stem and bottom ends trimmed, cut lengthwise into ¼-inch slices

1 pound zucchini, stem and bottom ends trimmed, cut lengthwise into ¼-inch slices

1½ pounds yellow squash, stem and bottom ends trimmed, cut lengthwise into ¼-inch slices

½ cup olive oil

Salt and freshly ground black pepper

10 ounces soft, mild goat cheese

2 tablespoons minced fresh basil leaves

2 tablespoons minced fresh parsley

2 tablespoons extra virgin olive oil

2 large red bell peppers (about 1 pound), roasted, cores, seeds, and skins removed, cut into 3 or 4 large pieces

16 ounces fresh spinach, washed, stems removed, then blanched, squeezed dry, and coarsely chopped

2 large yellow bell peppers (about 1 pound), roasted, cores, seeds, and skins removed, cut into 3 or 4 large pieces

1 recipe Sun-Dried Tomato Sauce (recipe follows)

Toasted croutons, for serving

1. Preheat the oven to 425°F.

2. Line 2 large baking sheets with aluminum foil and lightly grease with olive oil. Arrange some of the eggplant, zucchini, and yellow squash slices in a single layer on the

sheets, slightly overlapping them. Brush with olive oil and lightly season with salt and pepper. Bake until soft and just golden around the edges, 8 to 10 minutes. Remove from the oven and transfer to a plate to cool. Repeat with the remaining vegetable slices.

3. In a large bowl, combine the goat cheese with the basil, parsley, and extra virgin olive oil. Season to taste with salt and pepper and mix well.

4. In a 6-cup terrine (12 × 3 × 3 inches), arrange the eggplant slices crosswise over the bottom and up the sides, overlapping the slices to completely cover the terrine. The ends of the slices should overhang the sides of the terrine. Top the eggplant with thin layers of red bell pepper, zucchini, yellow squash, spinach, and yellow bell pepper. Crumble a layer of the goat cheese mixture on top of the yellow bell pepper, and repeat the layering with the remaining vegetable slices. Bring the overhanging eggplant slices up over the terrine. Wrap the terrine loosely in plastic wrap. Top with an equal-size terrine or a piece of cardboard wrapped in aluminum foil. Place a brick or heavy pot on top of the terrine and refrigerate for at least 8 hours or for up to 24 hours.

5. Remove the terrine from the refrigerator. Remove the weight and unwrap. Slice with a very sharp knife and serve 1 thick or 2 thin slices per person with Sun-Dried Tomato Sauce and toasted croutons.

• • • • • • • • • • • • • • • • • • • • • • • • • • • • • • • • • • • • • • • • • • •

## SUN-DRIED TOMATO SAUCE

MAKES ABOUT 2 CUPS

1 cup tightly packed sun-dried tomatoes (not oil packed), reconstituted in hot water and drained
1 teaspoon balsamic vinegar
4 garlic cloves, minced
¼ teaspoon salt
¼ teaspoon crushed red pepper
⅛ teaspoon freshly ground black pepper
1¼ cups extra virgin olive oil

In the bowl of a food processor, combine the sun-dried tomatoes, balsamic vinegar, garlic, salt, crushed red pepper, and black pepper and puree on high speed. With the motor running, gradually add the olive oil through the feed tube and process until well combined. Pour into a container until ready to serve.

# Emeril's Southwest Cheesecake

• MAKES 16 SERVINGS •

Oh, baby! This savory cheesecake is gonna knock your socks off! I've seasoned this with all of my favorite Southwest flavors, and have included a recipe for a simple salsa and a Cilantro Pesto to—well, you know, kick it up a notch or two. If I were you, I'd make this cheesecake a day or so ahead of time and then chill it, so the flavors have a chance to blend. Remember to bring the cheesecake to room temperature before serving. The salsa and pesto can also be made in advance and chilled.

1 cup finely crushed tortilla chips (about half of a 13½-ounce bag)

4 tablespoons unsalted butter, melted

3 tablespoons olive oil

1 cup diced onions

¾ cup chopped red bell peppers

¾ cup chopped yellow bell peppers

¼ cup minced jalapeños

2 tablespoons plus 2½ teaspoons Emeril's Southwest Essence

1 tablespoon plus ¼ teaspoon salt

1 tablespoon minced garlic

1½ pounds skinless, boneless chicken breasts, cut into ½-inch dice

2 pounds cream cheese, at room temperature

4 ounces sour cream

5 large eggs

6 ounces grated Cheddar cheese

½ cup grated Manchego or Parmesan cheese

1 recipe Simply Salsa (page 8)

1 recipe Cilantro Pesto (recipe follows)

1. Preheat the oven to 325°F.

2. Combine the chips and butter in a small bowl and mix to blend. Press the mixture into the bottom and slightly up the sides of a 10-inch springform pan. Set aside.

3. Heat 1 tablespoon olive oil in a large skillet over medium-high heat. Add the onions, bell peppers, jalapeños, 1 teaspoon Southwest Essence, and ¼ teaspoon salt.

Cook, stirring, until the vegetables are soft, 4 to 6 minutes. Add the garlic and cook until fragrant, about 30 seconds longer. Remove from the heat and set aside to cool.

4.    Season the chicken with 1½ teaspoons Essence. Heat the remaining 2 tablespoons olive oil in a large skillet over medium-high heat. Add the chicken and cook, stirring often, for 2 to 3 minutes. Remove from the heat.

5.    Add the cream cheese, sour cream, and eggs to a large bowl and beat with an electric mixer until very smooth. Using a rubber spatula, fold the vegetables, chicken, grated cheeses, remaining 2 tablespoons Essence, and remaining tablespoon salt into the cream cheese mixture. Pour the mixture into the springform pan and bake until the center has set, about 1 hour. Remove from the oven and set aside to cool on a wire rack. When cool, transfer to the refrigerator to chill thoroughly before serving.

## CILANTRO PESTO

MAKES 1¼ CUPS

2 cups tightly packed fresh cilantro leaves
¼ cup toasted pumpkin seeds or pine nuts
1 teaspoon minced garlic
¼ cup grated Manchego or Parmesan cheese
½ teaspoon freshly ground black pepper
½ teaspoon salt
1 cup extra virgin olive oil

Combine the cilantro, pumpkin seeds, and garlic in a food processor or blender. Puree on high speed. Add the cheese, black pepper, and salt and process to combine. Scrape down the sides of the processor. With the machine running, add the olive oil. Blend until well combined.

# SALADS

Salads are perfect for potluck events because most of them can be assembled in advance. Some salads actually like to sit around for a little while, and, you know—chill out! Take my eggplant salad, for example. Sure, it's good right after you make it, but give it a night of rest and—whoa, baby! A little downtime allows the flavors to develop. Some salads, like the endive salad and the Layered Tuna Niçoise Salad, are best assembled the day of your get-together and then tossed with the dressings just before serving.

# My Big Fat Greek Tomato Salad

• MAKES 6 CUPS, 6 TO 8 SERVINGS •

This Greek-inspired salad is the essence of summer to me. With bright flavors and colors—it is a showstopper. Use a good-quality feta cheese because that wonderful sweet-salty goodness really is the tie that binds. This salad is perfect for so many occasions—a picnic, casual dinner, or even brunch.

1 tablespoon red wine vinegar

1 tablespoon fresh lemon juice

½ teaspoon plus a pinch of salt, plus more to taste

½ teaspoon freshly ground black pepper, plus more to taste

6 tablespoons extra virgin olive oil

1 quart cherry tomatoes, halved

1 medium cucumber, peeled, halved lengthwise, and sliced crosswise ¼ inch thick

1¼ cups crumbled feta cheese (½ pound)

1 small yellow onion, halved and thinly sliced (1¼ cups)

1 teaspoon finely chopped fresh parsley

1 teaspoon finely chopped fresh basil

½ teaspoon finely chopped fresh mint

Combine the vinegar, lemon juice, salt, and pepper in a large serving bowl and whisk to blend. Gradually whisk in the olive oil. Add the remaining ingredients and toss to mix. Season with salt and pepper as necessary. Serve immediately.

# ENDIVE, PEAR, AND GORGONZOLA SALAD

• MAKES 6 TO 8 SERVINGS •

Some folks think of salad as something to be eaten in spring or summer, when many tender vegetables and lettuces are just coming into the market, but let me introduce you to the world of winter salads. All you need are some hearty greens, fruits, and nuts. And here is a perfect example. Endive, the ultimate winter green, begs to be tossed with some pears, walnuts, and Gorgonzola cheese.

4 large Belgian endive bulbs,
    14 to 16 ounces total, thinly
    sliced crosswise

6 ounces watercress or baby
    spinach

1 bunch (6 ounces) radishes, thinly
    sliced

4 cups diced pears (about 3)

6 ounces Gorgonzola (Italian blue
    cheese), crumbled

2 cups toasted walnuts

1 tablespoon honey

2 teaspoons minced shallots

1 teaspoon minced garlic

½ teaspoon Dijon mustard

¼ cup white wine vinegar

3 tablespoons cider vinegar

½ cup walnut oil

¼ cup olive oil

¼ teaspoon salt

¼ teaspoon freshly ground
    black pepper

1. Combine the endive, watercress, radishes, pears, and Gorgonzola in a large bowl. Sprinkle the walnuts on top, cover, and refrigerate until ready to serve.

2. Combine the honey, shallots, garlic, and mustard in a small bowl. Whisk to blend. Add the white wine and cider vinegars and whisk to incorporate. Gradually whisk in the walnut oil, followed by the olive oil. Season with the salt and pepper.

3. When ready to serve, drizzle the vinaigrette over the salad and toss to coat evenly. Serve immediately.

# — ENDIVE SALAD —

Like other green salads, this is best if tossed just before serving. But, hey—don't let that stop you from bringing this one to a friend's house for dinner. Transport the salad and the dressing separately. Just before serving, toss the salad with the dressing in a large bowl.

# Spinach, Orange, and Almond Salad

Hey, this is a super-easy salad to bring to a friend's house for dinner. Prepare the salad and dressing separately ahead of time. Keep the salad in a salad bowl, covered with plastic wrap and refrigerated, until you're ready to go. The dressing should be refrigerated in a nonreactive container with a tight-fitting lid. Then, when you get to your destination, dress the salad, season with a little salt and pepper, give it a good toss, and serve!

¼ cup plus 2 tablespoons sugar

½ cup sliced almonds

4 oranges

¼ cup Champagne or white wine vinegar

3 tablespoons vegetable oil

1 tablespoon extra virgin olive oil

½ teaspoon orange zest

¼ teaspoon salt, plus more for seasoning salad

⅛ teaspoon cayenne pepper

10 ounces baby spinach (6 cups), washed and dried

1 cup thinly sliced celery

½ cup thinly sliced red onions

Freshly ground black pepper, to taste

1. Lightly grease a 10-inch square of aluminum foil with butter or vegetable oil and set aside.

2. Combine 3 tablespoons sugar and 1 tablespoon water in a small saucepan and cook over medium-high heat, swirling occasionally, until the sugar turns a golden amber color, 3 to 4 minutes. Add the almonds and stir to coat. Continue cooking until the almonds are fragrant and golden brown, about 1 minute. Transfer to the prepared aluminum foil, using a spoon to spread into a thin layer, and set aside to cool completely.

3.  With a thin, sharp knife, cut the peel and bitter white pith from the oranges, one at a time. Working over a bowl to catch the juices, cut in between the membranes to release the segments. Reserve the segments in a separate bowl. Combine ¼ cup orange juice, the remaining 3 tablespoons sugar, the Champagne vinegar, vegetable oil, olive oil, orange zest, ¼ teaspoon salt, and the cayenne in a mixing bowl and whisk to blend. Transfer the dressing to a plastic container with a tight-fitting lid until you are ready to serve.

4.  Put the spinach in a large serving bowl, then top with the orange segments, celery, and red onions. Cover with plastic wrap and refrigerate until ready to serve.

5.  When ready to serve, break the caramelized almonds into bite-size pieces and scatter over the top of the salad. Drizzle the dressing over the salad and season with salt and black pepper to taste. Toss to coat evenly and serve immediately.

# LAYERED TUNA NIÇOISE SALAD

• MAKES 12 SIDE SALADS OR 6 TO 8 MAIN COURSE SALADS •

Talk about a salad that takes me back to days gone by. I first tasted this dish in the south of France, many years ago, when I worked there after cooking school. The salad highlights some of the flavors that this part of the world is known for—rich, fruity olives and olive oil, capers, anchovies, beautiful produce—and makes a wonderful main course salad for summer days when you long for lighter fare. Serve this with a loaf of fresh, crispy French or Italian bread, and you're set!

1 large head romaine lettuce, torn into bite-size pieces

1½ pounds red boiling potatoes, cooked until just tender and cut into ¼-inch-thick slices

Four 6-ounce cans solid white albacore tuna packed in spring water, drained

½ pound green beans, ends trimmed, blanched until crisp-tender

¾ pound ripe Roma tomatoes, cut into 1-inch cubes

6 hard-boiled eggs, peeled and halved lengthwise

1 medium red onion, thinly sliced (1 cup)

½ cup black olives, such as Niçoise or Kalamata, pitted and halved

½ cup green olives, pitted and halved

2 tablespoons capers, drained

4 to 6 anchovies (optional)

2 tablespoons thinly sliced fresh basil

French Vinaigrette (recipe follows)

1. Layer the ingredients in a large serving bowl in the order in which they are listed. (Note: a clear glass bowl works best for this salad.) Chill well until ready to serve, at least 2 hours and up to 4 hours. Make the salad dressing while the salad is chilling and refrigerate in a nonreactive container, or make the dressing up to 1 day in advance.

2. Just before serving, drizzle some of the dressing over the salad. Serve the remaining dressing on the side. (Alternatively, serve the dressing separately and allow

guests to dress their own salads— this way the salad will not become limp or soggy if it has to sit for any length of time.)

## FRENCH VINAIGRETTE

MAKES ABOUT 1 CUP

¼ cup red wine vinegar
4 teaspoons minced shallots
2 teaspoons Dijon mustard
½ teaspoon minced garlic
½ teaspoon salt
¼ teaspoon freshly ground black pepper
½ cup extra virgin olive oil
¼ cup vegetable oil

1. Combine the vinegar, shallots, mustard, garlic, salt, and pepper in a medium bowl and whisk to blend. Allow to sit for 15 minutes.

2. Add the oils in a thin, steady stream, whisking continuously, until the dressing thickens slightly. Taste and adjust seasoning if necessary.

# CURRIED CHICKEN SALAD

• MAKES 6 TO 8 SERVINGS •

This chicken salad is made with chicken that is marinated in oil and curry powder and other spices before it's seared. The cooked chicken is then combined with grapes, raisins, and toasted cashews, resulting in a chicken salad that makes a satisfying summertime addition to any potluck get-together.

2 pounds skinless, boneless chicken breasts, cut into 1-inch cubes

¼ cup vegetable oil

2 tablespoons curry powder

¾ teaspoon salt

¼ teaspoon cayenne pepper

1 medium red onion, finely chopped (1 cup)

2 tablespoons minced garlic

1 Granny Smith apple, cored and cut into ½-inch cubes

2 teaspoons fresh lime juice

⅓ cup Mayonnaise (page 6)

⅓ cup sour cream

½ pound seedless red or green grapes, halved (1½ cups)

⅔ cup raisins

½ cup roasted cashews

1. Place the chicken, 3 tablespoons of the vegetable oil, the curry powder, salt, and cayenne in a bowl and stir until the chicken is thoroughly coated with the oil and spices. Refrigerate, covered, for at least 1 hour and for up to 8 hours.

2. Heat a large skillet over high heat and, when hot, add the remaining tablespoon of vegetable oil. Add the chicken and cook, stirring occasionally, until golden brown around the edges and cooked through, 5 to 6 minutes. Using a slotted spoon, transfer the chicken to a clean large bowl and set aside to cool.

3. Lower the heat to medium-high and add the onion and garlic to the skillet. Cook, stirring occasionally, until the onion is translucent, 3 to 4 minutes. Add the onion and garlic to the chicken and set aside to cool before proceeding.

4. Add the apple, lime juice, mayonnaise, sour cream, grapes, and raisins to the bowl and stir to mix well. Serve immediately, or refrigerate, covered, until ready to serve. Garnish with the cashews just before serving. This salad is best served within 24 hours.

## — CURRIED CHICKEN SALAD —

Of course, chicken salad makes a great sandwich—so why not go way retro and make some finger sandwiches for your next lunch gathering. Just don't forget to cut the crust off the bread!

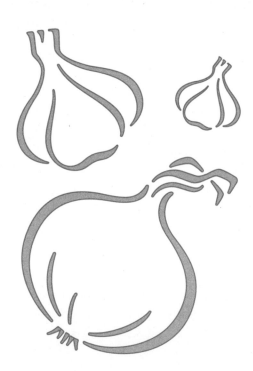

# ANTIPASTO PASTA SALAD

Here's your chance to enjoy two normally exclusive Italian favorites together in one dish! I've taken my favorite picks from an antipasto platter—provolone, salami, and prosciutto—and combined them with pasta, Italian herbs, and a simple oil-and-vinegar dressing to form one very kicked-up pasta salad. I think you'll agree that it's a marriage made in heaven. Just keep in mind, though, that this pasta salad doesn't benefit from refrigerator time—try to serve it as soon as you've finished assembling the ingredients. If you must refrigerate it, definitely bring it to room temperature before serving, and garnish with additional fresh herbs.

2 tablespoons plus ½ teaspoon salt

1 tablespoon olive oil

1 pound rotini pasta

2 teaspoons minced garlic

2 teaspoons balsamic vinegar

1 teaspoon Emeril's Italian Essence, or other dried Italian herb mixture

½ teaspoon freshly ground black pepper

¼ teaspoon crushed red pepper

¼ cup plus 2 tablespoons extra virgin olive oil

1½ cups ¼-inch cubes provolone

1 cup thinly sliced oil-packed sun-dried tomatoes, drained

1 cup thinly sliced salami (¼ pound)

1 cup thinly sliced prosciutto (¼ pound)

2 tablespoons finely chopped fresh parsley

2 tablespoons finely chopped fresh basil

1. Combine 2 tablespoons salt, the olive oil, and 4 quarts water in a large pot over high heat and bring to a boil. Add the rotini and cook, stirring occasionally to keep the pasta from sticking together, until just al dente, about 9 minutes.

2.   Meanwhile, mash together the garlic and remaining ½ teaspoon salt in a large bowl. Add the balsamic vinegar, Italian Essence, black pepper, and crushed red pepper. Whisk to blend. Gradually whisk in the olive oil.

3.   Drain the rotini and rinse under cold running water until cool. Add to the vinaigrette, along with the provolone, tomatoes, salami, prosciutto, parsley, and basil. Toss to mix. Serve immediately or cover and refrigerate until ready to serve. Let the salad return to room temperature before serving.

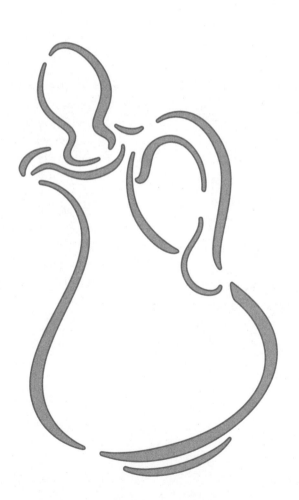

# ASIAN BROCCOLI SALAD

● MAKES 8 SERVINGS ●

Some version of broccoli salad always seems to show up at potluck gatherings—maybe a bit more often than some folks would like. But, hey, I've put a new twist on the classic recipe by uniting broccoli with some fresh Asian flavors, and I'm telling you—it's a knockout. Though you might see some unfamiliar ingredients listed here, don't panic: most of these ingredients are readily available in most supermarkets these days. If not, try your local specialty food store.

2 tablespoons soy sauce

2 teaspoons minced garlic

2 teaspoons minced fresh ginger

2 teaspoons minced green onions (white and green parts)

1 teaspoon Chinese hot mustard

1 teaspoon oyster sauce

½ cup rice wine vinegar

½ teaspoon crushed red pepper

¾ teaspoon salt

½ cup peanut, safflower, canola, or vegetable oil

2 tablespoons sesame oil

1½ cups thinly sliced carrots

1½ cups thinly sliced red bell peppers

4 pounds broccoli, cut into 1-inch florets

One 8-ounce can sliced water chestnuts

1 tablespoon toasted sesame seeds

8 wonton wrappers, cut into ⅛-inch strips

Vegetable oil, for frying

1. Combine the soy sauce, garlic, ginger, green onions, mustard, oyster sauce, rice wine vinegar, crushed red pepper, and salt in a medium bowl. Whisk to blend. Gradually whisk in the peanut oil and sesame oil until emulsified. Add the carrots and bell peppers and toss to coat. Cover and refrigerate overnight.

2. The next day, steam the broccoli until crisp-tender, about 5 minutes. Add the broccoli, water chestnuts, and sesame seeds to the carrot-pepper mixture. Toss to coat evenly and chill thoroughly before serving.

3. Fry the wonton strips in vegetable oil at 350°F for 45 to 60 seconds. Be sure to stir the wonton strips often to ensure even cooking and prevent sticking. Sprinkle the fried wonton strips on top of the salad just before serving.

# BLACK-EYED PEA SALAD

● MAKES 6 CUPS, 8 SERVINGS ●

In the deep South folks feel pretty strongly about their black-eyed peas! In fact, they love them so much that they even make a salad out of them! Here is my take on this contemporary Southern dish. This would be perfect to pack for a cookout or a picnic, especially with some cold fried chicken! Oh, baby!

5 cups cooked and drained dried black-eyed peas (see Note)

4 slices crisp cooked bacon, crumbled, fat reserved separately

½ cup plus 2 tablespoons red wine vinegar

½ cup olive oil

½ cup finely chopped red onions (½ medium onion)

½ cup finely chopped red bell peppers

3 tablespoons finely chopped green onions

2 tablespoons finely chopped jalapeños

2 tablespoons finely chopped fresh parsley

1½ teaspoons minced garlic

1½ teaspoons Emeril's Original Essence

¾ teaspoon salt

½ teaspoon freshly ground black pepper

1. Combine the black-eyed peas, bacon, 3 tablespoons reserved bacon fat, and all the remaining ingredients in a large bowl; toss well to combine. Cover and refrigerate for at least 4 hours or preferably overnight, stirring occasionally.

2. Allow the salad to sit at room temperature for 30 minutes before serving. Toss well just before serving.

NOTE    To make 5 cups cooked black-eyed peas: Soak 2 cups dried black-eyed peas for 4 hours. Drain the peas and place them in a large saucepan. Add water to cover by 2 inches and bring to a boil. Reduce the heat to a simmer and cook until just tender, 20 to 30 minutes. Drain and transfer to a bowl to cool.

— BETTER BEANS —

Bean dishes really improve with time. It takes a while for those babies to soak up all the flavors and really start kickin'. So make this salad (and really any bean dish) a day in advance for optimum performance!

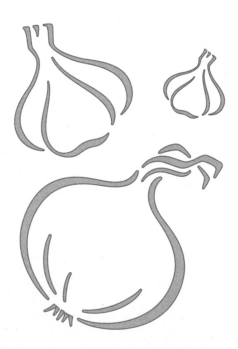

# CHARLOTTE'S
# GREEN BEAN SALAD

• MAKES 8 SERVINGS •

My friend Charlotte makes this salad in the summertime, when fresh green beans are widely available at markets and roadside stands. She says it is an updated, slightly more sophisticated version of a salad her grandmother made when she was a child.

2 pounds fresh green beans, ends
    trimmed
¼ cup red wine vinegar
2 teaspoons Dijon mustard
1½ teaspoons salt
¾ to 1 cup vegetable oil

Freshly ground black pepper,
    to taste
1 medium red onion, thinly sliced
6 large hard-boiled eggs, peeled and
    thinly sliced

1.   Fill a large heavy saucepan two-thirds full with salted water and bring to a boil. Add the green beans and blanch just until they are crisp-tender, 4 to 6 minutes. Transfer to an ice bath and set aside to cool. When the beans are cool, transfer them to a colander to drain.

2.   While the beans are draining, make the vinaigrette. In a large stainless steel or other nonreactive bowl, whisk together the vinegar, mustard, and salt. As you continue to whisk, add the oil in a thin, steady stream until the vinaigrette is emulsified. You may not need all the oil, depending on the acidity of the vinegar you are using. Season with pepper.

3.   Arrange the drained beans in a large shallow bowl or serving dish and scatter the sliced onion on top. Arrange the egg slices on top of the onion and pour the vinaigrette over all. The salad can be served immediately, or it can marinate in the vinaigrette, covered with plastic wrap and refrigerated, for up to several hours.

# Couscous Salad

· MAKES ABOUT 10 CUPS, 8 TO 10 SERVINGS ·

This light and refreshing salad has a surprising burst of flavor that comes from a combination of chopped vegetables and fruits. Cucumbers, apples, carrots, raisins, and pine nuts unite with other ingredients to make something that is truly delicious. Try it with the Olive-Stuffed Leg of Lamb for a traditional combination of Mediterranean flavors!

2 cups water

1 teaspoon salt

1 tablespoon olive oil

One 10-ounce package couscous

1 large or 2 small carrots, peeled and coarsely grated (¾ cup)

½ medium red bell pepper, seeded and finely minced (½ cup)

2 medium celery ribs, sliced thinly on the diagonal (1 cup)

½ medium red onion, finely chopped (½ cup)

1 sweet apple, such as Golden Delicious or Gala, cored and cut into ½-inch dice

1 medium cucumber, peeled, seeded, and chopped (1½ cups)

½ cup golden raisins

½ cup toasted pine nuts (3 ounces)

2 green onions, thinly sliced (⅓ cup)

¼ cup finely chopped fresh cilantro

### DRESSING

⅓ cup fresh lime juice

⅓ cup extra virgin olive oil

½ teaspoon ground cinnamon

½ teaspoon ground allspice

½ teaspoon ground cumin

¼ teaspoon salt

¼ teaspoon cayenne pepper

1. Combine the water, salt, and olive oil in a medium saucepan over medium-high heat and bring to a boil. Add the couscous and stir well. Cover and remove from the heat. Let stand 5 minutes, then toss gently with a fork. Let cool completely, tossing occasionally to ensure even cooling.

2.   Combine the cooled couscous in a large stainless steel or other nonreactive bowl with the carrots, bell pepper, celery, onion, apple, cucumber, raisins, pine nuts, green onions, and cilantro.

3.   Combine the ingredients for the dressing in a lidded jar and shake well to blend. Pour the dressing over the couscous mixture and toss to coat evenly. Taste and adjust seasoning if necessary. Let stand 30 minutes at room temperature before serving.

## — COUSCOUS —

Couscous is a grain-like pasta made from semolina (durum wheat) and can be used in salads, side dishes, or even desserts. It is used predominantly in North African cuisine with seasonings varying from country to country.

# EMERIL'S EGGPLANT SALAD

● MAKES ABOUT 6 CUPS, 8 SERVINGS ●

Eggplant. Some love it; others hate it. Some salt it; others don't. Well, I like eggplant; I don't salt it; and I'm happy! I am especially happy when I have a big bowl of this salad on hand. This is my version of the traditional Italian eggplant salad called caponata. I prefer to roast rather than sauté my eggplants—thus Emeril's Eggplant Salad. This is best made one day in advance—just be sure to taste before serving. You might want to add more salt and pepper.

- - - - - - - - - - - - - - - - - - - - - - - - - - - - - - - - - - - - - - - - - - - - - - - - - -

4 pounds eggplant, chopped
(about 18 cups)

1½ teaspoons freshly ground black
pepper

1 teaspoon salt

½ cup extra virgin olive oil

1 tablespoon olive oil

1½ cups chopped onions

1 tablespoon minced garlic

1 teaspoon Emeril's Italian Essence

3 cups coarsely chopped tomatoes

½ cup finely chopped oil-cured
black olives

2 tablespoons drained capers, plus
½ teaspoon caper juice

½ teaspoon red wine vinegar

2 tablespoons finely chopped fresh
parsley, plus more for garnish

1 tablespoon finely chopped fresh
basil, plus more for garnish

- - - - - - - - - - - - - - - - - - - - - - - - - - - - - - - - - - - - - - - - - - - - - - - - - -

1.    Preheat the oven to 400°F.

2.    Place the eggplant in a large roasting pan and season with 1 teaspoon black pepper and ½ teaspoon salt. Toss with the extra virgin olive oil. Roast until the eggplant is tender, 30 to 40 minutes. Remove from the oven and let cool.

3.    Meanwhile, heat the olive oil in a large skillet over medium heat. Add the onions and cook, stirring, until golden brown, about 10 minutes. Add the garlic and Italian Essence and cook until the garlic is fragrant, about 30 seconds. Add the tomatoes and cook until they begin to soften, about 2 minutes. Let cool.

4.    Once the eggplant and the onion mixture are cool, combine them in a large bowl. Add the olives, capers, caper juice, and vinegar. Stir to combine. Season with the remaining ½ teaspoon salt and ½ teaspoon black pepper and fold in the parsley and basil. Cover the salad and refrigerate for at least 6 hours.

5.    When ready to serve, let the salad return to room temperature. Just before serving, garnish with additional parsley and basil.

# Horseradish Coleslaw

• MAKES 8 TO 10 SERVINGS •

Have you ever tasted fresh horseradish? That's what makes this coleslaw special. That fiery root, tart apples, and a tangy dressing really shine together—cabbage never had it so good. Just be careful when you grate the horseradish—the fumes just might knock you off your feet! If you can't find fresh where you live, I've given instructions for using prepared horseradish, too.

5 cups shredded green cabbage

5 cups shredded red cabbage

2 cups shredded carrots

¼ cup finely sliced green onions

2 Granny Smith apples, cut into ¼-inch cubes

2 teaspoons fresh lemon juice

½ cup cider vinegar

¼ cup plus 1 tablespoon sugar

1½ teaspoons salt

1 teaspoon freshly ground black pepper

1 cup Mayonnaise (page 6)

¼ cup sour cream

6 tablespoons freshly grated horseradish or 3 tablespoons prepared horseradish

1 tablespoon Creole mustard or other coarse-grained mustard

1. Combine the green and red cabbages, carrots, and green onions in a large mixing bowl. In a small bowl toss the cubed apples with the lemon juice and add to cabbage mixture.

2. In a small mixing bowl combine the vinegar, sugar, salt, and pepper and whisk until the sugar is dissolved. Pour the seasoned vinegar mixture over the cabbage mixture and toss to thoroughly combine. Cover with plastic wrap and transfer to the refrigerator for 20 to 30 minutes.

3. In a small bowl combine the mayonnaise, sour cream, horseradish, and mustard and stir to combine. Add the mayonnaise mixture to the coleslaw and toss to combine thoroughly. Cover and refrigerate for at least one hour and up to overnight before serving.

# Emeril's Favorite Potato Salad

. MAKES 2 QUARTS, 8 TO 10 SERVINGS .

This is my all-time favorite potato salad—hence, the name. I just love this combination of flavors—salty bacon, creamy hard-boiled eggs, and tangy dressing. I do have a confession to make. Sometimes when I'm in a super rush I use bottled ranch dressing, and you know what?—it's okay. But it's not as good as when you make the dressing from scratch—I promise you you'll be glad you did.

14 small boiling potatoes, such as Red Bliss (about 2½ pounds), scrubbed well

8 slices crisp cooked bacon, crumbled

6 hard-boiled eggs, peeled and coarsely chopped

⅓ cup finely chopped red onions

⅓ cup finely chopped celery

1 recipe Homemade Ranch Dressing (recipe follows)

2 tablespoons finely chopped fresh parsley

1. Place the potatoes in a medium saucepan with enough water to cover by 1 inch. Bring to a boil over high heat, lower to a simmer, and cook until the potatoes are just tender, 15 to 20 minutes. Drain, let cool, then cut the potatoes into bite-size pieces.

2. In a large mixing bowl, combine the potatoes with all the remaining ingredients and gently toss. Refrigerate the salad several hours before serving to allow the flavors to blend.

# HOMEMADE RANCH DRESSING

MAKES ABOUT 1¼ CUPS

2 teaspoons minced garlic

1¼ teaspoons salt

¾ cup Mayonnaise (page 6)

½ cup buttermilk

1 tablespoon plus 1 teaspoon finely chopped celery leaves

1 tablespoon plus 1 teaspoon finely chopped green onions

1 tablespoon plus 1 teaspoon finely chopped fresh parsley

2 teaspoons fresh lemon juice

1 teaspoon Emeril's Original Essence

¾ teaspoon freshly ground black pepper

Mash together the garlic and ¼ teaspoon salt in a medium bowl. Add the mayonnaise and buttermilk and whisk to blend. Add the celery leaves, green onions, parsley, lemon juice, Essence, black pepper, and remaining 1 teaspoon salt. Stir to blend.

# ROASTED POTATO AND GARLIC SALAD

• MAKES 8 SERVINGS •

Roasting vegetables really brings out their underlying sugary side. Potatoes and garlic become especially sweet when roasted, and that's why they're a perfect match here. I add fresh rosemary and green onions to the roasted garlic in the dressing for an herbaceous flavor (but you could throw in a bit of sage as well!). This rather elegant potato salad even stands up to the grandeur of the Creole Mustard and Herb-Wrapped Beef Tenderloin (page 188). It is best when served warm or at room temperature.

4 pounds new potatoes, cut into bite-size pieces

1¼ cups extra virgin olive oil

1¼ teaspoons salt

1 teaspoon freshly ground black pepper

1 head garlic, top ½ inch cut off

1 tablespoon olive oil

2 cups chopped sweet onions, such as Vidalia

1 large egg

½ cup chopped green onions

1 tablespoon plus 1 teaspoon fresh lemon juice

2 teaspoons fresh rosemary

2 tablespoons finely chopped fresh parsley

1. Preheat the oven to 400°F.

2. Place the potatoes in a large roasting pan and toss with ¼ cup of the extra virgin olive oil. Season with ½ teaspoon salt and ½ teaspoon pepper. Wrap the garlic head in foil and add to the pan. Roast the potatoes and garlic until tender, 35 to 40 minutes. Remove from the oven and let stand until cool enough to handle.

3.   Meanwhile, heat the olive oil in a large skillet over medium heat. Add the onions and cook until golden brown, about 10 minutes. Remove from the heat.

4.   Once the garlic is cool enough to handle, squeeze as much pulp as possible from the head into the bowl of a food processor. Add the egg, green onions, lemon juice, rosemary, remaining ¾ teaspoon salt, and remaining ½ teaspoon pepper. Puree until smooth. With the machine running, slowly add the remaining 1 cup extra virgin olive oil. The mixture will thicken.

5.   Combine the potatoes and onions in a large bowl. Toss with 1 cup of the garlic dressing and the parsley. Serve immediately.

## — ROASTED POTATO AND GARLIC SALAD —

This salad makes use of one of my favorite kitchen tricks—roasting garlic. If you have never done this, then you should really try it. The garlic turns a beautiful nutty brown and tastes like candy. I like to use roasted garlic in salad dressings, sauces, and just smeared on bread. Use it to kick up everything!

# Retro Ambrosia

. MAKES ABOUT 8 CUPS, 8 SERVINGS .

Please, please, quit your crying about how you cannot stand ambrosia. This isn't your mama's ambrosia! While I like a lot of classic potluck dishes, classic ambrosia just needs a little something. I found that something by using fresh fruit. I kept that creamy dressing everyone loves, but when combined with fresh fruit and toasted nuts, the results are positively heavenly!

½ cup cream cheese, at room temperature (about 4 ounces)

½ cup sour cream

1 tablespoon plus 2 teaspoons light brown sugar

1 tablespoon fresh lemon juice

1 ripe pineapple, peeled, cored, and chopped (about 5½ cups)

1 pound ripe cherries, pitted and halved (about 2½ cups)

3 oranges, peeled and sliced (about 1 cup)

2 grapefruit, peeled and sliced (about ½ cup)

1 cup toasted pecans (7 minutes at 350°F)

1 cup toasted coconut (10 minutes at 350°F)

Combine the cream cheese, sour cream, brown sugar, and lemon juice in a large bowl. Whisk to blend. Add the pineapple, cherries, oranges, grapefruit, and pecans and stir to mix. Place in a serving dish, garnish with the coconut, and serve immediately.

## — AMBROSIA —

Bet you didn't know that *ambrosia* was the word used to describe the food and drink of the Greek and Roman gods. And its Latin root means "immortality"—so have some!

# SOUPS AND GUMBOS

I think of soups as having a lot of soul. By that I mean that these dishes have heart, spirit, and character made just so by the right combination of great ingredients. One of my favorites, Portuguese Tomato and Sausage Soup, combines tomatoes and sausage simmered with plenty of garlic and herbs. Make this for a potluck party and you are sure to be invited back!

That brings me to the other great thing about soups—they feed a crowd. What could be better than a big vat of Emeril's Classic Seafood Gumbo on a cold winter night? Or in the hot summer, cool off with chilled soups, like Gazpacho or Cold Cucumber Soup, both of which make the most of garden-fresh vegetables at their peak.

Soups can be made ahead of time, stored in airtight containers in the refrigerator, and then simmered while other dishes are being arranged for the rest of the meal. Most of them can be frozen and then given out as housewarming or get-well gifts—make someone happy, happy!

# BLACK BEAN SOUP

• MAKES 2 QUARTS, 8 SERVINGS •

Try this black bean soup for a taste of the islands—with hints of ginger, cinnamon, and orange, this vegetarian version is bound to inspire! Whip up a batch of the Simply Salsa on page 8; it's the perfect garnish for this soup and really makes the flavors come alive. Also, keep in mind that, like many soups, this soup is best when made a day in advance so that all the flavors have time to marry.

2 cups chopped onions

1 cup chopped celery

1 cup chopped carrots

1 cup chopped green bell peppers

2 tablespoons finely chopped seeded jalapeños

2 teaspoons minced fresh ginger

1 tablespoon olive oil

⅓ cup minced garlic

2 teaspoons ground cumin

¼ teaspoon ground cinnamon

1 pound dried black beans, picked over and rinsed

12 cups water

⅓ cup chopped cilantro stems and leaves

½ orange, unpeeled

1 tablespoon salt

1½ teaspoons Emeril's Kick It Up! Red Pepper Sauce, or more to taste

Simply Salsa (page 8)

Combine the onions, celery, carrots, bell peppers, jalapeños, and ginger in a large pot with the olive oil and cook over medium heat until the vegetables are soft, about 12 minutes. Add the garlic, cumin, and cinnamon and cook for 2 minutes. Add the beans, water, cilantro, orange, and salt. Bring to a boil and then reduce to a simmer. Cook, partially covered, for 2½ to 3 hours, or until beans are very tender and soup begins to get creamy. (Add more water if the soup becomes too thick.) Remove the orange before serving. Season with the hot sauce to taste. Serve with the salsa.

# CHEESE AND BEER SOUP

Now, this is my kind of soup—cheese *and* beer. This baby is rockin'! Of course, some of you folks might be a little intimidated by such an over-the-top combination, but let me assure you that this soup is good eating. I prefer less cheese than most recipes call for because this is soup, not a cheese dip, and the beer actually cuts the richness a bit. As for the sausage and the cheesy popcorn garnish—well, sometimes you just need to live a little! Test out my theory at your next cold weather–tailgating bash—you will make many mouths happy, happy.

½ pound kielbasa sausage, finely chopped

3 tablespoons olive oil

2 cups chopped yellow onions

1 teaspoon salt

½ teaspoon freshly ground black pepper

2 bay leaves

3 tablespoons minced garlic

½ cup all-purpose flour

6 cups Chicken Stock (page 4)

2 cups lager beer, preferably amber

1½ teaspoons chopped fresh thyme

3 cups grated Cheddar cheese
(12 ounces or ¾ pound)

Cheesy Popcorn (recipe follows)

2 tablespoons minced fresh chives,
for garnish

1. Cook the kielbasa in the olive oil in a large heavy soup pot over high heat until golden brown, 5 to 6 minutes. Add the onions, salt, black pepper, and bay leaves and cook, stirring, until the onions are slightly caramelized, 12 to 15 minutes. Add the garlic and cook, stirring, until fragrant, about 1 minute. Sprinkle the flour over the onions and cook, stirring constantly, for 2 minutes. Gradually whisk in the stock and the beer. Add the thyme and bring to a boil. Reduce the heat to medium-low and simmer uncovered, stirring occasionally, for 1 hour.

2. Add the cheese, a little at a time, stirring until nearly melted after each addition. Remove from the heat, taste, and adjust seasoning if necessary.

3. Ladle the soup into bowls and garnish with the Cheesy Popcorn and minced fresh chives.

## CHEESY POPCORN

MAKES ABOUT 10 CUPS

3 tablespoons olive oil
⅓ cup white popping corn
4 tablespoons unsalted butter, melted
½ teaspoon salt, or to taste
½ cup finely grated Parmesan cheese

In a large, partially covered saucepan, heat the olive oil and 1 kernel of popcorn until hot enough to make the corn pop. Add the remaining popcorn and cook, partially covered, shaking until all the corn is popped. Transfer to a large mixing bowl and toss with the remaining ingredients until evenly coated. Garnish each serving of the soup with a handful of the popcorn.

# Portuguese Tomato and Sausage Soup

• MAKES ABOUT 3 QUARTS, 12 SERVINGS •

This is a soup from my family's native country of Portugal. And, boy, is it good! As you might know, there are few foods I love more than sausage. Here I call for two of Portugal's most popular sausages—linguiça and chouriço, dry sausages with plenty of gaaahlic! If you cannot find them at your local specialty food store, then substitute a similar sausage, such as Spanish chorizo, for both.

4 slices bacon, diced

½ pound linguiça, finely chopped, and ½ pound linguiça, cut into ¼-inch-thick slices

½ pound chouriço, finely chopped, and ½ pound chouriço, cut into ¼-inch-thick slices

2 cups finely chopped red onions

1 tablespoon plus 1 teaspoon Emeril's Original Essence

½ teaspoon crushed red pepper

2 tablespoons minced garlic

2 bay leaves

8 cups chopped seeded tomatoes

6 cups Chicken Stock (page 4)

Salt and freshly ground black pepper, to taste

½ cup finely chopped fresh cilantro

Crusty bread, for serving

Cook the bacon in a medium pot over medium heat for about 2 minutes. Add the sausages and cook with the bacon until browned, about 5 more minutes. Add the onions and Essence and cook, stirring often, until the onions are softened, about 5 minutes. Add the crushed red pepper and garlic and cook until fragrant, about 30 seconds. Add the bay leaves, tomatoes, and Chicken Stock and stir to combine. Bring to a boil, reduce the heat, and simmer for about 30 minutes. Season to taste with salt and black pepper. Stir in the cilantro, ladle into warm soup bowls, and serve with crusty bread.

# — PORTUGUESE TOMATO AND SAUSAGE SOUP —

This soup hails from northern Portugal, where they specialize in sausage making. It calls for chouriço and linguiça—two of Portugal's most famous sausages. But if you're fortunate enough to have a source for other Portuguese sausages such as alheira, azedo, farinheira, morcela, and paio, try them.

# Roasted Garlic Soup

• MAKES ABOUT 2 QUARTS, 8 SERVINGS •

This soup is totally loaded with garlic, onions, and shallots, which are all alliums, members of the onion family. But, boy, is it good! All those intense flavors roast down to sweet, sweet goodness and make a soup that is out of this world. Don't skip the touch of balsamic vinegar at the end because it really balances the soup's flavors. This soup is elegant enough to serve at any dinner party.

4 to 6 large red onions (3½ pounds), quartered

Cloves from 2 large heads of garlic (about 1 cup), peeled

2 shallots (about ⅓ cup), peeled

2 tablespoons olive oil

2 tablespoons Emeril's Original Essence

6 cups Chicken Stock (page 4)

2 teaspoons finely chopped fresh sage

2 teaspoons finely chopped fresh thyme

¾ teaspoon salt

2 teaspoons balsamic vinegar

½ cup heavy cream

French bread, for serving

1. Preheat the oven to 400°F. Combine the onions, garlic, and shallots in a roasting pan just large enough to hold them in a single layer. Add the olive oil and Essence and toss to coat. Roast until well browned, about 1½ hours.

2. Remove the pan from the oven and set over two burners on medium-low heat. Add 2 cups of Chicken Stock, the sage, thyme, and salt and cook for 10 minutes, scraping up any browned bits from the bottom of the pan with a wooden spoon.

3. Transfer the mixture to a blender and puree until smooth, about 2 minutes.

4. Scrape the puree into a large pot over medium-low heat. Add the remaining 4 cups Chicken Stock and the balsamic vinegar and stir to combine. Bring to a simmer and stir in the cream. Serve with French bread.

# SOUTHERN-STYLE
# CORN CHOWDER

• MAKES 3 QUARTS, 10 TO 12 SERVINGS •

This is the perfect soup to make in the late summer months when corn is at its prime and you can find fresh ears for sale at roadside stands and farmers' markets. I've fashioned this version after traditional Southern-style corn soup, because it pairs corn with one of my very best friends, bacon. Oh, baby, talk about a match made in heaven! If you can't find fresh ears of corn, you could substitute frozen, but the taste won't be quite the same.

4 ounces bacon, chopped
1 cup finely chopped onions
½ cup finely chopped carrots
½ cup finely chopped celery
2 tablespoons minced garlic
¾ cup finely chopped red bell peppers
5 cups fresh corn kernels (from about 7 ears)
¼ cup all-purpose flour

2 quarts Chicken Stock (page 4) or canned low-sodium chicken broth
1½ cups ½-inch cubes peeled russet potatoes
1 tablespoon salt
¼ teaspoon cayenne pepper
1 cup heavy cream
Finely chopped fresh parsley, for garnish

Place an 8-quart stockpot over medium heat and cook the bacon until crispy, about 5 minutes. Remove the bacon and drain on paper towels. Add the onions, carrots, and celery and cook, stirring often, until vegetables are soft, about 5 minutes. Add the garlic and cook until fragrant, about 30 seconds. Add the bell peppers and corn to the pot and cook for 10 minutes, stirring often. Sprinkle the flour into the pot and cook, stirring constantly, for 5 minutes. Pour the Chicken Stock into the pot and stir to combine. Use a whisk if necessary to break up any lumps. Add the potatoes to the pot and bring to a boil, then reduce to a simmer and continue to cook for 20 minutes. Season the chowder with the salt and cayenne and stir in the cream. Serve with the bacon and parsley as garnish.

# NEW ENGLAND
# CLAM CHOWDER

• MAKES 4 QUARTS, 12 SERVINGS •

Nothing tastes better on a cold winter day than a big bowl of New England clam chowder. Talk about a dish that takes me back! Now, the chopping takes a bit of time, but the rest is easy. And you will not believe the result—a truly incredible soup fit for a simple lunch or an elegant dinner!

10 pounds small quahogs or large cherrystone clams, scrubbed and rinsed, open clams discarded

6 slices bacon, cut crosswise into ½-inch strips

4 tablespoons unsalted butter

2 medium leeks, white and light green parts only, halved lengthwise and thinly sliced crosswise (2½ to 3 cups)

1 cup finely chopped onions

1 cup finely chopped celery

2 teaspoons minced garlic

6 sprigs fresh thyme

2 bay leaves

2 pounds potatoes, peeled and cut into ½-inch cubes (about 5 cups)

2 cups heavy cream

½ teaspoon freshly ground black pepper

1¼ teaspoons salt, or to taste

6 tablespoons cold unsalted butter, cut into half-tablespoon pieces

¼ cup finely chopped fresh parsley

¼ cup finely chopped fresh chives or green onions

1.    In a large stockpot bring 3 cups of water to a boil. Add the clams, cover, and cook for 5 minutes. Uncover the pot and quickly stir the clams with a wooden spoon. Cover and cook 5 to 10 minutes longer (this will depend on the type and size of the clams), or until most of the clams are open.

2. Transfer the clams to a large bowl or baking dish and strain the broth twice through a fine-mesh sieve into a bowl, being careful to strain out the sand. (You should have about 8 cups of clam broth. If not, add enough water to bring the volume up to 8 cups.) When the clams are cool enough to handle, remove them from their shells and chop into ½-inch pieces. Set the clams and broth aside.

3. Cook the bacon in a large heavy pot over medium heat until crisp and the fat is rendered. Pour off all the bacon fat except 2 tablespoons. Add the 4 tablespoons butter, leeks, onions, and celery and cook until softened, about 5 minutes. Add the garlic, thyme, and bay leaves and cook until the vegetables are thoroughly wilted, about 3 minutes, being careful not to brown. Add the potatoes and reserved clam broth and bring to a boil. Lower the heat, cover, and simmer until the broth thickens slightly and the potatoes are very tender, about 30 minutes. (If you like a thicker broth, mash some of the potatoes against the side of the pot with a wooden spoon.) Remove from the heat, stir in the clams and cream, and season with the pepper and the salt to taste.

4. Set the chowder aside for 1 hour, covered, to allow the flavors to marry. Place the pot over low heat and slowly reheat, being careful not to let boil. Serve hot; garnish each bowl with a pat of butter and some parsley and chives.

# Manhattan Clam Chowder

• MAKES 3 QUARTS, 10 SERVINGS •

Sometimes Manhattan clam chowder, which is tomato based as opposed to the cream-based New England clam chowder, can be a bit blah. So I decided to kick mine up with some red pepper and cilantro. These bright flavors really bring out the beauty of this dish.

- - - - - - - - - - - - - - - - - - - - - - - - - - - - - - - - - - - - - - - - - - - - - - - - - - -

10 pounds small quahogs or large cherrystone clams, scrubbed and rinsed, open clams discarded

4 slices bacon, cut crosswise into ½-inch strips

2 cups finely chopped onions

1 cup finely chopped celery

½ cup finely chopped green bell peppers

¾ cup finely chopped carrots

1½ tablespoons minced garlic

3 bay leaves

1½ teaspoons dried oregano

4 sprigs fresh thyme

½ teaspoon crushed red pepper

1¼ pounds potatoes, peeled and cut into ½-inch cubes (about 3 cups)

1 cup Chicken Stock (page 4)

5 cups peeled and finely chopped tomatoes (about 4 large tomatoes), or one 28-ounce can whole tomatoes, finely chopped and juice reserved

¼ cup tomato paste

¼ cup plus 2 tablespoons finely chopped fresh cilantro, plus more for garnish

½ teaspoon freshly ground black pepper

Salt, to taste

- - - - - - - - - - - - - - - - - - - - - - - - - - - - - - - - - - - - - - - - - - - - - - - - - - -

1. In a large stockpot, bring 3 cups of water to a boil. Add the clams, cover, and cook for 5 minutes. Uncover the pot and quickly stir the clams with a wooden spoon. Cover and cook 5 to 10 minutes longer (this will depend on the type and size of the clams), or until most of the clams are open.

2. Transfer the clams to a large bowl or baking dish and strain the broth twice through a fine-mesh sieve into a bowl, being careful to strain out the sand. (You should have about 8 cups of clam broth. If not, add enough water to bring the volume up to 8 cups.) When the clams are cool enough to handle, remove them from their shells and chop into ½-inch pieces. Set the clams and broth aside.

3. Cook the bacon in a large stockpot over medium heat until golden and crispy, about 3 minutes. Pour off all the fat except 4 tablespoons. Add the onions, celery, bell peppers, and carrots and cook until softened, about 10 minutes. Add the garlic, bay leaves, oregano, thyme, and crushed red pepper and cook an additional 2 minutes. Increase the heat to high and add the potatoes, reserved clam broth, and Chicken Stock and bring to a boil, covered. Reduce to a simmer and cook until the potatoes are tender and the broth has thickened somewhat, about 20 minutes. Add the tomatoes and juice and tomato paste and continue to cook for 10 to 15 minutes. Remove the pot from the heat and add the reserved clams, the cilantro, and the black pepper and season to taste with salt.

4. Set the chowder aside for 1 hour, covered, to allow the flavors to marry. Place the pot over low heat and slowly reheat, being careful not to bring to a boil. Serve hot, garnished with more cilantro.

# Golden Shrimp Stew

This soup is a Peruvian dish with the unusual seasoning combination of turmeric, mustard, and saffron, which complements the shrimp. Host an international potluck dinner and serve this bright stew—your friends will be licking their bowls!

¼ cup olive oil

2 cups finely chopped onions

2 cups finely chopped red bell peppers

2 tablespoons minced jalapeños

2 tablespoons minced garlic

2 teaspoons turmeric

1 teaspoon mustard powder

½ teaspoon saffron threads, soaked in 1 tablespoon of water for 20 minutes

2 cups dry white wine

6 cups Shrimp Stock (page 10)

2 cups diced new potatoes

2 cups diced tomatoes

2 pounds medium shrimp, peeled and deveined

1 teaspoon salt

¼ cup plus 2 tablespoons finely chopped fresh cilantro

Heat the oil in a large stockpot or Dutch oven. Add the onions, bell peppers, and jalapeños and cook, stirring, until the vegetables begin to soften, about 5 minutes. Add the garlic and cook until fragrant, about 30 seconds. Add the turmeric, mustard, and saffron and stir to combine. Add the wine and cook another 2 minutes. Add the Shrimp Stock and potatoes and bring to a boil. Boil for 5 minutes. Lower to a simmer and add the tomatoes. Cook for 20 minutes. Add the shrimp and simmer until cooked through, about 4 minutes longer. Season with the salt. Stir in the cilantro, remove from the heat, and serve.

# OYSTERS ROCKEFELLER SOUP

• MAKES 2 QUARTS, 8 SERVINGS •

This soup is a popular takeoff on the legendary New Orleans dish Oysters Rockefeller. Both are found on menus all over, including NOLA, and for good reason—they are delicious! After all, how can you go wrong with oysters, spinach, and bacon? I top mine with some Crispy Brie Croutons. Talk about food of love!

- 4 slices bacon, chopped
- 1 small onion, finely chopped
- 2 teaspoons minced garlic
- 1 pint oysters with their liquor
- 4 cups heavy cream
- 1 pound fresh spinach, well washed and stems removed
- 4 teaspoons salt
- 2 teaspoons freshly ground white pepper
- ½ cup Herbsaint or other anise-flavored liqueur, such as Pernod or Ouzo
- Cripsy Brie Croutons (recipe follows), for serving

1. In a large heavy stockpot, cook the bacon, stirring constantly, over medium-high heat until browned, about 5 minutes. Add the onion, stirring occasionally, and cook until soft, about 5 minutes. Add the garlic and cook for 1 minute, stirring constantly. Add the oysters, the oyster liquor, and the cream and bring the mixture to a boil. Remove the pot from the heat.

2. Using an immersion blender, or working with batches in a blender, puree the ingredients, adding the spinach in batches as you puree. Season with the salt and white pepper and stir in the Herbsaint.

3. Serve with the Crispy Brie Croutons.

# CRISPY BRIE CROUTONS

MAKES 16 CROUTONS

Sixteen ¼-inch slices French bread
1 large garlic clove, peeled and smashed
½ pound Brie cheese, thinly sliced, divided evenly

1. Preheat the oven to 350°F.

2. Place the sliced bread in one layer on a large baking sheet and bake until lightly browned on both sides, turning once, about 4 minutes per side. Remove the bread from the oven and rub the garlic over one side of each slice. Top each bread slice with a slice of cheese and bake until the cheese is bubbly, about 4 minutes.

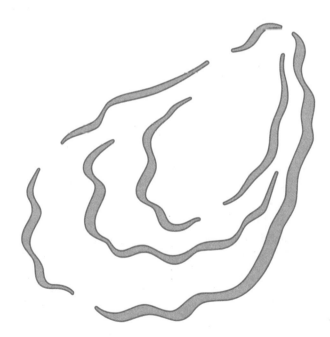

# SHRIMP, OKRA, AND TOMATO GUMBO

• MAKES 3 QUARTS, 10 TO 12 SERVINGS •

Now, I know that there are a lot of people out there who swear that they don't like okra. I am willing to bet that a lot of folks actually like okra and just don't know it. See, okra has an image problem, specifically a slimy image problem. And with this gumbo I want to set the record straight—okra is awesome when cooked correctly. Here the okra thickens the gumbo and flavors the shrimp and tomatoes to create a perfect union. Trust me—this gumbo might just make a believer out of you!

2 pounds okra

2 tablespoons olive oil

1 pound andouille or other smoked sausage, sliced into ¼-inch rounds

2 cups peeled, seeded, and finely chopped fresh tomatoes, or 2 cups finely chopped canned tomatoes

1 cup finely chopped onions

½ cup finely chopped green bell peppers

½ cup finely chopped celery

1 tablespoon minced garlic

2¼ teaspoons salt

¼ teaspoon cayenne pepper

2 bay leaves

½ teaspoon dried thyme

2 quarts Shrimp Stock (page 10), or water

2 pounds medium shrimp, peeled and deveined

2 teaspoons Emeril's Original Essence

Finely chopped fresh parsley and thinly sliced tender green onion tops, for garnish

White Rice (recipe follows), for serving

1. Wash the okra in cool water. Trim the stems and tips and cut into ¼-inch rounds.

2. Heat the olive oil in a large pot over medium-high heat. Add the sausage and cook, stirring often, to render out the fat, about 5 minutes. Add the okra and cook, stirring

constantly, for 10 to 12 minutes, or until most of the slime disappears. Add the tomatoes, onions, bell peppers, celery, and garlic and cook, stirring often, for 10 minutes, or until the okra and other vegetables are soft and the slime has completely disappeared. Add the salt, cayenne, bay leaves, thyme, and Shrimp Stock.

3. Season the shrimp with the Essence and set aside. Stir the pot and bring the contents to a boil. Reduce the heat to medium and simmer, uncovered, for 15 minutes. Add the shrimp and cook, stirring occasionally, for 30 minutes.

4. Remove the bay leaves, garnish with the parsley and green onion tops, and serve in shallow bowls over white rice.

• • • • • • • • • • • • • • • • • • • • • • • • • • • • • • • • • • • • • • • •

## WHITE RICE

MAKES 7 CUPS

2 cups long-grain white rice
4 cups water, Chicken Stock (page 4),
   or canned low-sodium chicken broth
1½ teaspoons salt
2 bay leaves

1. In a 2-quart saucepan, combine the rice, water, salt, and bay leaves and bring to a boil over high heat. Reduce the heat to low, cover, and simmer until all the liquid is absorbed, about 20 minutes. Remove the pan from the heat and let sit, covered, for 10 minutes.

2. Fluff the rice with a fork, and remove the bay leaves before serving.

• • • • • • • • • • • • • • • • • • • • • • • • • • • • • • • • • • • • • • • •

# EMERIL'S CLASSIC SEAFOOD GUMBO

• MAKES 3 QUARTS, 10 TO 12 SERVINGS •

There are a lot of seafood gumbo recipes out there, which is why I wanted to give you a classic, basic version that is ideal for a potluck party. Sometimes you don't need all those bells and whistles, just a good ol' dish, like this seafood gumbo.

¾ cup vegetable oil

1 cup all-purpose flour

1½ cups finely chopped onions

¾ cup finely chopped green bell peppers

¾ cup finely chopped celery

2 tablespoons minced garlic

One 12-ounce bottle amber beer

6 cups Shrimp Stock (page 10)

¼ teaspoon dried thyme

2 bay leaves

½ pound gumbo crabs (about 2)

2 teaspoons Worcestershire sauce

1 tablespoon salt

½ teaspoon cayenne pepper

1 pound medium shrimp, peeled and deveined

1 pound white fish fillets, such as catfish, grouper, snapper, or sole

1 tablespoon Emeril's Original Essence

2 cups shucked oysters with their liquor

¼ cup chopped fresh parsley

½ cup chopped tender green onion tops

White Rice (page 107), for serving

1. Place an 8-quart stockpot over medium heat, and add the oil. Allow the oil to heat for about 5 minutes, then add the flour to the pot. Stir the oil and flour together with a wooden spoon to form a roux. Continue to stir the roux for 20 to 25 minutes, or until the color of milk chocolate. Add the onions, bell peppers, and celery to the roux and stir to blend. Stir the vegetables for 5 minutes, then add the garlic. Cook the garlic for 30 seconds before adding the beer and Shrimp Stock to the pot. Season the gumbo with the thyme, bay leaves, gumbo crabs, Worcestershire, salt, and cayenne. Bring the gumbo to a boil and lower the heat to a simmer. Continue to simmer the gumbo for 1 hour, skimming the foam and any oil that rises to the surface.

2.	Season both the shrimp and the catfish with 1½ teaspoons Essence. Stir the shrimp and fish into the gumbo and cook for 2 minutes. Add the oysters to the pot and cook, stirring often, for an additional 5 minutes. Taste the gumbo and season if necessary.

3.	Garnish with the parsley and green onions and serve in shallow bowls over white rice.

## — SEAFOOD GUMBO —

I call this a "classic" seafood gumbo for a couple of reasons. First, I start with a roux, which is a mixture of cooked flour and fat that is often used to start and thicken soups and stews. Second, I use gumbo crabs, smaller crabs that do not yield as much meat for picking. Consequently, they are sold to use as flavoring in gumbo. If the gumbo variety are not available in your area, feel free to use larger crabs.

# POTATO AND LEEK SOUP

This classic French soup is great warm or cold—depending on your mood and the season. To serve warm, simply follow the recipe. To serve chilled, thin the cold soup with some milk or water and adjust the seasonings, because cold soups require a bit more salt and pepper. Either way this soup makes an impressive addition to a lunch or dinner party.

1 tablespoon olive oil
3 tablespoons unsalted butter
¼ cup diced cooked ham
1 cup chopped onions
½ cup chopped celery
½ cup chopped parsnips
1 tablespoon minced garlic
1½ pounds thinly sliced washed leeks (white part only; about 6 cups)

2 teaspoons chopped fresh thyme
2 quarts Chicken Stock (page 4)
1½ pounds russet potatoes, peeled and diced
2½ teaspoons salt
1¼ teaspoons freshly ground white pepper
1½ cups heavy cream
½ cup finely chopped fresh parsley, for garnish

Place an 8-quart stockpot over medium heat, and add the olive oil to it. Once the oil is hot, about 1 minute, add the butter. Once the butter has melted, add the ham and sear, browning on all sides, 3 to 4 minutes. Add the onions, celery, and parsnips to the pot and cook, stirring often, for 5 minutes. Once the vegetables are cooked, add the garlic to the pan and cook until fragrant, about 30 seconds. Follow with the leeks and thyme. Cook the leeks, stirring often, for 10 minutes. Pour the stock into the pot and bring the contents to a boil, then reduce to a simmer. Add the potatoes, salt, and white pepper and cook until the potatoes are tender, 20 to 25 minutes. Remove the pot from the heat, and puree the soup with an immersion blender, or in batches in a bar blender. Return the pureed soup to the stove and bring to a simmer. Add the cream to the soup and cook for 2 to 3 minutes. Taste the soup and season if necessary. Serve garnished with parsley.

# COLD CUCUMBER SOUP

● MAKES 2½ QUARTS, 8 TO 10 SERVINGS ●

Down here in New Orleans, we are always in search of new ways to cool off during the many hot months, and I think cold soups are the perfect solution. This vegetarian cucumber soup requires very little work; you don't even have to use the stovetop! Serve this at your next patio get-together and watch as everyone chills out.

6 pounds cucumbers (about 6), peeled, seeded, and coarsely chopped (12 cups)

2 yellow bell peppers, coarsely chopped

4 green onions, chopped (6 tablespoons)

2 minced jalapeños (3 tablespoons)

2 tablespoons finely chopped fresh cilantro

1 tablespoon finely chopped fresh mint

1 tablespoon finely chopped fresh dill

3 to 4 garlic cloves, mashed to a paste with 1 teaspoon salt

2 teaspoons Emeril's Original Essence

1½ teaspoons salt

½ teaspoon cayenne pepper

3 cups plain yogurt

3 cups sour cream

3 tablespoons extra virgin olive oil

2 teaspoons white wine vinegar

2 tablespoons minced fresh chives, for garnish

Combine the cucumbers, bell peppers, green onions, jalapeños, cilantro, mint, dill, garlic, Essence, salt, cayenne, yogurt, 2 cups of the sour cream, the olive oil, and white wine vinegar in a large bowl. Working in batches, puree the ingredients in a blender until very smooth. Transfer the soup to the refrigerator until well chilled, at least 2 hours. Taste and adjust the seasoning. Serve the soup in bowls, garnished with a dollop of the remaining sour cream and some of the minced chives.

# Gazpacho

MAKES 3 QUARTS, 10 TO 12 SERVINGS

Gazpacho is one of those dishes that has evolved so much that there are now countless variations. I prefer the lighter contemporary versions to the traditional bread-laden ones. Here I finely chop a bunch of sweet summer vegetables and marinate them in tomato juice, vinegar, and olive oil until they are positively dancing together! I do puree mine a bit to give the soup a little body—you could puree more or less according to your own taste. And you could also kick it up with some fresh seafood like crabmeat, boiled shrimp, or even boiled lobster. Play with your gazpacho and create your own evolution!

- 4 ripe medium tomatoes (about 2 pounds), cored and cut into ¼-inch cubes (about 5 cups), juice reserved
- 2 small red bell peppers (about 1 pound), cored, seeded, and cut into ¼-inch cubes (about 2 cups)
- 2 small cucumbers (about 1 pound), peeled, seeded, and cut into ¼-inch cubes (about 2 cups)
- ½ small sweet onion, peeled and minced (about ½ cup)
- 2 celery ribs, cut into ¼-inch cubes (about ½ cup)
- ¼ cup finely sliced green onions
- 2 medium garlic cloves, minced (about 1½ teaspoons)
- 1 tablespoon minced jalapeños
- 1 tablespoon plus 1 teaspoon finely chopped fresh herbs, such as cilantro or basil
- 3 tablespoons sherry vinegar
- 2½ teaspoons salt
- ½ teaspoon freshly ground black pepper
- 5 cups V8 juice
- 3 tablespoons extra virgin olive oil
- 1 teaspoon Emeril's Kick It Up! Red Pepper Sauce
- Crusty bread or croutons, for serving

EMERIL'S POTLUCK

112

Combine the tomatoes and their juice, bell peppers, cucumbers, onion, celery, green onions, garlic, jalapeños, herbs, vinegar, salt, and pepper in a large (at least 4-quart) nonreactive bowl or container. Let stand until the vegetables just begin to release their juices, about 5 minutes. Stir in the V8 juice, olive oil, and hot sauce. Transfer 6 cups of the mixture to a blender (working in batches if necessary) and puree until mostly smooth. Return the pureed mixture to the bowl and stir to combine. Cover tightly and refrigerate for at least 4 hours, or preferably overnight, to allow the flavors to marry. Adjust the seasoning if necessary and serve with crusty bread or croutons.

## — GAZPACHO —

Gazpacho comes from the Andalusian region of southern Spain. Originally, it was a peasant soup made primarily of leftover bread. In fact, the root of the word *gazpacho* is thought to mean "remainders."

# CASSEROLES

Now, you and I both know that there would be no such thing as potluck meals without casseroles, because you can prepare them in advance if desired, and reheat before serving; casseroles help make entertaining a breeze. We've assembled some of our favorites here with you in mind. You'll find both kicked-up versions of classics as well as some new twists. . . . How about Emeril's Favorite Choucroute Casserole for a tailgate party? Or Risotto and Wild Mushroom Casserole for a wine-tasting dinner? Or Tuna Tetrazzini for a retro night? From Creole Breakfast Bread Pudding to Puerto Rican–Style Beef and Plantain Pie, I love them all; deciding on just one is the hard part!

# Alden's Grandmother's Meat and Potato Casserole

This is kind of a Southern shepherd's pie thing that my wife's grandmother used to make for her when she was a child. Kids love it because all the stuff—ground beef, tender green beans, mashed potatoes, and such—is in the same dish. You can add cheese on top, but you don't have to. It's good either way! This would be a sure hit at a big family get-together.

1 pound fresh green beans, trimmed

2 pounds russet potatoes, peeled and cubed

1 tablespoon plus 1 teaspoon salt

5 tablespoons unsalted butter

1 tablespoon freshly ground black pepper

¾ cup whole milk

1 tablespoon olive oil

2 pounds ground beef

2 cups chopped yellow onions

1 cup chopped celery

1 tablespoon minced garlic

One 16-ounce can whole tomatoes, crushed with the juice

2 cups shredded Cheddar cheese (optional)

1. Preheat the oven to 350°F.

2. Bring a medium pot of water to a boil. Add the green beans and cook until tender, about 6 minutes. Drain the beans and put them in a large bowl filled with ice and water to cool. Drain again and reserve.

3.   Meanwhile, combine the potatoes and 1 teaspoon salt with water to cover in a medium saucepan over high heat and bring to a boil. Lower to a simmer and cook until tender, 20 to 25 minutes. Drain the potatoes and return to the pan. Add the butter, 1 teaspoon salt, 1 teaspoon black pepper, and ¼ cup milk. Mash the potatoes until smooth but slightly lumpy and reserve.

4.   Heat the olive oil in a large heavy skillet over medium-high heat. Add the ground beef, season with the remaining 2 teaspoons salt and 2 teaspoons black pepper, and cook, stirring, until well browned, about 6 minutes. Add the onions and celery and cook, stirring, until the vegetables begin to soften, about 2 minutes. Add the garlic and cook until fragrant, about 30 seconds. Add the green beans and cook for 5 minutes, stirring occasionally. Add the tomatoes and cook, stirring, for 5 minutes. Add the remaining ½ cup milk and cook, stirring, for 4 minutes. Remove from the heat and reserve for later use.

5.   Spread half of the potatoes in the bottom of a 9 × 13-inch baking dish. Pour in the meat mixture, then top with the remaining mashed potatoes. Sprinkle with the cheese and bake until bubbly and golden brown, about 1 hour. Remove from the oven and serve hot.

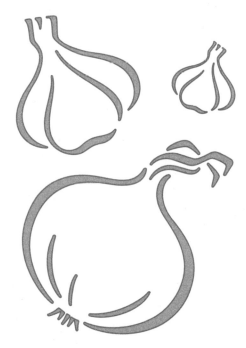

# PUERTO RICAN–STYLE BEEF AND PLANTAIN PIE

• MAKES 6 SERVINGS •

This unusual casserole, called *piñon* in Spanish, comes to us from Puerto Rico—and it's likely to become a favorite for you and your family. Accompany it with a salad and Nuevo Cubano Bread Pudding (page 284) and you've got an entire meal. Choose plantains that are semi-ripe, yellow with brown and black spots, for this dish—the all-green ones won't be sweet enough. But don't worry if you cannot find them semi-ripe—simply purchase plantains a few days in advance and allow them to ripen at room temperature before making the casserole.

FILLING
1½ pounds ground beef
1 large onion, chopped
⅓ cup chopped red bell peppers
⅓ cup chopped green bell peppers
½ teaspoon salt
½ teaspoon freshly ground black pepper
2 bay leaves
½ teaspoon ground achiote
One 16-ounce can whole tomatoes, drained, chopped, and juice reserved

½ cup halved drained pimiento-stuffed green olives
½ cup tomato sauce
¼ cup raisins
1½ tablespoons cider vinegar
6 semi-ripe plantains (yellow with some spots)
½ cup olive oil
2 large eggs
3 tablespoons water
½ cup freshly grated Parmesan cheese

1. To make the filling: Heat a large skillet over medium-high heat, add the beef and cook, stirring and breaking up clumps, until no pink remains, about 5 minutes. Add the onion, bell peppers, salt, black pepper, bay leaves, and achiote and cook until the vegetables are softened and the meat is browned, 6 to 8 minutes. Add the tomatoes

and reserved juice, olives, tomato sauce, raisins, and vinegar and simmer, stirring occasionally, until the sauce is flavorful and most of the liquid has evaporated, about 35 minutes. Transfer the filling to a bowl to cool and set aside.

2.   Peel the plantains and cut diagonally into ⅓-inch slices. In a large skillet, heat ¼ cup olive oil over medium-high heat and sauté the plantains in batches until golden brown, about 2 minutes on each side, adding remaining oil as needed. Transfer the cooked plantains to paper towels to drain.

3.   Preheat the oven to 350°F. Lightly oil a 3-quart baking dish or casserole.

4.   In a small bowl, whisk the eggs and water until blended.

5.   Pour half the egg-water mixture into the prepared baking dish and layer the bottom and sides of the dish with one-third of the plantains. Spread half the beef filling over the plantains and sprinkle with half the Parmesan. Top with half of the remaining plantains and then spread with the remaining beef filling, the remaining Parmesan, and ending with the remaining plantains. Pour the remaining egg-water mixture over the top of the pie, tilting to distribute evenly.

6.   Cover the baking dish with aluminum foil and bake in the middle of the oven until hot throughout and bubbly around the edges, about 1 hour. Cool for 10 minutes before serving. (The pie can be inverted onto a serving platter for a nice presentation.)

# — PUERTO RICAN–STYLE BEEF AND PLANTAIN PIE —

The meat filling used between the layers of this pie is called picadillo. Basically, it is a Latino version of chili and is found in many Spanish-speaking countries.

# CHARLOTTE'S LASAGNA BOLOGNESE

● MAKES 6 TO 8 SERVINGS ●

Anyone who knows me well knows that Bolognese is one of my favorite sauces. It's what I often prepare for my family on my days off from the restaurants. When my friend Charlotte shared this recipe with me, I became an instant convert. The sauce is rich and dense. Take note: Don't omit the chicken livers; they give the sauce depth of flavor. Charlotte usually makes this lasagna with sheets of fresh pasta, available at Italian groceries and pasta stores. If you can't find fresh pasta and don't want to make your own, substitute precooked lasagna noodles.

### BOLOGNESE SAUCE

2 tablespoons unsalted butter
6 strips bacon, diced
¼ pound ham, diced
½ pound ground veal or ground pork, or ¼ pound of each
1 pound ground beef
1½ cups chopped onions
½ cup finely chopped carrots
½ cup finely chopped celery
¼ pound thinly sliced mushrooms
3 garlic cloves, minced
Pinch of ground cloves
¼ teaspoon ground nutmeg
3 tablespoons tomato paste
1 cup dry white wine
3 cups Chicken Stock (page 4)
1½ teaspoons salt
¼ teaspoon freshly ground black pepper
4 chicken livers, finely chopped
½ cup heavy cream
¼ cup chopped fresh parsley

### BÉCHAMEL SAUCE

6 tablespoons unsalted butter
6 tablespoons all-purpose flour
4½ cups milk
1 teaspoon salt
¼ teaspoon ground nutmeg

1½ pounds fresh pasta sheets (spinach or regular or a combination), cut to fit the baking dish
1 cup freshly grated Parmesan cheese

1. To make the Bolognese Sauce: Heat the butter in a large pot over medium-high heat. Add the bacon and ham and cook, stirring often, until light brown, about 10 minutes. Add the ground meats and cook over high heat, stirring constantly, until well browned, about 20 minutes. Add the onions, carrots, celery, and mushrooms and cook, stirring often, until soft, about 5 minutes. Add the garlic, cloves, and nutmeg and cook for 2 minutes. Add the tomato paste and cook for 2 minutes. Add the wine and cook until almost evaporated. Add the Chicken Stock and simmer over medium-high heat until the sauce is thickened and flavorful, 45 minutes to 1 hour. Add the salt and black pepper. Add the chicken livers and cook 5 minutes. Stir in the cream and parsley and adjust the seasonings. Set aside until ready to assemble the lasagna.

2. Preheat the oven to 350°F.

3. To make the Béchamel Sauce: Melt the butter in a medium saucepan over low heat and stir in the flour, stirring constantly, until smooth, about 2 minutes. Slowly whisk the milk into the flour, stirring vigorously to blend. Increase the heat to high and quickly bring to a boil for 1 minute, stirring constantly. Allow the sauce to cook for another 5 minutes on medium heat, or until the floury taste is gone. Remove from the heat and add the salt and nutmeg.

4. Butter a 9×13-inch baking dish. Spoon ½ cup of the Bolognese Sauce onto the bottom of the dish. Cover with a layer of fresh pasta sheets. Top the pasta with another layer of meat sauce (making certain that the pasta is completely covered), then a layer of Béchamel Sauce, followed by a light dusting of Parmesan. Repeat the layering, using all of the ingredients and ending with a topping of Béchamel Sauce and Parmesan.

5. Bake the lasagna until it is bubbling and golden brown, about 1 hour. Let the lasagna rest for 10 minutes before serving.

# LAMB AND WHITE BEAN CASSEROLE

• MAKES 8 TO 10 SERVINGS •

The French dish cassoulet inspired me to create this lamb and bean casserole. A traditional cassoulet features all types of meat, such as duck confit, sausage, and pork, with the beans, but to keep things simple, I just use lamb. This heart-and-soul-warming dish is perfect on a cold winter's night with a green salad, some French bread, and a few bottles of red wine.

- 1 pound dried Great Northern beans, rinsed well and picked over
- 2 tablespoons bacon fat or olive oil
- 3 pounds boneless lamb stew meat, cut into 2-inch cubes
- 2 teaspoons salt
- 2 teaspoons freshly ground black pepper
- 3 cups chopped yellow onions
- 1 cup chopped celery
- 10 sprigs fresh thyme, tied with kitchen twine
- 3 bay leaves

- 2 teaspoons Emeril's Original Essence
- ¼ cup minced garlic
- 1 cup peeled whole tomatoes, coarsely chopped (canned is fine)
- 8 cups Chicken Stock (page 4), or canned low-sodium chicken broth
- ⅓ cup chopped green onions
- 2 tablespoons chopped fresh parsley
- 1 cup dried bread crumbs
- ½ cup freshly grated Parmesan cheese
- 3 tablespoons extra virgin olive oil

1. Preheat the oven to 400°F.

2. Combine the beans and 8 cups cold water in a large saucepan or soup pot and bring to a boil. Cover the pot and remove from the heat. Let sit for 1 hour. Drain the beans in a colander and discard the soaking liquid. Set the beans aside.

3.　　Meanwhile, heat the bacon fat in a large Dutch oven. Season the lamb with the salt and pepper and cook the lamb in batches until very brown on all sides, 8 to 10 minutes per batch. Using a slotted spoon, transfer the lamb to a bowl and set aside. Add the onions, celery, thyme, bay leaves, and Essence and cook, scraping up any browned bits from the bottom of the pan, until the vegetables are soft, 4 minutes. Add the garlic and cook for 2 minutes. Add the tomatoes and Chicken Stock and return the meat to the pot. Bring to a boil, reduce the heat to a simmer, and cook for 30 minutes.

4.　　Add the beans to the pot and continue cooking until the beans are tender but not mushy, 1 to 1½ hours. The cooking liquid should be slightly thickened, just enough to coat the beans and lamb. (If the sauce seems too thin, remove the meat and beans with a slotted spoon and cook until the liquid has reduced and is slightly thickened. Alternatively, if the cooking liquid has reduced too much, add a bit of water.) Add the green onions and parsley, taste, and season if necessary with additional salt and pepper.

5.　　Transfer the bean mixture to a 9 × 13-inch casserole and top with the bread crumbs and Parmesan cheese. Drizzle the top with the olive oil and bake, uncovered, until the casserole is golden brown on top and bubbly around the edges, about 30 minutes. Serve warm.

# CREAMY HAM AND POTATO PIES

• MAKES TWO 9-INCH PIES, 8 TO 10 SERVINGS •

Upon tasting this dish, one of my friends exclaimed, "Wow! This is the type of thing you should eat after a day of sledding." Ham and potatoes are such a natural combination; topping them with Gruyère and Parmesan cheeses puts this through the roof. This tastes just as good hot from the oven as at room temperature. Bake the piecrusts before starting the recipe.

2 recipes Savory Piecrust
(page 9), blind baked

2½ cups milk

2 cups water

1½ teaspoons salt

1 teaspoon minced garlic

2 bay leaves

3 pounds russet potatoes
(7 medium), peeled and thinly
sliced lengthwise just before
cooking

6 ounces ham, cubed

1½ cups heavy cream

1 cup grated Gruyère cheese

1 cup freshly grated Parmesan
cheese

1 teaspoon finely chopped fresh
thyme

4 tablespoons unsalted butter, cut
into small pieces

½ teaspoon freshly ground black
pepper

1.    Prepare the piecrusts as described on page 9. Roll out the 2 disks of dough and fit them into 9-inch pie pans. Crimp the edges. Refrigerate the piecrusts for at least 30 minutes. Preheat the oven to 350°F. Line the piecrusts with parchment paper or aluminum foil and fill each with pie weights. Bake until the crusts just set, about 20 minutes. Remove from the oven and remove weights. Allow to cool.

2.    Preheat the oven to 350°F.

3.    Combine the milk, water, 1 teaspoon salt, garlic, and bay leaves in a large saucepan over medium-high heat. Once the mixture is hot, add the potatoes and gently stir to

combine. Bring to a boil and cook, stirring occasionally, until the potatoes are tender, about 8 minutes. Drain the potatoes (the cooking liquid may be reserved to form the base of a soup).

4.    Line each of the baked piecrusts with half of the potatoes. Cover the potatoes with the cubed ham. Pour ¼ cup cream on top of the potatoes in each pie. Sprinkle ¼ cup Gruyère and ¼ cup Parmesan on top of the cream in each pie. Arrange 1 tablespoon butter on top of the cheese in each pie. Arrange the remaining half of the potatoes on top of the creamy mixture. Sprinkle ½ teaspoon thyme on top of the potatoes in each pie. Pour ½ cup of the remaining cream over each pie. Dot each pie with 1 tablespoon of the remaining butter. Sprinkle ¼ cup Gruyère and ¼ cup Parmesan on top of each pie. Sprinkle each pie with ¼ teaspoon salt and ¼ teaspoon black pepper. Bake the pies until golden brown and bubbly, about 30 minutes.

# CHEF DAVE'S POLENTA CASSEROLE

MAKES 8 TO 10 SERVINGS

My good friend and our Homebase culinary director—Chef Dave McCelvey—developed this recipe, which is a potluck standout. It reminds me of an Italian version of the classic New Orleans dish grillades and grits. (Grillades are thin pieces of beef or veal that are slow-cooked in a rich, flavorful gravy and then served over creamy grits). Here sweet Italian sausage takes the place of grillades and polenta takes the place of grits. Serve this as a brunch dish (as we do grillades and grits) or for a hearty winter dinner.

- 1 tablespoon extra virgin olive oil
- 1½ pounds sweet Italian sausage, removed from casings and crumbled
- 1 cup chopped onions
- 1 cup chopped green bell peppers
- ½ cup chopped red bell peppers
- 1 teaspoon minced garlic
- 1½ teaspoons Emeril's Italian Essence
- 2 cups canned whole tomatoes with their juice, crushed
- ¼ teaspoon freshly ground black pepper
- Salt to taste, depending on saltiness of sausage
- 1 recipe Creamy Polenta (recipe follows)
- 2 tablespoons cold unsalted butter, cut into small pieces
- ½ cup freshly grated Parmesan cheese

1. Preheat the oven to 350°F.

2. Heat the olive oil in a large skillet over high heat. Add the sausage and cook until browned, breaking up clumps with a wooden spoon, about 5 minutes. Transfer the sausage to a paper towel–lined plate. Add the onions and bell peppers to the pan and cook until they begin to soften, about 2 minutes. Add the garlic and Italian Essence and

CASSEROLES

127

cook for another 2 minutes. Return the sausage to the pan, stir to mix, and cook for another minute. Add the tomatoes and stir to mix. Cook until most of liquid has evaporated, about 7 minutes. Season with the black pepper and salt. Pour the sausage mixture into a 9 × 13-inch baking dish, distributing it evenly. Pour the polenta on top, spreading it evenly with a rubber spatula. Top the polenta with the butter and Parmesan. Bake until golden brown and bubbly, about 30 minutes.

. . . . . . . . . . . . . . . . . . . . . . . . . . . . . . . . . . . . . . . . . . . . . . .

## CREAMY POLENTA

4 cups milk
2 cups Chicken Stock (page 4), or canned low-sodium chicken broth
1 teaspoon salt
¼ teaspoon freshly ground white pepper
⅛ teaspoon plus a pinch of mace
1¾ cups polenta or fine yellow cornmeal
1 cup grated Parmesan cheese
3 large eggs
2 large egg yolks

1. Combine the milk, Chicken Stock, salt, white pepper, and mace in a large pot over high heat. Bring to a boil, stirring occasionally. Whisk in the polenta. Once the mixture begins to thicken, reduce the heat to medium-low. Cook until the polenta is tender, stirring constantly with a wooden spoon and scraping down the sides of the pot, about 10 minutes. Add the Parmesan and stir to blend. Remove from the heat and stir to cool for 3 minutes.

2. Meanwhile, combine the eggs and egg yolks in a medium bowl and whisk until frothy.

3. Add ½ cup of the polenta to the eggs (to temper) and whisk to blend. Gradually add the egg mixture to the rest of the polenta (in about 3 additions), stirring constantly. Continue to stir vigorously for another 2 minutes. Reserve for the casserole.

. . . . . . . . . . . . . . . . . . . . . . . . . . . . . . . . . . . . . . . . . . . . . . .

# EMERIL'S FAVORITE CHOUCROUTE CASSEROLE

Talk about a manly meal! A big plate of sausages and sauerkraut is right up my alley! This casserole makes it easy to serve this up for a crowd, because most of the cooking time takes place in the oven, leaving you free to do other things. Round out this meal with some crusty dark bread and your favorite beer and, hey, life doesn't get much better than this!

2 pounds fresh or jarred sauerkraut

4 tablespoons unsalted butter or duck, chicken, or goose fat

¼ pound pancetta or bacon, cut into ½ inch thick slices

3 medium yellow onions, peeled and sliced

4 sprigs fresh thyme

2 bay leaves

1½ teaspoons black peppercorns

8 juniper berries, lightly crushed

1 head garlic, split in half crosswise

2 ham hocks, scored

1 cup Chicken Stock (page 4)

2 cups dark or amber beer, such as Abita Amber

1 pound garlic sausage, kielbasa, or knockwurst

1 pound bratwurst or veal sausage

1½ pounds small red new potatoes, halved if large

Creole, whole-grain, or Dijon mustard, for serving

1.  Preheat the oven to 325°F.

2.  Place the sauerkraut in a colander and rinse briefly to remove some of the salt from the brine—don't rinse it too much, or you will lose a lot of the flavor. (Alternatively, if the sauerkraut is not excessively salty, use as is.) Press to release most of the excess liquid and set aside. In a large nonreactive skillet, melt 3 tablespoons of the butter over medium-low heat and add the pancetta. Cook for 5 minutes; don't let the pancetta

brown. Add the onions and continue to cook until they are soft but not browned, about 8 to 10 minutes. Transfer the bacon-onion mixture to a 3½- or 4-quart nonreactive casserole or ovenproof Dutch oven. Add the drained sauerkraut and toss to combine. Using a small piece of cheesecloth, make a bouquet garni with the thyme, bay leaves, peppercorns, juniper berries, and garlic and place in the baking dish. Add the ham hocks, Chicken Stock, and beer and stir to combine. Cover the casserole and bake, undisturbed, for 2 hours.

3.   Meanwhile, melt the remaining tablespoon of butter in a large skillet over high heat and brown the sausages on both sides. Set aside.

4.   Place the new potatoes in a saucepan and add water to cover. Bring to a boil, reduce the heat to a simmer, and cook until the potatoes are just tender, about 15 minutes. (This will depend on the size of your potatoes.) Drain and set aside.

5.   When the sauerkraut and ham hocks have baked for 2 hours and the hocks are tender, remove the casserole from the oven. Place the sausages and potatoes on top of the sauerkraut. If the liquid has reduced to less than two-thirds, add a bit more water. Cover the casserole and return it to the oven. Cook for about 30 minutes, or until the potatoes are very tender and the sausages are heated through. Remove the casserole from the oven and discard the bouquet garni. Serve immediately, with each person receiving some of each of the sausages, part of a hock, some potatoes, and sauerkraut. Pass the mustard at the table.

# — SAUERKRAUT —

Sauerkraut is often associated with German food (as in this dish), but the Chinese actually created sauerkraut more than two thousand years ago. Supposedly, the shredded cabbage was fermented in rice wine and eaten by men building the Great Wall. Once the dish made its way to Europe, it was a huge hit with the Germans, and they developed their own sauerkraut traditions.

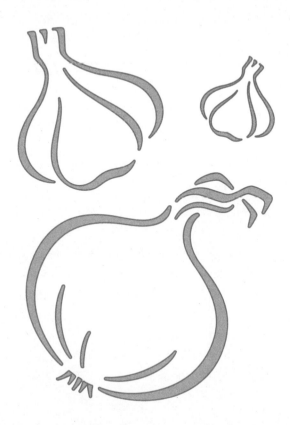

# PENNE À LA VODKA CASSEROLE

A bit of vodka in pasta sauces gives them a real flavor boost. I like vodka sauce so much that I make one that can be found on the pasta aisle at your local grocery. But you know what? This homemade version is slightly different. Try it the next time you're craving Italian food.

4 tablespoons extra virgin olive oil

1 pound sweet Italian sausage, cut crosswise into 1-inch slices

1 pound hot Italian sausage, cut crosswise into 1-inch slices

4 cups thinly sliced onions

1¾ teaspoons salt

¾ teaspoon freshly ground black pepper

¼ cup thinly sliced fresh basil leaves

1 tablespoon minced garlic

½ cup vodka

Two 16-ounce cans whole tomatoes, crushed with their juice

1 teaspoon Emeril's Original Essence

½ cup heavy cream

1 tablespoon olive oil

1 pound penne pasta

15 ounces ricotta cheese

1 cup grated Parmigiano-Reggiano cheese

1½ cups grated mozzarella cheese

Crusty bread, for serving

1. Preheat the oven to 350°F.

2. Heat 2 tablespoons extra virgin olive oil in a large skillet or saucepan over high heat. Add the sausages and cook, stirring, until browned, 4 to 5 minutes. Add the onions, ¾ teaspoon salt, and the black pepper. Cook, stirring occasionally, until the onions are just soft, about 4 minutes. Add the basil and garlic, and cook, stirring, for 2 minutes. Add the vodka and tomatoes, reduce the heat to medium-low, and simmer, uncovered, stirring occasionally, for 40 minutes. Add the Essence and heavy cream, stir to mix, and simmer for 5 minutes. Remove from the heat.

3.    To cook the pasta, combine 4 quarts water, the olive oil, and the remaining teaspoon salt in a large pot over high heat. Bring to a boil, add the pasta, and cook until al dente, 12 to 14 minutes. Remove from the heat and drain well. Combine half of the ricotta cheese and half of the Parmigiano-Reggiano with the remaining 2 tablespoons extra virgin olive oil in a large mixing bowl. Add the pasta and toss to coat evenly. Add the sausage mixture and mix well. Add the remaining ricotta cheese and the remaining Parmigiano-Reggiano and mix well.

4.    Transfer the mixture to a 9 × 13-inch baking dish. Sprinkle with the mozzarella cheese. Bake until bubbly and golden, about 45 minutes. Remove from the oven. Serve warm with crusty bread.

# MEXICAN BREAKFAST CASSEROLE

• MAKES ABOUT 10 SERVINGS •

I've eaten a lot of breakfast casseroles in my day, and I have to say that this is one of the best. Roasted peppers and spicy sausage provide the perfect backdrop for the eggs. Now, don't be intimidated by roasting the peppers. It's really quite easy, and their smoky flavor is essential. Great after a big night, serve this casserole for brunch on New Year's Day!

6 poblano chile peppers (about 1½ pounds)

1 teaspoon unsalted butter

1½ pounds Mexican chorizo or other hot sausage, removed from casings and crumbled

1 cup chopped yellow onions

½ cup chopped red bell peppers

1 tablespoon plus 1 teaspoon minced garlic

1 tablespoon plus 1 teaspoon chili powder

1 tablespoon plus 2 teaspoons vegetable oil, or more as needed

5 flour tortillas

10 large eggs

3 cups half-and-half

½ teaspoon Emeril's Kick It Up! Red Pepper Sauce, or other hot sauce

½ teaspoon salt

½ teaspoon freshly ground black pepper

½ cup chopped green onions, green tops only

¼ cup chopped fresh cilantro

1½ cups grated Pepper Jack cheese

1½ cups grated medium Cheddar cheese

Simply Salsa (page 8)

Sour cream, for garnish

1. Preheat the oven to 350°F.

2. Roast the chile peppers by placing them on an open gas flame, turning them frequently with tongs until all sides are charred black, 7 to 10 minutes. (Alternatively, the peppers can be roasted under a broiler or on top of a gas or charcoal grill.) Place the

blackened peppers in a bowl and cover with plastic wrap. Let rest until cool enough to handle, about 15 minutes. Peel the peppers, split in half lengthwise, and discard the seeds and stems.

3.  Grease a 9 × 13-inch baking dish with the butter. Spread the poblanos in a flat layer across the bottom of the dish.

4.  In a large skillet, cook the sausage over medium-high heat, stirring to break up the meat, until browned. Add the onions and bell peppers and cook, stirring, for 4 minutes. Add the garlic and chili powder and cook, stirring, for 1 minute. Remove from the heat.

5.  In a separate skillet, heat about 1 teaspoon of vegetable oil over medium-high heat. Add 1 tortilla and cook until softened, about 30 seconds per side. Remove from the pan and cut into quarters. Add more oil to the pan and repeat with the remaining tortillas.

6.  Combine the eggs, half-and-half, hot sauce, salt, and black pepper in a large bowl and whisk. Combine the green onions, cilantro, and cheeses in a medium bowl and mix well.

7.  Spoon one-third of the sausage mixture over the poblanos in the baking dish, top with one-third of the tortilla quarters, and then one-third of the cheese mixture. Repeat the layering, ending with a cheese layer. Pour the egg mixture over the ingredients. Let rest, covered, in the refrigerator for at least 6 hours, or overnight.

8.  Bake the casserole, uncovered, until bubbly and golden brown, and a knife inserted into the custard comes out clean, about 1 hour and 10 minutes. Remove from the oven and let rest 10 minutes before serving. Serve with the salsa and sour cream.

# CREOLE BREAKFAST BREAD PUDDING

· MAKES 8 TO 10 SERVINGS ·

This dish is ideal for any breakfast or brunch menu, and equally good at suppertime when served with a nice green salad and a simple soup to start. Linguiça sausage adds the right savory touch to kick this bread pudding up a notch or two. If you can't find linguiça where you live, substitute any garlicky smoked pork sausage.

½ pound linguiça sausage, removed from casings and chopped
½ cup minced yellow onions
¼ cup minced green bell peppers
⅓ cup sliced green onions
⅓ cup dry white wine
8 cups 1-inch cubes day-old French bread
2½ cups milk
½ cup heavy cream
¼ cup melted unsalted butter

8 large eggs, beaten
½ pound Pepper Jack cheese, grated
½ pound Monterey Jack cheese, grated
¾ teaspoon salt
⅛ teaspoon freshly ground black pepper
⅛ teaspoon cayenne pepper
¾ cup sour cream
½ cup grated Parmesan cheese

1. Preheat the oven to 325°F.

2. Heat a skillet over medium-high heat. Add the sausage and cook until golden brown and the fat is rendered, about 5 minutes. Add the onions and bell peppers, and sauté until soft, 3 minutes. Add the green onions and stir well. Add the white wine and reduce slightly, stirring, about 1 minute over high heat. Remove from the heat.

3. Place the bread in a large mixing bowl. Add the milk and cream and stir well. Let sit for 5 minutes.

4.    Pour the melted butter into a 9 × 13-inch casserole dish, and coat the sides and bottom evenly. Pour any extra butter into the bread mixture.

5.    Mix the sausage and bread mixtures. Add the eggs, grated Pepper Jack and Monterey Jack cheeses, salt, black pepper, and cayenne, and quickly fold together. Cover with aluminum foil and bake for 1 hour. Uncover and bake for 15 minutes. Remove the casserole from the oven and increase the temperature to 375°F. Spread the sour cream evenly over the top and cover with the Parmesan. Bake uncovered for 10 to 15 minutes, or until the casserole is lightly browned on top. Serve hot.

## — DO AHEAD —

Just the ticket for the busy holiday season, because you can assemble the dish a day ahead, refrigerate, and then bake the next morning. Come to think of it, it benefits from a night's rest in the fridge.

# Eggplant, Sausage, and Ziti Casserole

• MAKES 8 TO 10 SERVINGS •

This casserole has all the stuff that I love—eggplant, Italian sausage, tomatoes, black olives, cheese, and just the right blend of herbs and spices. Cooked to perfection, this dish is an excuse for a party!

¼ cup plus 3 tablespoons plus 1 teaspoon olive oil

1 large eggplant, halved lengthwise and cut crosswise into ⅓-inch-thick half circles

1 tablespoon salt, possibly more or less depending on saltiness of sausage

2 teaspoons Emeril's Italian Essence or Italian herb blend

1¼ teaspoons freshly ground black pepper

1 pound Italian sausage, removed from casings

1 cup chopped yellow onions

2 tablespoons tomato paste

1 tablespoon minced garlic

One 28-ounce can whole Italian tomatoes, crushed with their juice

½ cup pitted black olives, coarsely chopped

¼ teaspoon crushed red pepper

¼ cup minced fresh basil leaves

4 tablespoons unsalted butter

4 tablespoons all-purpose flour

2 cups whole milk

⅛ teaspoon freshly grated nutmeg

1 pound ziti pasta

1 cup grated mozzarella cheese

½ cup freshly grated Parmesan cheese

1.  Preheat the oven to 375°F. Grease a 9 × 13-inch casserole with 1 teaspoon olive oil and set aside.

2.  Heat ¼ cup plus 2 tablespoons olive oil in a medium Dutch oven over medium-high heat. Add the eggplant in batches, seasoning on both sides with ½ teaspoon salt, 1 teaspoon Italian Essence, and ½ teaspoon pepper. Cook until golden brown, adding

more olive oil if needed. Transfer the eggplant slices to a plate as they cook and set aside.

3.    Heat the same Dutch oven over medium-high heat. Add the sausage and cook, stirring to break up with a wooden spoon until browned, about 5 minutes. Add the onions, tomato paste, and garlic and season with ½ teaspoon salt and ¼ teaspoon black pepper. Cook, stirring frequently, until the paste begins to brown, about 5 minutes. Add the tomatoes with their juice, the remaining teaspoon Italian Essence, the black olives, and the crushed red pepper. Reduce the heat to medium-low and gently simmer, uncovered, until the flavors marry and the sauce slightly thickens, about 20 minutes. Remove from the heat. Add the basil and adjust the seasoning to taste.

4.    Meanwhile, melt the butter in a medium saucepan over medium-high heat. Stir in the flour and cook, stirring constantly, until the mixture is thickened and forms a light roux, about 2 minutes. Whisk in the milk and cook, whisking frequently, until the sauce is thick and smooth, about 4 minutes. Remove from the heat and season with the nutmeg, 1 teaspoon salt, and the remaining ½ teaspoon pepper.

5.    Combine 4 quarts water seasoned with the remaining 1 teaspoon salt and 1 tablespoon olive oil in a large heavy pot over high heat. Bring to a boil. Add the ziti and cook, stirring occasionally, until al dente, 8 to 10 minutes. Remove from the heat and drain in a colander.

6.    Arrange half of the eggplant slices on the bottom of the casserole, overlapping as necessary. Top with half of the cooked pasta, then half of the sausage-tomato sauce. Place another layer of eggplant slices on top of the sauce, then layers of pasta and sausage-tomato sauce. Pour the white sauce evenly over the mixture, then top with the mozzarella and Parmesan cheeses.

7.    Bake the casserole until puffed and golden brown, 30 to 35 minutes. Remove from the oven and serve hot.

# PEGGY'S CHICKEN POTPIES

• MAKES TWO 9-INCH DEEP-DISH POTPIES, 12 SERVINGS •

My friend Mindy's mother, Peggy, makes the best potpie I've ever had. For starters, it's loaded with tender chicken chunks and surrounded by plenty of good-for-you veggies. But here's the clincher: her potpie is so super-stuffed with filling that it actually sets up and cuts as slices after being baked. This potpie is really a pie! Though it might appear complicated, it's really just a number of simple steps, many of which can be prepared ahead of time. The pie can be assembled and baked just before serving. These potpies are also just as good if prepared and baked a day or two in advance and simply reheated in a low oven until ready to serve. The trick to getting your piecrust cooked through and crispy on the bottom is to make sure that it is thoroughly chilled before baking, and then to bake on the lowest rung of the oven at a high temperature for the first 20 minutes, as instructed. Try this version of a true American classic . . . you won't be sorry!

4 recipes Savory Piecrust (page 9)

One 3½- to 4-pound frying chicken, cut into 8 pieces

1¼ teaspoons salt

½ teaspoon freshly ground black pepper

2 tablespoons olive oil

3 cups Chicken Stock (page 4), or canned low-sodium chicken broth

1 bay leaf

1 teaspoon poultry seasoning

2 teaspoons Emeril's Chicken Rub

1 large russet baking potato, cut into ½-inch cubes (about 2 cups)

2 cups sliced carrots (¼-inch-thick slices)

1 cup coarsely chopped onions

1 cup fresh corn kernels (from 2 medium ears)

1 cup white button mushrooms, quartered

1 cup frozen lima beans

¼ cup heavy cream

3 tablespoons all-purpose flour

1½ tablespoons unsalted butter, at room temperature

1 large egg, lightly beaten

1.     Prepare the piecrusts as described on page 9. Divide the dough into 4 parts and form into 4 disks. Wrap each disk in plastic wrap and refrigerate for at least 30 minutes before rolling 2 disks out to fit into two 9-inch deep-dish pie pans. Trim the edges of the dough so that ½ inch hangs over the sides of the pans. Roll the remaining 2 disks out and refrigerate (placed on a baking sheet with plastic or parchment between the crusts), along with the fitted piecrusts, until you are ready to bake the potpies.

2.     Season the chicken pieces with the salt and black pepper. Heat a Dutch oven or other large heavy pot over high heat and brown the chicken pieces on both sides in the olive oil, working in batches if necessary, about 5 minutes on each side. Drain all the fat from the Dutch oven and add the Chicken Stock, bay leaf, poultry seasoning, and Chicken Rub. Bring to a boil, cover, reduce the heat to low, and simmer until the chicken is very tender and falling from the bone, about 1 hour. Using a slotted spoon, transfer the chicken pieces to a plate and set aside until cool enough to handle. When the chicken is cool enough to handle, remove the meat from the bones and tear into bite-size pieces. Set aside.

3.     Meanwhile, add the potato, carrots, onions, corn, mushrooms, lima beans, and heavy cream to the Dutch oven and return to a boil. Cover the pot, reduce the heat to a simmer, and cook until the vegetables are very tender, about 30 minutes.

4.     Combine the flour and butter in a small bowl to form a thick paste. Ladle some of the hot chicken broth into the bowl and whisk to combine with the flour-butter paste. When smooth, add to the pot and stir to combine well. Bring the sauce to a low boil and continue to cook until the sauce is thick and smooth, about 5 minutes. Add the reserved chicken meat, stir to combine, and remove from the heat. Discard the bay leaf, taste and adjust the seasoning if necessary. Set aside to cool completely. Once cooled, refrigerate until thoroughly chilled.

5.     Preheat the oven to 400°F and position an oven rack on the lowest rung of the oven.

6.     Divide the chilled filling between the two chilled pastry-lined pie pans and, using a spatula, smooth the filling to the edges. Place the egg in a small bowl and beat with 1 tablespoon of water. Lightly brush the edges of the overhanging pastry with some of the egg wash. Top each potpie with a rolled-out crust and trim the edges to match those

of the bottom crusts. Using your fingers, pinch the edges of dough together and roll inward so they sit inside the edges of the pie pans; decoratively crimp. Using the tip of a sharp knife, cut several decorative slits in the top of each pie to allow steam to escape while cooking. Brush the top of each potpie with some of the egg wash.

7. Bake the potpies for 20 minutes. Reduce the oven temperature to 350°F and continue baking the potpies until the crusts are golden brown and the filling is heated through, about 40 minutes longer.

8. Remove the potpies from the oven and allow to cool slightly before serving. Cut the potpies into wedges and serve.

— PEGGY'S CHICKEN POTPIES —

These potpies are the best because they are easily made a day in advance. After baking and cooling them, simply cover and refrigerate until ready to reheat in a moderate oven.

# Chicken and Olive Pasta Casserole

This is much like chicken (or turkey) tetrazzini, but with a little added kick. You can also make it, freeze it, and pull it out for reheating as needed when unexpected company drops by.

- 2 chickens (about 3½ pounds each), quartered
- 2 tablespoons plus 2½ teaspoons salt
- ½ teaspoon cayenne pepper
- 1 pound pasta, such as angel hair or linguine, cooked and drained
- 1 tablespoon plus ½ teaspoon olive oil
- 6 tablespoons unsalted butter
- 6 tablespoons all-purpose flour

- 2 cups chopped yellow onions
- ½ cup chopped celery
- ½ cup chopped black olives
- ½ cup chopped pimiento-stuffed green olives
- ½ teaspoon Emeril's Original Essence
- 2 tablespoons chopped pickled jalapeños
- 2 cups freshly grated Parmesan cheese

1. Put the chickens in a large heavy pot with 2 tablespoons salt and the cayenne. Add enough water to cover. Bring to a boil, then reduce the heat to medium-low and cook until the chickens are very tender, about 1 hour. Remove the chickens from the pot and reserve 3 cups of the stock. Set aside.

2. Bring a large pot of water with 1 teaspoon salt and 1 tablespoon olive oil to a boil over high heat. Add the pasta and cook until al dente, about 7 minutes. Remove from the heat, drain, and rinse under cold water. Toss the pasta with the remaining ½ teaspoon olive oil and set aside.

3.    When the chicken is cool, remove the meat from the bones, discarding the rest.

4.    Preheat the oven to 350°F.

5.    Combine the butter and flour in a heavy saucepan over medium heat and whisk to blend. Cook, whisking, for 2 minutes. Add the onions and celery and cook, stirring, until just soft, 2 to 3 minutes. Gradually add the reserved chicken stock and whisk to blend. Cook, stirring, until smooth and slightly thickened. Add the chicken and olives and season with the remaining 1½ teaspoons salt, the Essence, and the jalapeños. Remove from the heat. Add 1 cup Parmesan and stir to blend.

6.    Spread half of the pasta in a 9 × 13-inch baking dish. Spoon half of the chicken mixture over the pasta and sprinkle with ½ cup of the Parmesan. Spread the remaining pasta over the Parmesan and top with the remaining chicken mixture. Sprinkle the casserole with the remaining ½ cup Parmesan.

7.    Bake until bubbly and the cheese has melted, about 20 minutes. Remove from the oven and serve warm.

# Cowboy Chicken Casserole

This awesome chicken casserole makes a great addition to a Southwestern-themed potluck or buffet: everyone, kids and adults, will enjoy it. Skinless, boneless chicken breasts are poached, combined with a mushroom-béchamel sauce, and piled on a bed of crunchy tortilla chips. Now you're talkin'!

2 pounds skinless, boneless chicken breasts

2½ cups Chicken Stock (page 4)

½ cup dry white wine

¼ cup coarsely chopped fresh cilantro

1½ tablespoons fresh lime juice

2 garlic cloves, smashed

1 teaspoon black peppercorns

1¼ teaspoons salt

¼ teaspoon dried Mexican oregano

2 bay leaves

6 tablespoons unsalted butter

1 pound white button mushrooms, wiped clean and stems trimmed, quartered

Pinch of freshly ground black pepper

4 tablespoons all-purpose flour

1½ cups whole milk

12 cups tortilla chips

2 cups finely chopped onions

1 cup finely chopped bell peppers

2 jalapeños, stems and seeds removed, finely chopped (optional)

8 ounces grated Pepper Jack cheese

8 ounces grated Cheddar cheese

1 tablespoon Emeril's Southwest Essence

2 teaspoons chili powder

1 teaspoon ground cumin

1 cup chopped drained canned tomatoes

One 4-ounce can diced green chiles, drained

1.  Combine the chicken, Chicken Stock, wine, cilantro, lime juice, garlic, peppercorns, 1 teaspoon of the salt, the oregano, and bay leaves in a medium saucepan

and bring to a boil. Reduce the heat to a simmer and cook, uncovered, for 10 minutes. Remove from the heat and allow the chicken to cool in the poaching liquid for 45 minutes. Remove the chicken from the cooking liquid and tear or cut into bite-size pieces. Reserve the chicken. Strain the cooking liquid and reserve.

2.    Preheat the oven to 350°F.

3.    Heat the butter in a large skillet over high heat until foamy. Add the mushrooms, the remaining ¼ teaspoon salt, and the black pepper and cook, stirring occasionally, until the mushrooms release their liquid. Continue to cook until the mushrooms are golden brown and all the liquid has evaporated, about 6 minutes. Sprinkle the mushrooms with the flour, stir to blend, and cook for 1 minute. Add the milk and stir, scraping up any bits from the bottom of the pan. Cook until the mixture begins to thicken. Add 1½ cups of the reserved chicken cooking liquid, stir, and cook until very thick and flavorful, about 10 minutes. Remove from the heat.

4.    Place the tortilla chips in the bottom of a 9 × 13-inch glass casserole. Crush the chips with your hands so they form a thin layer on the bottom of the dish. Pour 1 cup of the reserved cooking liquid over the tortilla chips and allow them to soak up the liquid. Scatter the chicken over the top of the tortilla layer. Spread the chopped onions, bell peppers, and jalapeños evenly over the chicken. Top with half of the grated cheeses. Sprinkle with the Southwest Essence, chili powder, and cumin. Spoon the reserved mushroom mixture evenly over the top of the spices, then top with the tomatoes and green chiles. Cover with the remainder of the cheeses. Bake uncovered for 40 to 45 minutes, or until the cheese is bubbly and the casserole is heated through. Let sit for 5 minutes before serving.

TIP    This casserole may be prepared in advance and frozen until ready to use— simply allow it to thaw 1 day in the refrigerator and come to room temperature before baking.

Watermelon Daiquiri (PAGE 18), Green Vodka Cooler (PAGE 16),
Orange Emeril (PAGE 22), Spiced Nuts (PAGE 37)

Classic Blue Cheese Dip  (PAGE 30)

Alain's Sweet and Spicy Asian Wings (PAGE 45),
Cocktail Crawfish Turnovers (PAGE 49)

Layered Tuna Niçoise Salad (PAGE 69)

Golden Shrimp Stew (PAGE 103)

Emeril's Favorite Choucroute Casserole (PAGE 129)

Penne à la Vodka Casserole (PAGE 132)

Creole Breakfast Bread Pudding (PAGE 136)

Chicken in a Box (PAGE 166), Buttermilk Biscuits
(PAGE 249), Emeril's Favorite Potato Salad (PAGE 85)

Creole Mustard and Herb-Wrapped Beef Tenderloin  (PAGE 188)

Paul's "Make the Whole Crew Happy" Sausage
Meatballs with Red Gravy (PAGE 199)

Slow-Cooked Pork Roast with Barbecue Sauce
(PAGE 204), Horseradish Coleslaw (PAGE 84)

Serious Southern Cornbread (PAGE 247),
Cajun Maque Choux (PAGE 240)

Prosciutto Breadsticks (PAGE 254)

Gigi's Carrot Cake (PAGE 263)

Glazed Lemon Pound Cake (PAGE 267)
with Summer Fruit Salad (PAGE 291)

Chocolate Peanut Butter Pie (PAGE 286)

# Swedish Salmon and Potato Casserole

. MAKES 10 TO 12 SERVINGS .

This is my take on a Swedish dish that combines smoked salmon, potatoes, eggs, and cream in one casserole. Light but satisfying, it would be perfect at brunch or lunch.

½ cup plus 3 tablespoons unsalted butter, melted

½ cup dried bread crumbs

3 pounds russet potatoes, peeled and cut into ⅛-inch-thick slices

1 teaspoon salt

¾ teaspoon freshly ground white pepper

1 pound smoked salmon, cut into thin slices (about 20)

1 tablespoon plus 1 teaspoon finely chopped fresh dill

6 large eggs

3 cups heavy cream

Lemon wedges, for serving

1. Preheat the oven to 425°F.

2. Lightly grease a 9 × 13-inch casserole dish with 1 tablespoon melted butter. Coat the greased casserole with 3 tablespoons bread crumbs. Lay about a third of the potatoes in the casserole dish—overlapping them in a shingle pattern. Season the potato layer with ¼ teaspoon salt and ¼ teaspoon white pepper. Lay half the salmon slices over the potatoes and sprinkle the salmon with 1 teaspoon chopped dill. Lay half the remaining potatoes over the salmon—once again in a shingle pattern—and season with another ¼ teaspoon salt and ¼ teaspoon white pepper. Lay the remainder of the salmon over the potatoes, and sprinkle with 1 teaspoon chopped dill. Arrange the rest of the potatoes over the salmon and season with the remaining ½ teaspoon salt and ¼ teaspoon white pepper.

3. Combine the eggs with the heavy cream and 2 tablespoons melted butter in a medium bowl. Whisk to combine. Pour the egg and cream mixture over the casserole and wrap with aluminum foil. Place the casserole dish in the oven and bake on the middle rack of the oven for 30 minutes. Remove the casserole from the oven, peel away the foil, and sprinkle the remaining bread crumbs over the top. Place the casserole back in the oven and bake until the top is golden brown and the potatoes are tender, about 30 minutes more.

4. Remove the casserole from the oven and allow to cool for 15 to 20 minutes before serving. Sprinkle the remaining 2 teaspoons of chopped dill over the casserole. Serve, drizzled with the remaining ½ cup melted butter and garnished with lemon wedges.

## — SLICING POTATOES —

I use a mandoline for even, thinly sliced potatoes. Mandolines are available at kitchen and houseware stores.

# Shrimp and Mirliton Casserole

The combination of shrimp and mirlitons is a popular one in southern Louisiana, where mirlitons are available during the late summer and early fall. Mirlitons are known as chayotes in Latino markets and are called *christophenes* in France. Traditionally, mirliton halves are filled with the shrimp mixture, but for potluck meals, I suggest boiling them until tender and serving in a casserole as described.

- 5 pounds (about 8) medium mirlitons (chayotes)
- 2 pounds medium shrimp, peeled and deveined
- 4 tablespoons olive oil
- 1½ tablespoons Emeril's Bayou Blast Essence
- 2 cups chopped yellow onions
- ½ cup chopped green bell peppers
- 1 large jalapeno, seeded and minced (about ¼ cup)
- ½ teaspoon dried thyme
- ¼ cup minced garlic

- 1½ teaspoons salt
- ½ teaspoon freshly ground black pepper
- ½ cup finely chopped green onions
- ¼ cup finely chopped fresh parsley
- 3 large eggs, lightly beaten
- 1 cup plus 1 tablespoon dried fine bread crumbs
- 1 teaspoon Emeril's Kick It Up! Red Pepper Sauce, or other hot sauce
- ¾ pound freshly grated American cheese

1. Bring a large pot of water to a boil. Add the mirlitons and cook until tender, 45 minutes to an hour. Remove from the heat, drain, and set aside to cool completely.

2. Meanwhile, combine the shrimp with 2 tablespoons olive oil and 1 tablespoon Bayou Blast in a mixing bowl and toss to coat evenly. Cover and refrigerate until ready to use.

3.    When the mirlitons are cool, cut them in half lengthwise, remove the seeds, peel, and coarsely chop. Set aside.

4.    Preheat the oven to 350°F.

5.    Heat the remaining 2 tablespoons olive oil in a large heavy pot or Dutch oven over medium-high heat. Add the onions, bell peppers, and jalapeño. Add the remaining ½ tablespoon Bayou Blast and the thyme. Cook, stirring, until the vegetables are soft and lightly golden, 4 to 6 minutes.

6.    Add the garlic and cook, stirring, for about 2 minutes. Add the mirlitons and cook, mashing them with a potato masher, until very tender and most of the liquid has evaporated, about 30 minutes. Add the shrimp, salt, black pepper, green onions, and parsley. Cook, stirring, until the shrimp turn pink, 3 to 4 minutes. Remove from the heat.

7.    Add the eggs, 1 cup of the bread crumbs, and the pepper sauce. Mix well. Spoon the mixture into a 9 × 13-inch casserole dish. Sprinkle the cheese evenly over the top, then sprinkle with the remaining tablespoon bread crumbs. Bake until the topping is lightly browned and bubbly, about 30 minutes. Serve warm.

# Risotto and Wild Mushroom Casserole

The intense flavor of mushrooms marries perfectly with the creamy risotto in this rich dish. It's one of those dishes that would be ideal on a cold, blustery night while watching a football game on the tube. Maybe you had better make two batches!

- ¾ ounce dried porcini mushrooms, soaked in ½ cup warm water until soft
- 4 tablespoons unsalted butter
- 2 tablespoons extra virgin olive oil
- 2 cups Arborio rice
- 3 tablespoons chopped shallots
- 1 tablespoon minced garlic
- 5 to 6 cups hot Chicken Stock (page 4) or low-sodium chicken broth
- 1½ teaspoons salt
- 1 teaspoon finely chopped fresh thyme
- ½ teaspoon finely chopped fresh rosemary
- ½ teaspoon plus a pinch freshly ground black pepper
- 2 pounds white button mushrooms, wiped clean and stems removed, coarsely chopped
- 1 tablespoon soy sauce
- 2 tablespoons chopped fresh parsley
- ¼ cup dry white wine
- 1 cup freshly grated Parmesan cheese
- 2 large eggs
- 1 cup heavy cream

1.    Strain the porcini mushrooms in a fine-mesh sieve and reserve the soaking liquid. Chop the mushrooms and set aside.

2.    Heat 2 tablespoons butter with the olive oil in a large Dutch oven or saucepan until foamy. Add the Arborio rice and cook, stirring frequently, until the rice is well coated and fragrant, 1 to 2 minutes. Add 1½ tablespoons shallots and ½ tablespoon garlic and cook, stirring, until fragrant, about 1 minute. Add the reserved porcini soaking liquid and cook until it evaporates. Reduce the heat to medium and add 2 cups Chicken Stock and ¾ teaspoon salt. Cook, stirring constantly, until the broth has been absorbed. Continue to cook, adding more broth, ½ cup at a time, until it is absorbed and the rice is al dente, 16 to 18 minutes total cooking time. (You may not need all 6 cups of the broth.) Add the thyme, rosemary, and ¼ teaspoon black pepper. Set aside while you prepare the mushrooms.

3.    Heat the remaining 2 tablespoons butter in a large skillet until foamy, 1 to 2 minutes. Add the remaining 1½ tablespoons shallots and the remaining ½ tablespoon garlic and cook until fragrant, about 1 minute. Add the white button mushrooms, ½ teaspoon salt and ¼ teaspoon black pepper and cook, stirring frequently, until the mushrooms release their liquid, about 4 minutes. Add the reserved porcini mushrooms and continue to cook, stirring, for 6 minutes, or until all the liquid evaporates and the mushrooms are golden brown around the edges. Add the soy sauce and parsley and cook for 1 minute. Add the white wine and cook until evaporated, 2 minutes. Remove from the heat.

4.    Layer half of the reserved risotto in a 9 × 9-inch casserole or baking dish and sprinkle with half of the Parmesan. Top with the mushroom mixture. Add the remaining risotto and top with the remaining Parmesan.

5.    In a small bowl, whisk together the eggs, cream, the remaining ¼ teaspoon salt and pinch of black pepper. Pour the mixture evenly over the top of the casserole and bake, uncovered, for 30 minutes or until golden brown. Remove from the oven and let stand for 5 minutes before serving.

# Spinach Enchiladas

Enchiladas are perfect for a Mexican-style potluck feast because you can assemble them ahead of time and then just pop them in the oven before serving. This recipe calls for one slightly esoteric ingredient—queso fresco. This is a salty, fresh white cheese from Mexico, and it can be found in most Latino markets. If you have trouble finding it, then just substitute mozzarella, but, boy, it is good—so look hard!

- 4 poblano chile peppers (about 1 pound)
- 4 pounds fresh spinach, stems removed, well rinsed
- 8 tablespoons (1 stick) unsalted butter
- 1 cup chopped yellow onions
- 1 tablespoon chopped garlic
- 2 teaspoons chili powder
- ¾ teaspoon salt
- ¼ teaspoon freshly ground black pepper
- Pinch of cayenne pepper
- ½ cup all-purpose flour

- 2 cups half-and-half
- 2 cups Pepper Jack cheese, 1 cup cubed and 1 cup freshly grated
- 1 cup cubed queso fresco or mozzarella cheese
- 1 cup freshly grated Parmesan cheese
- 2 tablespoons vegetable oil, plus more as needed
- 12 corn tortillas
- 1 cup Chicken Stock (page 4), or canned low-sodium chicken broth
- 1 cup heavy cream

1. Roast the peppers by placing them on an open gas flame, turning them frequently with tongs until all sides are charred black, 7 to 10 minutes. (Alternatively, the peppers can be roasted under a broiler or on top of a gas or charcoal grill.) Place the blackened peppers in a plastic or paper bag and let rest until cool enough to handle, about 15 minutes. Peel the peppers, split in half lengthwise, and discard the seeds and stems. Roughly chop and set aside.

2.   Bring a large pot of salted water to a boil. In 3 batches, add the spinach and blanch for 15 seconds. Remove with a slotted spoon and cool in an ice bath. Remove from the ice bath and squeeze out the excess water. Chop and set aside.

3.   In a large saucepan, melt 4 tablespoons butter over medium-high heat. Add the onions and cook, stirring, until very soft, 3 to 4 minutes. Add the garlic, chili powder, salt, black pepper, and cayenne and cook, stirring, for 45 seconds. Add ¼ cup flour and cook, stirring with a wooden spoon, to make a light roux, 2 minutes. Gradually add the half-and-half and cook, stirring, until thick, 2 to 3 minutes. Add the spinach and stir to incorporate. Remove from the heat and fold in half of the chopped poblanos. Adjust the seasoning to taste. Fold in the cubed Pepper Jack and queso fresco cheeses and set aside.

4.   In a small bowl, combine the grated Pepper Jack and Parmesan cheeses. Set aside.

5.   Preheat the oven to 350°F.

6.   In a medium skillet, heat 2 tablespoons vegetable oil over medium heat. Add the tortillas, 1 at a time, to the hot oil and cook, turning, until soft and pliable, 15 seconds per side, adding more oil as needed. Remove from the pan and place on a work surface.

7.   Place about ½ cup of the spinach mixture into the center of each tortilla and roll up into a cylinder. Place the cylinders, seam side down, in a single layer across the bottom of a 9 × 13-inch casserole.

8.   In a medium saucepan, melt the remaining 4 tablespoons butter over medium heat. Add the remaining ¼ cup flour and cook, stirring constantly with a wooden spoon, to make a light roux. Slowly add the Chicken Stock and cook, stirring, until thickened, 3 to 4 minutes. Add the cream and cook, stirring, until thick, about 2 minutes. Add the remaining poblanos and cook for 1 minute.

9.   Pour the sauce over the filled enchiladas and bake for 20 minutes. Remove from the oven and cover evenly with the remaining grated cheeses. Return to the oven and bake until the cheeses are melted and bubbly and the enchiladas are completely warmed through, 10 to 15 minutes. Remove from the oven and let sit for 5 minutes before serving.

# TUNA TETRAZZINI

I love Tuna Tetrazzini! I've jazzed things up just a bit to make a slightly more modern version of this potluck classic. No canned condensed soups here—this version is made with a deceptively simple mushroom béchamel that truly makes it come to life. The crushed potato chips that top the casserole bring this tuna tetrazzini up to another level!

1½ cups chopped onions

½ cup chopped red bell peppers

7 tablespoons unsalted butter

1 teaspoon minced garlic

1 pound white button mushrooms, ends trimmed, sliced

1½ teaspoons Emeril's Original Essence

½ teaspoon chopped fresh thyme

¼ cup all-purpose flour

¼ cup dry white wine

2 cups Chicken Stock (page 4)

1¾ cups heavy cream

12 ounces wide egg noodles

Three 6-ounce cans solid white tuna, drained and broken up

1 tablespoon chopped fresh parsley

1½ teaspoons salt

¾ teaspoon freshly ground black pepper

⅓ cup freshly grated Parmesan cheese

One 5½-ounce bag potato chips, crushed

1. Sauté the onions and bell peppers in 6 tablespoons butter in a large skillet or Dutch oven over high heat until soft, about 4 minutes. Add the garlic and cook for 2 minutes, stirring. Add the mushrooms, Essence, and thyme and cook, stirring occasionally, until the mushrooms are soft and have released their liquid, about 6 minutes. Sprinkle with the flour and cook, stirring, for 2 minutes. Add the wine and Chicken Stock and cook, stirring, until smooth and thick, about 2 minutes. Add the heavy cream and bring to a boil. Reduce the heat to medium and simmer, stirring occasionally, until the sauce is thick enough to coat the back of a spoon and very flavorful, 15 to 20 minutes.

2. Preheat the oven to 375°F.

3. Meanwhile, bring a large pot of salted water to a boil and cook the egg noodles until al dente, about 10 minutes. Drain in a colander and set aside. Butter a 9 × 13-inch casserole or baking dish with the remaining tablespoon of butter and set aside.

4. When the sauce has thickened, add the noodles, tuna, parsley, salt, black pepper, and Parmesan to the skillet and stir until thoroughly combined. Transfer to the prepared casserole and top with the potato chips. Bake uncovered until bubbly and golden brown, about 30 minutes. Serve immediately.

# GRILLED VEGETABLE LASAGNA WITH PUTTANESCA SAUCE AND PESTO OIL

• MAKES 8 TO 10 SERVINGS •

This hearty lasagna—which includes grilled vegetables paired with one of my favorite Italian pasta sauces—will please vegetarians and carnivores alike. Everything can be made in advance and then assembled as time allows. The Puttanesca Sauce will be even better if made a day in advance. Grill the veggies and make the sauce the day before, and then assemble the lasagna the next day. Make life easy on yourself—hey, it's not rocket science! Even better, this lasagna is made with uncooked dried lasagna noodles. This method works well (especially in this lasagna, where the vegetables tend to produce a lot of liquid during cooking) and eliminates one step from the preparation

## PUTTANESCA SAUCE

¼ cup olive oil

1 medium onion, finely chopped

6 garlic cloves, minced

Two 28-ounce cans Roma tomatoes, broken into pieces, with their juice

1 cup tightly packed pitted Kalamata olives, coarsely chopped

2 tablespoons tomato paste

2 tablespoons drained capers

2 tablespoons minced anchovy fillets (about 8)

½ teaspoon dried basil

½ teaspoon crushed red pepper

Salt, to taste

## PESTO OIL

2 garlic cloves, minced

2 cups loosely packed basil leaves

1 cup extra virgin olive oil

1 teaspoon salt, or to taste

### GRILLED VEGETABLES

4 medium zucchini, cut lengthwise
  into ¼-inch slices
4 red or yellow bell peppers,
  roasted, seeded, and peeled, cut
  into large pieces (page 153)
2 medium eggplants (about 1½
  pounds), cut into ¼-inch rounds
2 large yellow onions, cut into
  ¼-inch rounds

¼ cup extra virgin olive oil
1 tablespoon salt

2 pounds ricotta cheese
1¼ pounds uncooked dried lasagna
  noodles
8 ounces coarsely grated mozzarella
  cheese (about 2 cups)

1. Make the Puttanesca Sauce: Heat the olive oil in a large pot over medium-high heat. Add the onion and cook until soft and slightly caramelized, about 6 minutes. Add the garlic and cook for 2 minutes, stirring frequently. Add the tomatoes and the remaining ingredients and simmer until the sauce is thickened and slightly reduced, about 40 minutes. Adjust the seasoning to taste, cover, and set aside.

2. Make the Pesto Oil: Combine the garlic and basil in the bowl of a food processor or blender and process on high while adding the olive oil in a steady stream. Continue to process until well blended, season with salt to taste, and set aside until ready to assemble the lasagna.

3. Grill the vegetables: Light the grill or preheat the broiler. In a large shallow bowl, toss the zucchini, bell peppers, eggplants, and onions with the olive oil and salt. If using the broiler, arrange the vegetables in a single layer on 2 lightly greased or nonstick baking sheets. Grill or broil in batches, turning the vegetables once, until they are tender, lightly browned, and have released most of their moisture, 5 to 6 minutes per side.

4. Preheat the oven to 350°F and lightly grease a 9 × 13-inch baking dish.

5. Combine the ricotta cheese with ½ cup Pesto Oil in a medium bowl and set aside.

6.    Spoon ½ cup of the Puttanesca Sauce onto the bottom of the prepared baking dish. Cover with a single layer of lasagna noodles, making sure they do not overlap. Top the lasagna with a layer of ricotta cheese, then a layer of grilled vegetables—eggplants, zucchini, onions, and bell peppers—a layer of grated mozzarella, and a layer of Puttanesca Sauce. Continue layering the lasagna, ricotta, vegetables, mozzarella, and sauce until all the ingredients have been used, ending with mozzarella.

7.    Cover the lasagna with aluminum foil and bake for 45 minutes. Remove the foil and continue to bake until the lasagna is bubbling and golden brown, 15 to 30 minutes longer. Let the lasagna rest for 10 minutes before serving, drizzled with some of the remaining Pesto Oil.

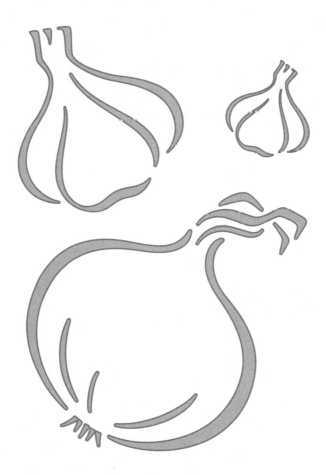

# SHELLFISH-STUFFED CANNELLONI

• MAKES ABOUT 8 SERVINGS •

Sometimes a classic needs to be kicked up a little bit. Now, you might think I went a little overboard by stuffing these cannelloni with shrimp, crab, *and* lobster. But you know what? There's a time and place for everything. And if you want to really treat some friends right, then this dish is your answer. If you prefer, kick it up a bit more with a drizzle of truffle oil in the sauce. Or you could simplify and just use shrimp.

2 tablespoons plus 2 teaspoons olive oil

2¼ teaspoons salt

One 8-ounce package cannelloni (about 14 cannelloni)

12 tablespoons unsalted butter

½ cup all-purpose flour

5 cups milk

½ teaspoon freshly ground white pepper

⅛ teaspoon freshly grated nutmeg

2 cups finely chopped onions

2 teaspoons minced garlic

1 pound cooked deveined shrimp, coarsely chopped

1 pound jumbo lump crabmeat

½ pound cooked lobster meat, coarsely chopped (from one 1¼-pound lobster)

¼ cup finely chopped mixed fresh herbs, such as tarragon, parsley, and basil

½ cup finely grated Parmesan cheese

1.  Preheat the oven to 375°F. Grease a 9 × 13-inch casserole with 1 teaspoon olive oil.

2.  To cook the pasta, combine 6 quarts water, 1 tablespoon olive oil, and 1 teaspoon salt in a large pot over high heat. Bring to a boil, add the pasta, and cook until al dente, about 8 minutes. Remove from the heat, drain, and rinse. Toss with 1 teaspoon olive oil; reserve.

3.  Meanwhile, melt 8 tablespoons butter in a medium saucepan over medium heat. Whisk in the flour and cook for 2 minutes, stirring frequently. Add the milk and whisk to combine well. Bring to a boil, stirring frequently, and cook for 5 minutes, until very thick and the floury taste is gone. Season with ¾ teaspoon salt, ¼ teaspoon white pepper, and the nutmeg. Remove from the heat and press plastic wrap onto the surface of the sauce so that a skin will not form; reserve.

4.  Combine the remaining 4 tablespoons butter with the remaining 1 tablespoon olive oil in a medium skillet over medium-high heat. Add the onions and cook until softened, about 6 minutes. Add the garlic and cook for 2 minutes longer. Transfer to a mixing bowl and add the shrimp, crabmeat, lobster, herbs, and ½ cup of the sauce. Gently toss to combine. Season with the remaining ½ teaspoon salt and ¼ teaspoon white pepper.

5.  Stuff each of the cannelloni with ¼ cup of the shellfish filling and place them side by side in the prepared casserole. Sprinkle any remaining filling on top of the cannelloni. Pour the sauce over the cannelloni, sprinkle with the grated Parmesan, and bake until heated through, bubbly, and golden brown, about 30 minutes.

# CAJUN QUICHE

• MAKES ONE 9-INCH QUICHE, ABOUT 8 SERVINGS •

This isn't your same old, boring quiche. Would I do that? I loaded this baby up with big Cajun flavors like tasso and crawfish, but you could substitute another type of smoked ham and shrimp.

1 recipe Savory Piecrust (page 9)

1 large egg white, lightly beaten

2 tablespoons unsalted butter

1 cup finely chopped yellow onions

½ cup finely chopped green bell peppers

2 teaspoons Emeril's Original Essence

½ cup finely chopped green onions

2 teaspoons minced garlic

¾ pound cooked crawfish tails, with the fat

¼ pound tasso or other smoked ham, chopped

1 tablespoon tomato paste

½ cup grated Swiss or Monterey Jack cheese (2 ounces)

3 large eggs, beaten

1 cup half-and-half

1 teaspoon finely chopped fresh thyme

1 teaspoon salt

½ teaspoon freshly ground black pepper

⅛ teaspoon cayenne pepper

1. Preheat the oven to 400°F.

2. Roll out the piecrust on a lightly floured surface to fit a deep 9-inch pie pan. Place the pastry in the pie pan and crimp the edges decoratively. Refrigerate the pastry for at least 30 minutes, then line with aluminum foil. Fill with pie weights and bake for 12 to 15 minutes, or until lightly golden around the edges. Remove the foil and pie weights and return the crust to the oven for 3 to 5 minutes. Remove from the oven and brush the surface of the piecrust with a light coating of egg white; allow to cool.

3. In a large skillet, melt the butter over medium-high heat. Add the onions, bell peppers, and Essence and cook until the vegetables soften, about 4 minutes. Add the green onions and garlic and cook for 1 minute. Add the crawfish tails with their fat, tasso, and tomato paste and cook for 2 minutes longer. Transfer to a bowl and let cool. Once cool, stir in the cheese.

4. In a large bowl, whisk together the eggs, half-and-half, thyme, salt, black pepper, and cayenne. Pour the crawfish mixture into the pie shell, and pour the egg mixture over the top. Bake on the bottom rack of the oven until the custard is set and the quiche is golden brown on top, about 30 minutes. Allow to cool slightly before serving.

## — TASSO —

Tasso, a Cajun specialty, is smoked pork shoulder that has been heavily seasoned with the usual Louisiana suspects such as cayenne and black pepper. It's diced and used in gumbos, jambalayas, and other local dishes. Since tasso is difficult to find outside the state, substitute any other lean smoked ham.

# BEYOND CASEROLES

I don't think anyone wants to live off casseroles alone—so I scoured my mind for other tasty entrée options that would work well for potlucks. Now, of course, there are plenty of delicious entrées out there, but I wanted to give you dishes that are easily prepared, easily transported, and easily served. For example—Chicken in a Box, my tried-and-true recipe for fried chicken. Just fry up some chicken, place it in a wax paper–lined cardboard box, and you're on your way! (Everyone knows that fried chicken tastes better at room temperature.) Or try Rhena's Stuffed Peppers, which are cooked at your house and then reheated in a low oven when you reach your destination. Then there are the Dutch oven wonders such as Smothered Pork Chops, where you just need to pick up your Dutch oven and go. I'll meet you there!

# CHICKEN IN A BOX

• MAKES 8 SERVINGS •

Making good fried chicken is an art. Since many home cooks don't own a deep fryer, which makes the best fried chicken, I fiddled around and finally came up with a foolproof recipe. There are just a few tricks—soak the chicken in a salty marinade, rest the chicken once it's floured, and keep the oil at a steady temperature. Though many cooks suggest cooking fried chicken at a higher temperature, I find that if I do that the coating burns before the chicken is cooked through. I prefer a lower heat. Buy a clip-on thermometer to control the temperature and you will become a master. And, hey—make life easy on yourself and fry up a batch before your party starts, because this chicken is just as good at room temperature as it is hot. I bring it over to friends' houses in a wax paper–lined cardboard box—talk about making folks happy, happy!

- - -

1 quart buttermilk

½ cup Emeril's Original Essence

2 tablespoons salt

2 tablespoons sugar

1 head garlic, cloves peeled and crushed

Two 3½- to 4-pound chickens, cut into 8 pieces each

4 cups all-purpose flour

2 tablespoons cayenne pepper

Peanut oil, for frying

- - -

1. Combine the buttermilk, ¼ cup Essence, salt, sugar, and garlic in a large non-reactive bowl. Stir to blend. Immerse the chicken in the mixture and refrigerate for at least 4 hours and for up to 24 hours.

2. Combine the flour, the remaining ¼ cup Essence, and the cayenne in a large doubled brown paper bag or plastic freezer bag and shake to blend. Drop the chicken, a few pieces at a time, into the flour mixture and shake thoroughly to completely coat. Remove the chicken and shake off the excess flour. Repeat the coating process with the

remaining chicken pieces. Place the coated chicken on a large wire rack set over a sheet pan and let rest until ready to fry, at least 20 minutes.

3.  Heat 4 inches of oil to 300°F over medium-high heat in a medium Dutch oven or heavy pot. Fry the chicken in batches, skin side down, until golden brown, about 10 minutes. Turn and fry until golden brown on the second side, 8 to 10 minutes longer. Remove the chicken and drain on paper towels. (Note: An even oil temperature is the key to success; a clip-on candy/deep-fry thermometer should be kept in the pot at all times. And the temperature should remain between 280°F and 300°F at all times.) Allow the chicken to rest at least 5 minutes before serving.

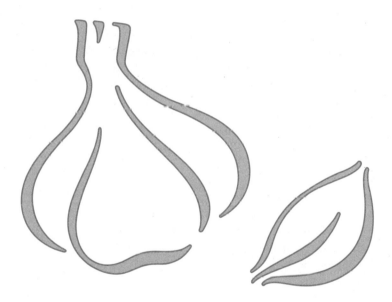

# Classic Chicken Jambalaya

### • MAKES 6 TO 8 SERVINGS •

Jambalaya, like gumbo, is a Louisiana specialty that comes in a zillion variations. One of my favorites is a simple but classic chicken jambalaya. But don't be fooled, there's more than chicken in there—some ham and some sausage for flavor, of course! This dish is a meal in itself, but serve it with a nice green salad and a loaf of crusty French bread and let your guests take a trip down the bayou!

One 3½-pound chicken, cut into 8 pieces

2 tablespoons plus 1 teaspoon Emeril's Original Essence

½ teaspoon salt

¼ cup vegetable oil

1 cup chopped celery

1 cup chopped green bell peppers

1 cup chopped onions

1 tablespoon minced garlic

1 pound andouille sausage, cut crosswise into ¼-inch slices

½ pound boneless smoked ham, cut into ¼-inch cubes

2 cups rice

2 cups Chicken Stock (page 4), or canned low-sodium chicken broth

1 cup canned whole tomatoes, drained and crushed

1 tablespoon tomato paste

1 teaspoon Worcestershire sauce

½ teaspoon Emeril's Kick It Up! Red Pepper Sauce, or other hot sauce, plus more for serving

4 bay leaves

4 sprigs fresh thyme

2 tablespoons finely sliced green onions, for garnish

1. Preheat the oven to 375°F.

2. Season the chicken with 2 tablespoons Essence and the salt. Heat the oil in a small Dutch oven or heavy lidded pot over medium-high heat. Add the chicken and cook until browned on all sides, working in batches if necessary, 8 to 10 minutes per batch. Transfer the chicken to a plate and set aside. Add the celery, bell peppers, and onions

and cook until they begin to soften, about 2 minutes. Add the garlic and cook for another 2 minutes. Add the sausage and ham and cook for another 2 minutes. Add the rice, stir to blend, and cook for another 2 minutes. Add the Chicken Stock, tomatoes, tomato paste, Worcestershire, the remaining 1 teaspoon Essence, the pepper sauce, bay leaves, and thyme. Stir to combine and return the chicken to the pot, nestling the pieces in the rice mixture.

3.    Cover the pot and bake until the chicken and rice are tender, about 40 minutes. Remove from the oven and let stand, still covered, for 5 minutes. Garnish with the green onions and serve with hot sauce.

# COUNTRY CAPTAIN

• MAKES 8 TO 10 SERVINGS •

My friend Sarah Etheridge says this Southern classic was often served at family gatherings and potluck dinners in her hometown of Columbus, Georgia. Rumors abound about this dish's legendary status. Some associate it with President Franklin D. Roosevelt, who kept a home in Warm Springs, Georgia. Still others associate it with General George S. Patton, who would pass through Columbus on the train. Obviously, it's popular! Try it and you'll see why.

1½ cups all-purpose flour

1 tablespoon paprika

2 teaspoons salt

1 teaspoon freshly ground black pepper

Two 3½-pound chickens, cut into serving pieces

3 tablespoons vegetable oil

2 tablespoons unsalted butter

2 cups chopped yellow onions

2 cups chopped green bell peppers

1 cup chopped celery

1 bay leaf

1 tablespoon curry powder

½ teaspoon ground dried thyme

¼ teaspoon crushed red pepper

1 tablespoon minced garlic

6 cups canned whole peeled tomatoes, crushed with their juice

1 cup Chicken Stock (page 4), or canned low-sodium chicken broth

1 tablespoon dark brown sugar

1 cup dried currants

Steamed white rice, for serving (page 107)

6 ounces toasted slivered almonds, for garnish

1. Combine the flour, paprika, 1 teaspoon salt, and the black pepper in a large shallow dish and stir to blend. Dredge the chicken pieces in the flour mixture, coating evenly. Shake off any excess. Set aside.

2.   Heat the oil and 1 tablespoon butter in a large heavy saucepan over medium-high heat. Cook the chicken, in batches, until lightly browned, 3 to 4 minutes per side. Transfer the chicken to paper towels to drain; set aside.

3.   Add the remaining tablespoon butter to the saucepan and add the onions, bell peppers, celery, bay leaf, curry powder, thyme, and crushed red pepper. Cook, stirring, until the vegetables are soft, about 5 minutes. Add the garlic and cook, stirring, until fragrant, about 30 seconds.

4.   Add the tomatoes, Chicken Stock, brown sugar, and the remaining teaspoon salt. Stir to blend, and then reduce the heat to medium. Add the chicken and cook, stirring occasionally, until very tender but not falling off the bones, about 50 minutes. Add the currants and cook 10 minutes longer. Serve hot over steamed white rice. Garnish with the almonds.

# Chicken Chili with Cornbread Topping

• MAKES 8 SERVINGS •

Chicken chili topped with cornbread will make you feel like you are home on the range. If you have a cast-iron Dutch oven, use it for this dish. This is crowd-pleasing potluck at its best.

3 tablespoons vegetable oil

4 pounds skinless, boneless chicken thighs, cubed

2 tablespoons Emeril's Southwest Essence

4 teaspoons chili powder

2 teaspoons ground cumin

2½ cups chopped yellow onions

1½ cups chopped red bell peppers

¼ cup minced jalapeños

2 tablespoons minced garlic

2 bay leaves

1¼ teaspoons salt

½ teaspoon cayenne pepper

2 cups fresh corn kernels (from about 3 ears)

Two 28-ounce cans chopped tomatoes with their juice

2 cups Chicken Stock (page 4)

½ cup chopped fresh cilantro

1 recipe Cornbread Topping (recipe follows)

1 cup grated Cheddar cheese

½ cup chopped green onions, for garnish

2 cups sour cream, for serving

1.   Preheat the oven to 400°F.

2.   Heat 2 tablespoons oil in a medium Dutch oven (preferably cast-iron) over high heat. Add the chicken, Southwest Essence, chili powder, and cumin and cook, stirring, until browned on all sides, about 5 minutes. Transfer to a bowl and set aside.

3.   Add the remaining tablespoon oil to the Dutch oven along with the onions, bell peppers, and jalapeños and cook, stirring, for 3 minutes. Add the garlic, bay leaves, salt, and cayenne and cook, stirring, for 30 seconds. Add the corn and cook until starting to

color and pop, about 3 minutes. Add the reserved chicken, tomatoes and their juice, and the Chicken Stock and bring to a boil. Reduce the heat to a simmer and cook, stirring occasionally, until the mixture has thickened and is chili consistency, 30 to 40 minutes.

4.    When the chili has thickened, remove from the heat and discard the bay leaves. Stir in the cilantro and adjust the seasoning to taste. Spoon the Cornbread Topping over the chicken mixture, leaving a ½-inch border around the sides.

5.    Bake until the topping is golden brown, 15 to 20 minutes. Remove the chili from the oven and sprinkle the cheese on top. Return to the oven until melted, 2 minutes. Remove from the oven and garnish with the chopped green onions. Serve hot with the sour cream alongside.

• • • • • • • • • • • • • • • • • • • • • • • • • • • • • • • • • • • • • • • • • • • • • • • • • • • • • • • • • • • • • • • •

### CORNBREAD TOPPING
¾ cup cornmeal
¼ cup all-purpose flour
1½ teaspoons baking powder
½ teaspoon salt

½ cup buttermilk
1 large egg
2 tablespoons bacon grease, melted,
    or vegetable oil

• • • • • • • • • • • • • • • • • • • • • • • • • • • • • • • • • • • • • • • • • • • • • • • • • • • • • • • • • • • • • • • •

1.    Combine the cornmeal, flour, baking powder, and salt in a mixing bowl.

2.    Beat together the buttermilk, egg, and bacon grease in a small mixing bowl. Add to the dry ingredients and mix until just blended, being careful not to overmix.

## — DO AHEAD —

Make the chili a day ahead to make things easy on yourself. The next day, when you're ready to serve, reheat the chili, dollop the cornmeal batter over the top, and stick it in the oven.

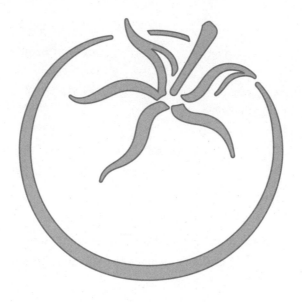

# CHEESY CHICKEN TAMALES

MAKES APPROXIMATELY 18 TAMALES, 4 TO 6 SERVINGS

When you say *tamale,* most people think of the more common beef- or chili-filled variety—but these cheesy chicken tamales are gonna knock your socks off! They're different, too, in that the outer tamale coating contains grits in addition to the masa harina—and this works well with the cheese, chicken, and poblano filling. Now, this recipe serves 4 to 6, but once you've mastered the art of tamale making, you might want to make a bigger batch for a party, and you'll find that this recipe can be scaled up proportionately with no problem.

One 8-ounce package dried corn husks
⅔ cup quick-cooking or old-fashioned grits (not instant)
1¼ cups Chicken Stock (page 4), plus more for tamale batter if needed
¾ cup masa harina
2 teaspoons ground cumin
1 cup lard or vegetable shortening

1 teaspoon baking powder
½ teaspoon salt
1½ cups shredded cooked chicken meat
½ pound Monterey Jack or mild Cheddar cheese, coarsely grated
4 poblano chiles, roasted, seeded, peeled, and coarsely chopped

1. Combine the corn husks and enough water to cover in a medium saucepan and bring to a boil. Top the husks with a heavy plate or bowl to keep them submerged, and boil for 10 minutes. Remove the pan from the heat and steep until the husks are soft and pliable, 1 to 1½ hours. Drain the husks, remove any corn silk, and pat dry before assembling the tamales.

2. Process the grits in the bowl of a food processor for 1 minute. Bring the Chicken Stock to a low boil in a small saucepan. Transfer the grits to a large bowl and add the hot stock. Let stand, uncovered, for 10 to 12 minutes. Add the masa harina and cumin and mix until evenly combined. Cool to room temperature before proceeding.

3. In the bowl of an electric mixer fitted with the paddle attachment, whip the lard until smooth, light, and creamy, about 2 minutes. Stir in half of the masa mixture and whip until well blended. Add the remaining masa mixture, little by little, until the batter resembles thick cake batter, adding additional Chicken Stock if needed. Add the baking powder and salt and whip for 1 to 2 minutes, or until well incorporated and smooth.

4. Lay 1 corn husk on a work surface with the narrow end closest to you. Top with a second corn husk so that the fat ends overlap in the middle and the narrow ends point in opposite directions. Spoon ¼ cup of the masa batter into the center of the husks and, with the back of a spoon, spread it into a 4-inch square. Place about 1 generous tablespoon each of the chicken, grated cheese, and chopped poblanos in the center of the masa square.

5. Fold 1 side of the corn husk over the filling, fold the other side over the filling, and then the top and bottom ends. With a piece of kitchen string or a thin strip of leftover corn husk, tie the tamale together loosely so that it resembles an oblong rectangular package. Repeat with the remaining corn husks and filling.

6. Once the tamales are assembled, line a steamer basket with any remaining corn husks and layer the tamales inside the steamer basket, leaving enough room for the tamales to expand slightly while cooking. Cover the tamales with another corn husk, cover the steamer with a tight-fitting lid and steam for 1½ hours, or until the tamales are tender and pull away easily from the corn husks. Let sit for 10 to 15 minutes before serving.

# — TAMALES —

Traditionally tamales are wrapped in a softened corn husk or banana leaf, but sometimes you will see them wrapped in paper instead. While the paper is a lot easier to use, it lacks that wonderful flavor imparted by husks or leaves.

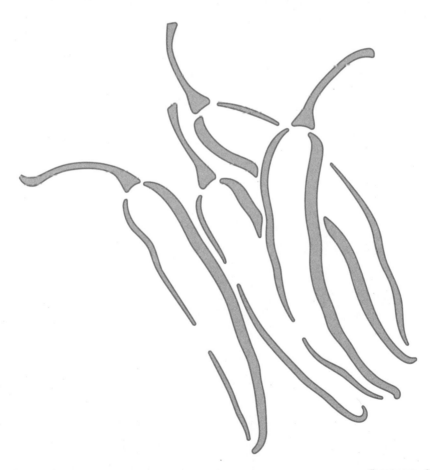

# Shrimp Étouffée

MAKES 3 QUARTS, ABOUT 10 SERVINGS

If you have ever been to southern Louisiana, then you probably have tasted an étouffée. Though it may sound very fancy, *étouffée* is French for "smothered"— and generally refers to a sort of stew in which the main ingredient is cooked in a rich gravy and served over white rice. Some purists use only butter and seasonings in their étouffée—for a very rich dish—while others use a roux as the basis of the sauce, as I do here. The most popular type of étouffée is crawfish, but since crawfish can be difficult to find, I've decided to give you a shrimp version. And, boy, is it good! A perfect dish for a big family gathering.

6 tablespoons unsalted butter

½ cup all-purpose flour

4 cups chopped onions

2 cups chopped green bell peppers

2 cups chopped celery

2 tablespoons minced garlic

One 14.5-ounce can diced tomatoes

2 bay leaves

2 teaspoons salt

½ teaspoon cayenne pepper

2 tablespoons Emeril's Original Essence

1 quart Shrimp Stock (page 10)

3 pounds medium shrimp (21 to 25 per pound), peeled and deveined

¼ cup chopped fresh parsley

Steamed white rice, for serving (page 107)

½ cup thinly sliced tender green onion tops, for garnish

1.  In a large Dutch oven set over medium heat, melt the butter. Add the flour and stir continuously to make a roux. Stir the roux over medium heat until the color of peanut butter, 5 to 7 minutes. Add the onions, bell peppers, celery, and garlic to the roux, and cook, stirring often, for 10 minutes. Add the tomatoes to the pot and season with the bay leaves, salt, cayenne, and 1 tablespoon Essence. Cook the tomatoes for 2 to 3 minutes and then whisk in the Shrimp Stock.

2.   Bring the pot to a boil, and reduce to a simmer. Cook the étouffée, stirring occasionally, for 45 minutes. Season the shrimp with the remaining tablespoon Essence and add them to the pot, stirring to evenly distribute. Cook the shrimp for 5 to 7 minutes, or until they are cooked through. Add the chopped parsley to the pot and stir to combine. Serve the étouffée with steamed white rice. Garnish with the green onion tops.

# Oven-Poached Salmon with Pink Grapefruit and Tarragon Sauce

• MAKES 6 TO 8 SERVINGS •

2 cups Shrimp Stock (page 10) or
    Chicken Stock (page 4)

1 cup dry white wine

3 cups pink grapefruit juice

1 bay leaf

2 smashed garlic cloves

1½ teaspoons whole black
    peppercorns

1 sprig fresh thyme

3 sprigs fresh tarragon

3 tablespoons minced shallots

One 6- to 7-pound side of salmon,
    trimmed, and pin bones removed

1 tablespoon kosher salt

1 teaspoon fresh cracked white
    pepper

1. Preheat the oven to 300°F.

2. In a medium saucepan, combine the Shrimp Stock, white wine, grapefruit juice, bay leaf, garlic, peppercorns, thyme, tarragon, and shallots. Bring to a boil over medium-high heat, then reduce the heat to a simmer. Simmer the infusion for 15 minutes, then remove from the heat.

3. Take two pieces of aluminum foil, 2 feet long, and lay them, overlapping, side by side lengthwise. Lay the salmon perpendicular to the seam, and pick up the salmon by grabbing both ends of foil right at the point where they meet. Place the salmon in a roasting pan (we used one 11.5 × 15 inches) or another large baking dish with high sides that is just long enough to hold the side of salmon. Season the salmon with the kosher salt and white pepper and pour the hot poaching liquid over the top of the salmon. The liquid should come at least halfway up the side of the salmon. Cover the roasting pan with aluminum foil and place in the oven. Cook the salmon for 18 minutes, remove from the oven, and remove the aluminum foil cover. Using the two sheets of aluminum

foil underneath the salmon, carefully grasp the sheets on both sides where the edges overlap in order to lift the salmon out of the poaching liquid. Lay the salmon on a large platter, and strain the poaching liquid into a saucepan and place over medium-high heat. Bring the liquid to a boil, reduce the heat to medium, and continue to boil and reduce the liquid until you have 1 cup left, 20 to 25 minutes. Remove from the heat and reserve the liquid for making the sauce.

FOR THE SAUCE
3 tablespoons unsalted butter
2 tablespoons minced shallots
1 teaspoon minced garlic
¼ cup dry white wine

1 cup reduced poaching liquid
2 cups heavy cream
¼ teaspoon freshly ground black pepper
2 tablespoons all-purpose flour

Set a 1-quart saucepan over medium heat. Add 1 tablespoon of the butter to the pan, and when it melts and turns frothy, add the shallots and garlic to the pan. Stir continuously for 1 minute, then deglaze with the white wine. When the wine has nearly completely evaporated, add the reduced poaching liquid, heavy cream, and black pepper. In a small mixing bowl, combine the remaining 2 tablespoons of butter with the flour, and mash together to form a paste; this is also known as a beurre manié. Once the saucepan comes to a boil, add the beurre manié and whisk vigorously to incorporate. Cook the sauce for 20 minutes, or until any floury taste is gone. Taste and reseason the sauce if necessary. Remove the sauce from the stovetop and let cool before serving with the salmon. The salmon and sauce may be served warm, at room temperature, or even chilled.

# EMERIL'S POT ROAST

• MAKES ABOUT 10 SERVINGS •

**M**any of us have cherished memories of Sunday pot roast dinners . . . well, here's my version of this comfort food classic. It's a good, simple pot roast made just the way I like it—and I think you'll approve.

Two 3-pound boneless chuck roasts
1 head garlic, cloves peeled and
    sliced in half if very large
2½ teaspoons salt
2½ teaspoons freshly ground black
    pepper
4 tablespoons vegetable oil
2 teaspoons Emeril's Original
    Essence
⅓ cup all-purpose flour

2 cups chopped onions
1 cup chopped celery
1 cup chopped carrots
Three 14-ounce cans low-sodium
    beef broth
¼ cup tomato paste
2 bay leaves
2 pounds russet potatoes, peeled
    and quartered

1. Preheat the oven to 300°F.

2. With a small, sharp knife, make 1½-inch-deep slits around the outside of the roasts. Insert the cloves of garlic into the slits. Rub the roasts with the salt and black pepper on all sides.

3. Heat a large Dutch oven or other heavy, wide pot over high heat. Add 2 tablespoons oil and heat. Add the roasts and sear on all sides, about 4 minutes per side. Remove the roasts from the pan and sprinkle with Essence on all sides. Reduce the heat to medium-high. Add the remaining 2 tablespoons oil and the flour and cook, stirring constantly, until chocolate brown in color, about 5 minutes. Add the onions, celery, and carrots and cook until the vegetables begin to soften, about 5 minutes. Add the beef broth, tomato paste, and bay leaves and stir to blend. Return the roasts to the pan and top with the potatoes.

4. Cover and bake for 3 to 4 hours, depending on how tender you prefer your meat. Remove the pot from the oven and remove the meat and potatoes; set aside. Place the pot on the stove over medium-high heat and cook until the gravy is reduced slightly and begins to thicken, about 10 minutes. Remove the bay leaves. Puree the gravy with an immersion blender or in batches in a bar blender. Slice the meat and cut the potatoes into bite-size pieces; return to the pot with the gravy. Serve warm.

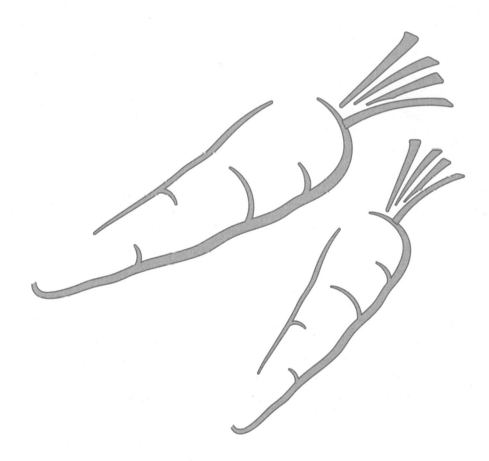

# PASSOVER BRISKET

• MAKES ABOUT 8 SERVINGS •

A while back I was looking for a really good Passover recipe, and our Web designer, Damion Michaels, stepped forward to say he knew just the one—a Passover brisket made by his mother-in-law, Harriet. Well, Harriet was nice enough to share the recipe with us; we changed it just a bit so as not to reveal all her secrets. Thank you, Harriet!

One 6-pound brisket

1 head garlic, cloves peeled

1 quart beef stock (unsalted or low-sodium)

3 tablespoons vegetable oil

4 cups sliced onions

1 cup ketchup

1 cup chili sauce

1 cup packed brown sugar

2 teaspoons salt

2 teaspoons Emeril's Original Essence

1 teaspoon freshly ground black pepper, or to taste

1 teaspoon onion powder

1 teaspoon garlic powder

1. Preheat the broiler to high.

2. Using a paring knife, make slits all over the brisket and stuff with garlic cloves. Place the brisket in a baking dish or casserole and broil until browned on top, about 10 minutes. Remove the baking dish from the oven, turn the brisket, and return the dish to the oven until the brisket is browned on the other side, about 10 more minutes. Reduce the oven temperature to 350°F. Add enough beef stock to the casserole to come up 1 inch on the sides, cover with foil, and bake 1 hour.

3. While the brisket is cooking, heat the oil in a large skillet over medium-high heat. Add the onions and cook, stirring occasionally, until caramelized and most of the liquid has evaporated, about 20 minutes; reserve.

4.  Add the remaining ingredients to a small bowl and stir to combine; reserve.

5.  Remove the baking dish from the oven after 1 hour and arrange most of the onions on top of the brisket and the rest around it. Pour the ketchup mixture over and around the brisket. Cover and continue to cook until the meat is very tender but not falling apart, about 3 more hours. Remove the brisket to a carving board and slice. Serve the sliced brisket with the pan juices alongside. (The brisket is better if made a day in advance; simply reheat covered in a low oven.)

## — BRISKET SANDWICHES —

Talk about good leftovers! This stuff is good any time of year and makes killer sandwiches the next day. Just cover and reheat in a low oven.

# EMERIL'S BEEF STROGANOFF

When I decided to write this cookbook I knew I had to include a recipe for beef Stroganoff. It's one of my favorite dishes and I daresay I'm not alone! This recipe yields enough to feed a small army, or at least quite a few very hungry friends. I've kicked it up a bit with some red wine and a variety of onions. And, hey, it tastes even better after a day in the fridge.

1 pound bacon, chopped

3½ pounds beef top sirloin, trimmed and sliced into strips about 1 × 3 inches

2½ teaspoons salt

1½ teaspoons freshly ground black pepper

4 cups thinly sliced onions

1 tablespoon minced garlic

½ cup all-purpose flour

1 cup dry red wine

Two 14-ounce cans beef broth

1 teaspoon Emeril's Original Essence

1 pound large white button mushrooms, wiped clean, trimmed, and sliced

½ cup finely chopped red onions

½ cup finely chopped green onions

1 tablespoon olive oil

1 pound wide egg noodles

1 cup sour cream

2 cups grated white Cheddar cheese

1. Preheat the oven to 350°F.

2. Cook the bacon in a large heavy skillet or Dutch oven over high heat until slightly crispy, about 7 minutes. Meanwhile, season the beef with 1 teaspoon salt and 1 teaspoon black pepper. Add the beef to the bacon and cook, stirring, for 3 minutes. Add the onions and cook, stirring, until soft, about 8 minutes. Add the garlic and the flour. Cook, stirring, for 3 minutes. Add the red wine and the beef broth. Stir to blend and bring to a boil. Add ½ teaspoon salt, the remaining ½ teaspoon black pepper, and the Essence. Reduce the heat to medium and simmer for 5 minutes. Add the mushrooms, red and green onions and cook, stirring occasionally, for 4 minutes. Remove from the heat.

**3.** Combine 4 quarts water, the olive oil, and the remaining 1 teaspoon salt in a large pot. Bring to a boil, add the noodles, and cook until al dente, 5 to 6 minutes. Drain well and transfer to a large mixing bowl. Add the beef sauce and the sour cream and toss to coat evenly. Pour the mixture into a deep 9 × 13-inch baking dish. (This will be a tight fit.) Sprinkle the cheese evenly over the top of the noodle mixture. Place the baking dish on a large baking sheet and bake until bubbly and golden, about 20 minutes. Remove from the oven and serve warm.

# CREOLE MUSTARD AND HERB-WRAPPED BEEF TENDERLOIN

• MAKES 8 TO 10 SERVINGS •

Filet of beef always impresses a crowd. Easy to prepare and serve, it will make everyone think that you slaved hours over the stove. (Let them!) The secret is not to overcook the meat. Filet is an elegant addition to a buffet table. Pair this with the Roasted Potato and Garlic Salad (page 87) and a green salad.

3 tablespoons vegetable oil

1 beef tenderloin, trimmed and tied (3½ to 4 pounds)

1 tablespoon salt

2 teaspoons coarsely ground black pepper

½ cup Creole mustard or other spicy whole-grain mustard

8 garlic cloves, finely minced or pressed

1 bunch fresh rosemary, finely chopped

1 bunch fresh thyme, finely chopped

1. Preheat the oven to 425°F.

2. Heat the oil in a large skillet over high heat until almost smoking. Season the beef on all sides with the salt and pepper and transfer to the skillet. Cook until well browned on all sides, turning with tongs when necessary, 8 to 10 minutes. Transfer the beef to a cutting board or platter and, using a rubber spatula or spoon, rub it all over with Creole mustard and garlic. Cover the meat with the chopped herbs, using your hands to evenly pat them into the mustard coating. Place the prepared filet in a shallow roasting pan and cook until a meat thermometer inserted in the thickest part registers 125°F for medium

rare, 20 to 25 minutes. Remove the meat from the oven and let stand for at least 10 minutes before slicing.

NOTE   The meat may also be served at room temperature; but don't slice it until just before serving.

# Poor Man's Beef Wellington

• MAKES 6 SERVINGS •

Try my simplified rendition of this classic dish—it's made with ground beef, mashed potatoes, and mushrooms instead of tenderloin and foie gras. Hey, all wrapped up in puff pastry and then baked to golden brown goodness, it's a beautiful thing.

- - -

1 pound ground beef

1½ cups chopped yellow onions

2 tablespoons minced garlic

2 teaspoons Emeril's Original Essence

½ teaspoon crushed red pepper

½ teaspoon salt

2 tablespoons tomato paste

¼ cup heavy cream

2 tablespoons unsalted butter

½ pound white button mushrooms, chopped

¼ teaspoon dried thyme

1 tablespoon Worcestershire sauce

1 large egg

2 tablespoons water

One 17.3-ounce package frozen puff pastry (2 sheets), thawed in the refrigerator

Mashed Potatoes (recipe follows)

¾ cup diced smoked Gouda cheese

1 cup grated sharp Cheddar cheese

- - -

1.  Preheat the oven to 400°F.

2.  Heat a large skillet over high heat. Add the beef and cook, stirring, until well browned, about 5 minutes. Add the onions, garlic, Essence, crushed red pepper, and ¼ teaspoon salt and cook, stirring, until the onions are soft and lightly caramelized, about 7 minutes. Add the tomato paste and heavy cream and cook until the cream is evaporated, 1 to 2 minutes. Remove from the heat and spread on a plate to cool.

3.  In a large skillet, melt the butter over medium-high heat. Add the mushrooms, thyme, Worcestershire, and the remaining ¼ teaspoon salt and cook, stirring often, until

most of the liquid has evaporated, 8 to 10 minutes. Remove from the heat and spread on a plate to cool.

4. Combine the egg and water in a small bowl to make an egg wash. Whisk to combine.

5. On a lightly floured surface, roll out the puff pastry sheets, 1 at a time, to a ⅛-inch thickness about 11 inches square. Brush 1 short edge of 1 sheet with egg wash and overlap with the other. With the rolling pin, press down on the seam to make 1 large sheet. Spread the cooled Mashed Potatoes along the lower third of the pastry, leaving a 1-inch border on 3 sides. Top with the beef and the mushrooms, then sprinkle the Gouda cubes over the top. Brush the border with egg wash and fold the pastry over the filling to completely enclose. Press to seal the edges tightly with the tines of a fork. Transfer to a large baking sheet and brush with the egg wash. Cut 5 small steam vents in the top of the pastry. Bake until starting to turn golden brown, 15 to 16 minutes. Sprinkle the top with the Cheddar and bake until the pastry is golden brown and the cheese is melted, about 4 minutes.

6. Remove from the oven and let rest for 5 minutes. Transfer to a large serving platter. Slice and serve warm.

# MASHED POTATOES

MAKES ABOUT 2½ CUPS

¾ pound Idaho potatoes, peeled and cut into large dice
¾ teaspoon salt
6 tablespoons heavy cream
2 tablespoons unsalted butter
⅛ teaspoon freshly ground white pepper
1 tablespoon minced fresh parsley

1. Combine the potatoes, ½ teaspoon salt, and enough water to cover by 1 inch in a medium saucepan. Bring to a boil and cook until just fork-tender, about 12 minutes. Remove from the heat and drain. Return to the pan and cook for 1 minute, mashing with a potato masher or heavy whisk over medium heat. Add the cream, butter, remaining ¼ teaspoon salt, and white pepper and mash until smooth. Stir in the parsley.

2. Remove from the heat and spread on a plate to cool. (The potatoes can be made in advance and refrigerated until ready to use.)

# Kickin' Chili

Everyone has an opinion about chili. I can't keep track of all the itty-bitty differences between this chili and that chili. So I take a little bit from each one and make just real good chili the way I like it.

2 tablespoons vegetable oil

4 pounds ground beef

4 cups chopped yellow onions

3 tablespoons chili powder

1 tablespoon ground cumin

2 teaspoons Emeril's Southwest Essence

2 teaspoons cayenne pepper

1 teaspoon ground cinnamon

¼ teaspoon crushed red pepper

1 bay leaf

2 tablespoons minced garlic

Four 12-ounce bottles dark beer

Two 28-ounce cans whole tomatoes, crushed

2 tablespoons tomato paste

1 tablespoon salt

1 tablespoon plus 1 teaspoon dark brown sugar

1 ounce (1 square) unsweetened chocolate

6 cups cooked red kidney beans (see Note) or four 15-ounce cans, drained and rinsed

1 cup grated Cheddar cheese, for garnish

1 cup finely chopped green onions, for garnish

½ cup chopped fresh cilantro, for garnish

Heat the oil in a large heavy pot over high heat. Add the beef and brown well, about 10 minutes. Add the onions, chili powder, cumin, Southwest Essence, cayenne, cinnamon, crushed red pepper, and bay leaf and cook, stirring often, until the onions soften, about 8 minutes. Add the garlic and cook until fragrant, about 30 seconds. Add the beer and cook until the foam subsides, about 1 minute. Add the tomatoes, tomato paste, salt, brown sugar, and chocolate to the pot. Stir well and bring to a boil. Reduce to a simmer and cook until slightly thickened, about 1 hour, stirring occasionally to prevent the chili from sticking to the bottom of the pot. Skim off as much fat as possible. Add the beans, return to a simmer, cover, and cook until thickened, about 1½ hours longer. Serve with the cheese, green onions, and cilantro alongside as garnish.

NOTE    To make 6 cups cooked red kidney beans: Soak 1 pound dried beans for 6 hours or overnight. Drain the beans and place them in a large saucepan. Add water to cover by 2 inches and bring to a boil. Reduce the heat to a simmer and cook until just tender, 30 to 45 minutes. Drain and set aside to cool.

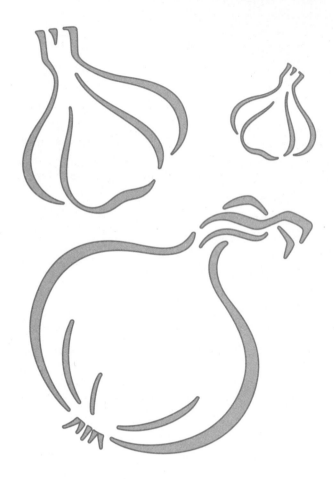

# RHENA'S STUFFED PEPPERS

· MAKES 10 LARGE STUFFED PEPPERS, 10 SERVINGS ·

My friend Marcelle Bienvenu shared her mother Rhena's recipe for this traditional Louisiana dish. Her mother did more than her share of cooking for crowds, because theirs was a family that knew no strangers when it came to get-togethers. The eggplant and ground meat stuffing can be served on its own or with rice. No sauce is necessary for these peppers, since the stuffing itself is moist. If you prefer a drier stuffing, simply increase the amount of bread crumbs added at the end, but taste and adjust the seasoning as needed. You eggplant lovers out there are gonna love this one! They are even better the next day!

1 tablespoon plus ½ teaspoon salt
10 large green bell peppers
¼ cup vegetable oil
1⅔ cups chopped yellow onions
⅔ cup chopped celery
1 tablespoon minced garlic
2 pounds ground beef
3 large eggplants (about 3¾ pounds total), peeled and cut into ½-inch cubes

1½ teaspoons Emeril's Original Essence
½ teaspoon cayenne pepper
1 cup plus 2 tablespoons bread crumbs
¼ cup freshly grated Parmesan cheese

1. Bring a large pot of water to a boil. Season with ½ teaspoon salt.

2. Slice the tops off the bell peppers and reserve, discarding the stems. Remove the seeds and ribs and discard. Blanch the bell pepper bottoms in the boiling water, working in batches if necessary, until crisp-tender, about 3 minutes. Remove the peppers from the water and set aside to cool.

3. Chop the reserved pepper tops; you should have about 1⅓ cups. Heat the oil in a medium pot over medium-high heat. Add the chopped pepper tops, onions, and celery and cook until the vegetables are soft, about 5 minutes. Add the garlic and cook for 1 minute. Add the ground beef and cook, stirring, until the beef is browned and all the pink has disappeared, about 5 minutes. Add the eggplant and season with the remaining 1 tablespoon salt, Essence, and cayenne. Cook, stirring occasionally, until the eggplant is very soft, about 30 minutes. The filling should be moist—if it begins to dry out and stick to the bottom of the pan, add a bit of water. Remove the eggplant mixture from the heat and add 1 cup of the bread crumbs—this should be just enough to bind the mixture lightly. Cool the mixture for about 10 minutes.

4. Fill the bell pepper bottoms with the eggplant stuffing and place in a large casserole or baking dish. Combine the remaining 2 tablespoons bread crumbs with the Parmesan and divide this mixture evenly among the tops of the peppers. Add enough water to just cover the bottom of the casserole and bake the peppers, uncovered, for about 30 minutes, or until heated through and the tops are lightly golden.

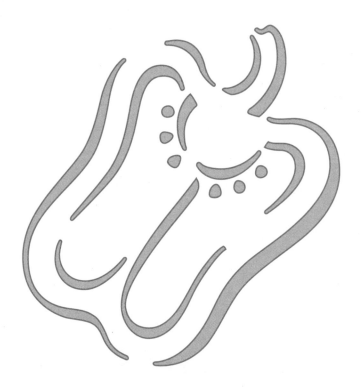

# KICKED-UP CABBAGE ROLLS

Many people turn up their noses at the very idea of trying a cabbage roll. Hey, don't be so quick to judge! I cannot imagine a better cold-weather meal than some of these and a good dark beer—you'd better believe it!

- 2 teaspoons olive oil
- 2½ cups chopped onions
- 2 tablespoons Emeril's Original Essence
- 2 tablespoons minced garlic
- One 35-ounce can whole tomatoes, broken into pieces, with their juice
- One 15-ounce can tomato sauce
- 1 tablespoon apple cider vinegar
- 2 teaspoons sugar
- ½ teaspoon salt
- ¼ teaspoon crushed red pepper
- ½ cup heavy cream
- ½ pound ground beef
- ½ pound bulk pork breakfast sausage
- 2 cups cooked long-grain white rice
- ¼ teaspoon freshly ground black pepper
- 1 large egg
- 1 head cabbage, cored and blanched in hot water until the leaves are soft and easy to separate

1.   Heat the olive oil in a large saucepan over medium-high heat. Add 1¼ cups onions and 1 tablespoon Essence and cook, stirring, for 3 minutes. Add 1 tablespoon garlic and cook, stirring, for 1 minute. Add the tomatoes, tomato sauce, vinegar, sugar, salt, and crushed red pepper and cook, stirring occasionally, for about 20 minutes, or until the sauce thickens. Add the heavy cream and cook for 5 to 10 minutes, or until thickened and flavorful. Taste the tomato sauce and adjust the seasoning if necessary. Set aside.

2.   Heat a medium skillet over high heat. Add the ground beef, breakfast sausage, the remaining 1¼ cups onions, and the remaining tablespoon Essence and cook over high heat, breaking the meat into pieces with the back of a spoon, until the meat is golden brown and the onions are very soft, about 8 minutes. Add the remaining 1 tablespoon garlic and cook, stirring, for 1 minute. Remove from the heat and let cool slightly. Add

the rice, black pepper, egg, and ¼ cup of the tomato sauce and stir until thoroughly blended.

3.     Preheat the oven to 350°F. Ladle 1 cup of the tomato sauce onto the bottom of a nonreactive 9 × 13-inch casserole or baking dish.

4.     Separate the cabbage leaves and cut off the thickest part of the hard spine from each leaf. Spread the leaves on paper towels and pat dry. Working with one at a time, spoon about ¼ cup of the filling into the center of a leaf. Roll up egg-roll fashion, tucking in the ends, and place the roll onto the sauce in the casserole dish, seam side down. Repeat with the remaining leaves (fit the rolls into the casserole in 1 layer.) Pour the remaining tomato sauce over the rolls, cover tightly with aluminum foil, and bake until the rolls are very tender and heated through, 45 minutes to 1 hour.

# Paul's "Make the Whole Crew Happy" Sausage Meatballs with Red Gravy

• MAKES 6 HEARTY SERVINGS, PLUS LEFTOVER MEATBALLS FOR SANDWICHES THE NEXT DAY •

My friend Paul is a New Orleans firefighter who likes to cook and often makes this for the guys at the engine house. Let me tell you, these are some serious meatballs. I suggest you do as Paul and the guys do and use any leftover meatballs to make meatball po'boys the next day.

### RED GRAVY

3 tablespoons vegetable oil

5 cups chopped yellow onions

2 teaspoons Emeril's Italian Essence

1 teaspoon salt

½ teaspoon crushed red pepper

20 cloves garlic, minced (about ⅓ cup)

2 tablespoons whole anise seeds

Two 6-ounce cans tomato paste

Four 15-ounce cans tomato sauce

One 28-ounce can whole tomatoes, pureed with their juice

2 teaspoons Emeril's Original Essence

### SAUSAGE MEATBALLS

1½ pounds ground chuck

1½ pounds sweet Italian sausage, removed from casings

1 pound fresh hot sausage, removed from casings

10 cloves garlic, minced

2 large eggs, lightly beaten

4 teaspoons Emeril's Original Essence

½ teaspoon salt

½ teaspoon freshly ground black pepper

1 pound spaghetti, cooked according to package directions

1 cup grated Parmesan cheese, for serving

1. Make the Red Gravy: In a very large saucepan or Dutch oven, heat the oil over medium-high heat. Add the onions, Italian Essence, salt, and crushed red pepper and cook, stirring, until the onions are soft, 6 minutes. Add the garlic and anise seeds and cook, stirring, for 2 minutes. Add the tomato paste and cook, stirring frequently, until the paste begins to brown, about 5 minutes. Add the tomato sauce, pureed tomatoes, 2½ cups of water, and the Original Essence and bring to a boil. Reduce the heat and simmer for 45 minutes, stirring occasionally.

2. Make the Sausage Meatballs: In a large bowl, combine the ground chuck, Italian sausage, hot sausage, garlic, eggs, Original Essence, salt, and black pepper, and mix briefly but thoroughly to distribute the seasonings. Shape into about 20 large meatballs, about ⅓ cup each, and set aside in the refrigerator.

3. Add the Sausage Meatballs to the Red Gravy and do not stir until the meatballs float to the surface, about 10 to 12 minutes. Stir well and simmer the meatballs in the sauce for 30 minutes, stirring occasionally, and skimming off any fat that rises to the surface. Taste, adjust the seasoning if necessary, and serve immediately over hot pasta. Pass the grated Parmesan at the table.

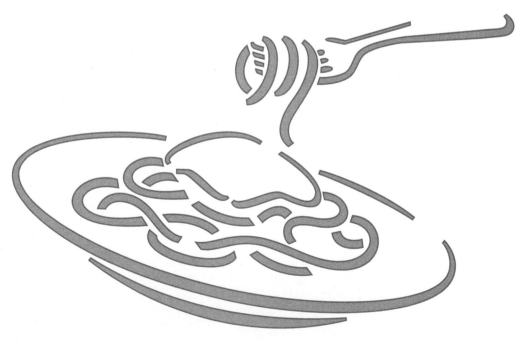

# Asian Pork Tenderloins

Pork tenderloins are great cooked on the grill or in the oven. Just don't overcook them, or you will end up with cardboard tubes instead! Don't worry—I'll tell you how long to cook them. The temperature might seem a bit low to all you pork police out there, but the meat continues cooking while it rests. The Asian flavors are noticeable whether the meat is served warm or at room temperature, making this dish perfect for a potluck affair!

½ cup soy sauce

¼ cup pineapple juice

¼ cup coarsely chopped green onions

¼ cup coarsely chopped shallots

¼ cup loosely packed fresh cilantro leaves

2 tablespoons coarsely chopped fresh ginger

2 tablespoons honey

2 tablespoons rice wine vinegar

2 tablespoons Emeril's Asian Essence

2 tablespoons chopped garlic

1 tablespoon sesame oil

1 tablespoon crushed red pepper

2 pork tenderloins (about 2 pounds total)

1. Combine all the ingredients except the tenderloins in a food processor and pulse several times to puree. Put the tenderloins in a large plastic storage bag and pour in the marinade. Seal the bag and refrigerate for 1 hour.

2. Preheat the oven to 400°F. Heat a large nonstick ovenproof skillet over high heat. When the skillet is hot, add the tenderloins and sear, turning to ensure even browning, about 4 minutes. Transfer to the oven and cook for 18 to 20 minutes, or until an instant-read thermometer inserted in the thickest part reads 145°F. Remove from the oven and let rest for 5 minutes. Alternatively, heat a grill to medium-hot. Grill the tenderloins, turning several times, for 25 minutes, or until an instant-read thermometer inserted in the thickest part reads 145°F. Remove from the grill and let rest for 5 minutes.

# FUNKY SOUTHWEST PORK LOIN

• MAKES 8 TO 10 SERVINGS •

Follow the same rules as in the Asian Pork Tenderloins: Don't overcook; the meat will continue to cook when removed from the oven, and will taste great straight from the oven or at room temperature. But wait—that's not all—let me tell you why this pork loin is so special. It's all in the Mojo Paste with its zesty Southwest flavors. For serving, go with the Southwestern theme and serve the sliced pork with flour tortillas, sour cream, guacamole, and Simply Salsa (page 8). Start off with the Fresh and Fierce Margaritas (page 17), of course.

One 3¾-pound boneless loin pork
  roast
1 tablespoon plus 2 teaspoons
  Emeril's Southwest Essence

Mojo Paste (recipe follows)

1. Preheat the oven 350°F. Line a shallow baking pan with aluminum foil.

2. Place the roast in the pan and rub the Southwest Essence evenly all over it. Spread ½ cup of the Mojo Paste on each side of the roast. Bake, uncovered, for 45 minutes, or until an instant-read thermometer inserted in the thickest part reads 110°F. Remove from the oven and spread the remaining ⅓ cup Mojo Paste on the top of the roast. Return the roast to the oven and bake for 15 to 20 minutes longer, or until the thermometer reads 145°F. Let stand for about 10 minutes before slicing crosswise to serve.

## Mojo Paste

MAKES 1⅓ CUPS

2 jalapeños, stemmed, seeded, and coarsely chopped (about ½ cup)
½ cup coarsely chopped onions
½ cup chopped green onions
½ cup chopped fresh cilantro
½ cup vegetable oil
3 tablespoons canned chipotle peppers in adobo sauce
1 teaspoon salt

Put all the ingredients in a food processor and pulse several times to make a smooth paste.

# Slow-Cooked Pork Roast with Barbecue Sauce

• MAKES 10 TO 12 SERVINGS (SANDWICHES) •

This is the easiest way I know to end up with finger-lickin', delicious, oven-made barbecue. It does take six hours of slow cooking to end up with a roast that is tender enough to be shredded in this manner, which is what you want for pulled-pork barbecue sandwiches. The pork shoulder is a must; don't substitute another cut. Make the barbecue sauce while the pork is roasting so that once the meat comes out of the oven, you're ready to go. All of this can be done a day or two in advance and then reheated—simply make sure that you reheat any shredded meat in a covered dish with some barbecue sauce so it doesn't dry out.

1 pork shoulder roast (Boston butt or picnic roast; 6 to 8 pounds)

4 teaspoons Emeril's Original Essence

1 tablespoon salt

1 teaspoon cayenne pepper

Barbecue Sauce (recipe follows)

Sandwich buns, for serving

1. Remove the pork from the refrigerator and let it come to room temperature before proceeding. Preheat the oven to 350°F and line a roasting pan with aluminum foil. Season the roast well on all sides with the Essence, salt, and cayenne. Place a rack inside the roasting pan and place the seasoned pork on the rack, fat side up. Cover with aluminum foil and bake for 4 hours.

2. Remove the foil from the pan and continue to bake until the roast is very tender and will pull apart easily with a fork, about 2 hours longer. Remove the pork from the oven and set aside to cool slightly. Remove any excess fat from the roast and discard (if desired—I just love the crunchy bits of skin left on top!). Using 2 forks or your hands, shred the pork into bite-size pieces. Serve with the sauce and buns.

# BARBECUE SAUCE

MAKES 3 CUPS

4 tablespoons unsalted butter
1½ cups finely chopped onions
6 cloves garlic, finely chopped
2¼ teaspoons sweet paprika
2 teaspoons Emeril's Bayou Blast
2 teaspoons ground mustard
1¼ teaspoons salt
½ teaspoon crushed red pepper
½ teaspoon freshly ground black pepper
¼ teaspoon cayenne pepper
One 6-ounce can tomato paste
1½ cups water
¾ cup cider vinegar
6 tablespoons dark brown sugar

1. In a medium nonreactive saucepan set over medium-high heat add the butter and, when melted, add the onions and cook until they are very soft, about 4 minutes. Add the garlic, paprika, Bayou Blast, ground mustard, salt, crushed red pepper, black pepper, and cayenne and cook for 2 minutes. Add the tomato paste and cook, stirring frequently, for 2 minutes, or until the tomato paste begins to brown. Add the water, cider vinegar, and dark brown sugar and stir to combine. Reduce the heat to low and cook until the sauce has thickened and the flavors have come together, 15 to 20 minutes.

2. Set aside to cool before serving.

3. The sauce may be made up to one week in advance and refrigerated in an airtight, nonreactive container.

# SMOTHERED PORK CHOPS

● MAKES 4 SERVINGS (2 CHOPS EACH) OR 8 SERVINGS ●

This is one of my favorite dinners to make at home on my nights off from the restaurants—my wife, Alden, goes crazy for these. It's best to use the thinly cut pork chops that are easy to find in any grocery store. Cooked this way, with sausage and onions in a deceptively rich roux-based gravy—oh, baby, you're playing with my emotions.

8 thinly cut (about ½ inch thick) pork chops (about 3 pounds total)

2 teaspoons Emeril's Original Essence

½ cup olive oil

¼ cup plus 2 tablespoons all-purpose flour

4 cups thinly sliced onions

½ teaspoon salt

½ teaspoon freshly ground black pepper

1 tablespoon chopped garlic

4 bay leaves

Two 14½-ounce cans low-sodium chicken broth, or 3½ cups Chicken Stock (page 4)

1½ cans water (measured in the chicken broth cans)

1 pound smoked sausage or andouille, cut crosswise into 1-inch slices

1 pound russet potatoes, peeled and cut into 1-inch cubes

Steamed white rice or rice pilaf, for serving (page 107)

1. Season both sides of the chops with the Essence.

2. Heat the olive oil in a large heavy pot or Dutch oven over high heat. Add the pork chops, 3 or 4 at a time, and lightly brown, about 2 minutes per side. Remove the pork chops and transfer to a platter. Set aside.

3.    Reduce the heat to medium. Add the flour and stir constantly until the roux is the color of peanut butter, about 4 minutes. Add the onions, salt, and black pepper. Cook, stirring, until the onions are slightly soft, about 5 minutes. Add the garlic, bay leaves, chicken broth, and water and bring to a boil. Return the pork chops to the pot. Reduce the heat to medium-low, cover, and simmer for 45 minutes. Add the smoked sausage and the potatoes. Bring to a boil, then reduce the heat to medium-low, and cook, uncovered, stirring occasionally, for 30 minutes. Remove the bay leaves.

4.    Remove from the heat. Serve with either steamed white rice or rice pilaf.

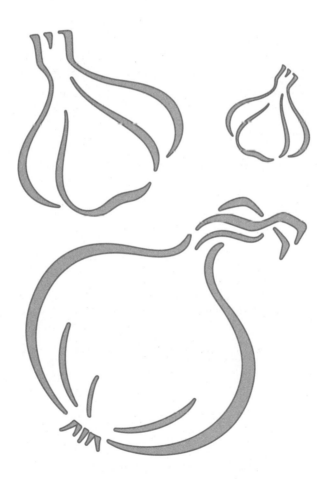

# Emeril's Oven-Braised Osso Buco with Orzo Risotto

. MAKES 8 SERVINGS .

This very kicked-up dish will impress your friends and family alike: melt-in-your-mouth veal shanks just love keeping company with the orzo risotto that is baked in the same dish! A perfect meal for special occasions, serve this with a green salad, some crusty French bread, and a nice bottle of red wine.

4 tablespoons olive oil

½ cup all-purpose flour

1½ tablespoons Emeril's Original Essence

8 veal shanks about 1½ inches thick, tied tightly around the middle with kitchen string

3 cups chopped onions

1½ cups chopped celery

1½ cups chopped carrots

3 tablespoons minced garlic

3 bay leaves

1½ tablespoons chopped fresh thyme

1½ tablespoons chopped fresh rosemary

1 tablespoon salt

1½ teaspoons coarsely ground black pepper

2¼ cups dry red wine

1½ quarts rich veal or beef stock

½ cup chopped fresh parsley

1½ pounds orzo pasta

¾ cup finely grated Parmesan cheese, for serving

1. Preheat the oven to 350°F.

2. Heat a large Dutch oven over medium heat. Add the olive oil and heat until very hot. In a shallow bowl or plate, combine the flour with the Essence and dredge the shanks in the seasoned flour. Shake the shanks to remove any excess flour, then transfer to the pot and cook until well browned on all sides, working in batches if necessary, 6 to 8 minutes. Remove the shanks to a roasting pan or deep lasagna pan large enough to hold the shanks in one layer and set aside. Add the onions, celery, and carrots to the Dutch oven and cook until softened and lightly browned around the edges, 4 to 6 minutes. Add the garlic, bay leaves, thyme, rosemary, salt, and black pepper and cook for 1 minute. Deglaze the pan with the red wine, scraping up any browned bits from the bottom of the pan. Transfer to the roasting pan along with the stock and bring to a boil on the stovetop. Cover the roasting pan with aluminum foil and transfer to the oven. Cook for about 2½ hours, or until the shanks are very tender.

3. Remove from the oven and add the parsley and orzo to the pan; stir to distribute evenly. Replace the cover and return the pan to the oven for 20 minutes. Remove the pan from the oven and stir gently. Cover and let sit for 10 minutes. Serve 1 shank per person on top of a bed of orzo risotto. Garnish with some of the Parmesan.

# Olive-Stuffed Leg of Lamb

Greeks really know how to cook lamb. Here I borrow some traditional Greek ingredients such as yogurt, mint, and garlic for a marinade, and then I stuff a boneless leg of lamb with olives, pine nuts, and herbs. The result is an impressive main course that can be served right out of the oven or at room temperature. Impress your friends at a spring lunch or dinner, with the Couscous Salad (page 80) on the side.

MARINADE

32 ounces plain yogurt

½ cup coarsely chopped fresh mint leaves

¼ cup minced garlic

2 tablespoons fresh lemon juice

1 tablespoon coarsely chopped fresh marjoram leaves

2 teaspoons lemon zest

2 teaspoons freshly ground black pepper

LAMB

One 5½-pound leg of lamb, boned and butterflied

1 tablespoon plus 1 teaspoon salt

1¾ teaspoons freshly ground black pepper

¾ cup plain bread crumbs

½ cup plus 2 tablespoons pitted brine-cured black olives, such as Kalamata

¾ cup extra virgin olive oil

3 tablespoons fresh lemon juice

3 tablespoons pine nuts

2 tablespoons coarsely chopped fresh marjoram leaves

2 tablespoons coarsely chopped fresh mint leaves

1 tablespoon minced garlic

¼ teaspoon lemon zest

1.  Combine the ingredients for the marinade in a large plastic freezer bag. Add the lamb and seal the bag. Shake to evenly distribute the marinade over the lamb. Refrigerate for 8 hours, turning occasionally.

2.  Preheat the oven to 400°F.

3.    Remove the lamb from the marinade and wash quickly under running water to remove most of the marinade. Pat dry and season with 2 teaspoons salt and ½ teaspoon black pepper on all sides. Spread the lamb, smooth side down, on a large baking sheet and set aside.

4.    Combine the bread crumbs, olives, ¼ cup olive oil, 1 tablespoon lemon juice, the pine nuts, marjoram, mint, garlic, 1 teaspoon salt, ¾ teaspoon black pepper, and the lemon zest in the bowl of a food processor. Pulse 2 to 3 times. Do not puree. Set the stuffing aside.

5.    Combine the remaining ½ cup olive oil, 2 tablespoons lemon juice, 1 teaspoon salt, and ½ teaspoon black pepper in a medium bowl and whisk to blend. Set this sauce aside for basting.

6.    Spread the olive mixture evenly over the lamb. Starting at 1 long side, roll the lamb up tightly. Tie the rolled lamb at several places with kitchen string to hold its shape. Brush the outside of the lamb liberally with the basting sauce; reserve the remainder.

7.    Roast the lamb until an instant-read thermometer inserted in the center registers 140°F for medium rare, about 1 hour and 30 minutes. Brush occasionally with the remaining basting sauce. Let stand 15 minutes. Slice the lamb and serve warm or at room temperature.

> NOTE    The cooking time will vary depending on the thickness of the meat. Start checking the temperature at 1 hour and don't forget that the meat will continue to cook once removed from the oven. Also, don't forget those tasty bits on the baking sheet. These can be spooned over individual slices of lamb as a sauce.

# SIDES

When I go to a really big potluck deal—you know, where every course has its own table—well, my favorite table is the one with all the side dishes. Those babies rock! From my mother's specialties—Miss Hilda's Baked Beans and Miss Hilda's Portuguese Dressing—to timeless classics—like Carrot Soufflé and Rice Pilaf, I savor them all. I even created some originals, like the Twice-Baked Potato Casserole. Need I say more?

# JUST RIGHT STUFFING

Here is my favorite basic stuffing. You could make it even more basic by skipping the bacon, but you know how I feel about pork fat! Regardless, the proportions have been worked out to perfection. So you will end up with a stuffing that is not too wet and not too dry—but just right!

½ tablespoon unsalted butter, softened, plus 3 tablespoons, melted

2 cups Chicken Stock (page 4), or canned low-sodium chicken broth

2 large eggs

½ cup finely chopped fresh parsley

¼ cup finely sliced green onions

¼ cup heavy cream

2 tablespoons finely chopped fresh sage leaves

12 to 14 cups ½-inch cubes day-old French bread

½ pound bacon (about 8 slices), cut into ½-inch pieces

3 cups chopped yellow onions

2 cups chopped celery

1 tablespoon Emeril's Poultry Rub

1 teaspoon salt

1 teaspoon freshly ground black pepper

2 tablespoons minced garlic

1. Preheat the oven to 400°F. Grease a 9 × 13-inch baking dish with ½ tablespoon butter.

2. Combine the Chicken Stock, eggs, parsley, green onions, heavy cream, and sage in a large bowl and whisk to combine. Add the bread and stir to combine; reserve.

3.     Heat a large skillet or medium pot over high heat. Add the bacon and cook, stirring frequently, until crisp and golden brown, about 5 minutes. Add the onions, celery, Poultry Rub, salt, and black pepper and cook, stirring occasionally, until the vegetables soften, about 10 minutes. Add the garlic and cook until fragrant, about 30 seconds. Remove from the heat and add to the bread mixture. Stir to combine. Pour the mixture into the prepared baking dish. Drizzle the remaining 3 tablespoons melted butter over the top of the bread mixture. Bake until golden brown, about 30 minutes. Cool if using as stuffing or serve warm as a side dish.

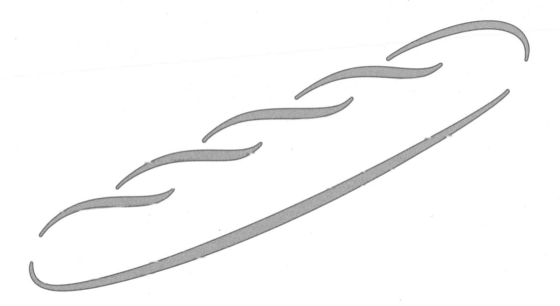

# CREOLE CORNBREAD STUFFING

• MAKES 10 TO 12 SERVINGS •

The secret to making top-notch cornbread stuffing is to start with leftover cornbread or fresh cornbread that has been dried in the oven. That way you end up with just the right amount of bite in your stuffing instead of a soggy mess. This one has all the classic Creole ingredients and it goes especially well with fried turkey.

1 baked Basic Cornbread (page 246), broken into 1-inch pieces (12 cups)

½ tablespoon unsalted butter

4 cups Chicken Stock (page 4), or canned low-sodium chicken broth

1 cup heavy cream

1 cup milk

2 large eggs

1 tablespoon plus 2 teaspoons Emeril's Original Essence

1 pound andouille sausage or other smoked sausage, cut crosswise into 1-inch pieces

3 tablespoons vegetable oil

3 cups chopped yellow onions

2 cups chopped celery

2 cups chopped green bell peppers

1 teaspoon salt

½ teaspoon freshly ground black pepper

Pinch of cayenne pepper

2 tablespoons minced garlic

4 teaspoons finely chopped fresh thyme

1. Preheat the oven to 250°F. Spread the cornbread in an even layer on a large baking sheet. Bake until dry and crispy, about 45 minutes. Remove and set aside.

2. Increase the oven temperature to 400°F. Grease a 10 × 15-inch baking dish or two 9-inch square baking dishes with the butter.

3. Combine the Chicken Stock, cream, milk, eggs, and 1 tablespoon Essence in a large bowl and whisk to blend. Add the dried cornbread and stir to mix, breaking up the pieces with a wooden spoon. Cover and refrigerate for 1 hour.

4. Meanwhile, heat a large skillet or medium pot over high heat. Add the andouille and cook until browned, about 5 minutes. Add the vegetable oil and reduce the heat to medium-high. Add the onions, celery, bell peppers, remaining 2 teaspoons Essence, the salt, black pepper, and cayenne and stir to mix. Cook the vegetables, stirring occasionally, until very soft and golden, about 15 minutes. Add the garlic and thyme and cook until fragrant, about 30 seconds. Remove from the heat and add to the cornbread mixture. Stir to mix well. Pour into the prepared baking dish and bake until golden brown, 35 to 40 minutes.

5. Remove from the oven. Cool if using as stuffing or serve warm as a side dish.

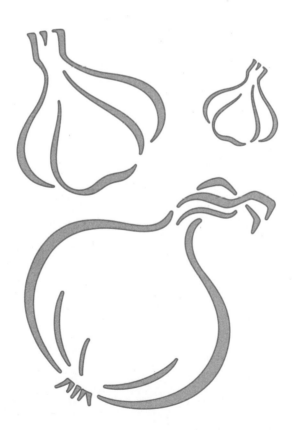

# MISS HILDA'S PORTUGUESE DRESSING

• MAKES 10 TO 12 SERVINGS •

It wouldn't be a holiday without my mother's Portuguese-style dressing, or stuffing—whatever you call it. This is more like a savory bread pudding, and it goes with just about anything—turkey, ham, you name it! The standout ingredient is a gaahlicky Portuguese sausage called chouriço, but its Spanish cousin, chorizo, which is much easier to find, will work just as well. Make plenty of this—you're gonna love it!

12 to 14 cups ½-inch cubes day-old French bread

4 cups milk

4 tablespoons extra virgin olive oil

¼ pound ground beef

1 pound chouriço, chaurice, or chorizo sausage, coarsely chopped

1½ cups chopped onions

1 cup chopped green bell peppers

½ cup chopped celery

1 bay leaf

1 teaspoon salt

1 teaspoon crushed red pepper

½ teaspoon freshly ground black pepper

1 tablespoon minced garlic

2 large eggs, lightly beaten

¼ cup chopped fresh parsley

1. Preheat the oven to 350°F.

2. Put the bread into a large mixing bowl and add the milk. Press the bread into the milk and let sit until the milk is absorbed and the bread is soft, about 15 minutes.

3. Heat 3 tablespoons olive oil in a 12-inch skillet over medium-high heat. Add the ground beef and cook, stirring, until lightly browned, about 1 minute. Add the sausage and cook, stirring until browned, about 3 minutes. Add the onions, bell peppers, celery,

and bay leaf. Season with the salt, crushed red pepper, and black pepper. Cook, stirring occasionally, until the vegetables are slightly softened, about 4 minutes. Add the garlic and cook, stirring, until fragrant, about 30 seconds.

4.   Add the meat mixture to the bread mixture and stir to mix well. Add the eggs and parsley and stir to blend. Remove the bay leaf and discard.

5.   Grease a 9 × 13-inch (3 quart) shallow baking dish with the remaining tablespoon olive oil. Pour the mixture into the prepared pan and spread evenly with a rubber spatula. Bake until bubbly and golden brown, about 1 hour. Remove from the oven and serve warm.

# SAVORY SPINACH AND ARTICHOKE BREAD PUDDING

• MAKES 10 TO 12 SERVINGS •

Compared to many traditional stuffings, this one is light in flavor. The bright notes of the spinach and lemon really shine and perfectly complement the tangy artichoke hearts. And the Brie just sends it through the roof. Serve with grilled leg of lamb on a spring evening.

¼ cup extra virgin olive oil

3 pounds spinach, washed, stems removed

2 cups chopped yellow onions

1 tablespoon coarsely chopped garlic

1 tablespoon plus 2 teaspoons Emeril's Italian Essence or other Italian seasoning blend

2½ teaspoons salt

1¼ teaspoons freshly ground black pepper

Three 8½-ounce cans quartered artichoke hearts, tough outer leaves removed

6 large eggs

3 cups heavy cream

2 cups milk

2 tablespoons fresh lemon juice

12 to 14 cups 1-inch cubes day-old French bread

1 pound Brie cheese, rind removed, cut into ½-inch cubes

½ cup freshly grated Parmesan cheese

¼ cup minced fresh parsley

1. Preheat the oven to 350°F. Grease a 9 × 13-inch baking dish with 1 tablespoon olive oil.

2. Bring a medium pot of water to a boil. Add the spinach and cook until just wilted, about 30 seconds. Drain and rinse with cold water. Once cool, squeeze as much water as possible from the spinach, then coarsely chop and reserve; you should have about 3 cups.

3.    Heat 1 tablespoon olive oil in a large skillet over medium-high heat. Add the onions and cook until golden brown and tender, about 5 minutes. Add the garlic, 2 teaspoons of Italian Essence, ½ teaspoon salt, and ¼ teaspoon black pepper and cook, stirring, until the garlic is fragrant, about 30 seconds. Add the artichokes and cook, stirring, another 2 minutes. Remove from the heat and reserve.

4.    Combine the eggs, cream, milk, lemon juice, remaining 1 tablespoon Italian Essence, remaining 2 teaspoons salt, and remaining 1 teaspoon pepper in a large bowl. Whisk to combine. Add the bread cubes, spinach, artichoke mixture, Brie, ¼ cup Parmesan, and parsley and stir to combine. If the bread does not absorb all of the liquid immediately, then let rest until it does, about 20 minutes.

5.    Pour the bread pudding mixture into the prepared dish, sprinkle the remaining ¼ cup Parmesan over the top, and drizzle with the remaining 2 tablespoons olive oil. Bake until firm in the center and golden brown, about 1 hour. Serve warm.

# CORN PUDDING

I know that often I repeat myself, but usually there's good reason. So let me say it again—I love corn! This is a traditional Southern-style corn casserole where the main ingredient is pretty much the only ingredient—CORN! If you are not as crazy about corn as I am, then here are a couple of suggestions. Replace the butter with some bacon fat—a little pork fat adds a great flavor. And if a smoother, less kernely texture is what you're after, puree half of the corn.

3½ tablespoons unsalted butter

2 cups thinly sliced yellow onions and 1 cup finely chopped yellow onions

Salt

6 large eggs

2 tablespoons yellow cornmeal

2 cups heavy cream

½ cup milk

6 cups fresh corn kernels (from about 8 ears)

1 cup finely sliced green onions

1½ teaspoons salt

1 teaspoon freshly ground white pepper

¼ teaspoon cayenne pepper

1. Preheat the oven to 350°F. Grease a 9 × 13-inch casserole with ½ tablespoon butter and set aside.

2. Melt the remaining 3 tablespoons butter in a large skillet over medium heat. Add the sliced onions and cook until tender and beginning to caramelize, about 20 minutes, stirring frequently, and adding a bit of water if the onions begin to brown before they have softened. Season with a pinch of salt, remove from the heat, and set aside.

3. Add the eggs, cornmeal, heavy cream, and milk to a large bowl and whisk to combine. Stir in the remaining ingredients, including the finely chopped onions, and pour the mixture into the prepared casserole. Top with caramelized sliced onions and bake on the middle rack for 45 minutes, or until the pudding is golden brown on top. Serve warm.

# Potatoes à la Boulangère

• MAKES 10 TO 12 SERVINGS •

This is a classic French dish that I love. Once you taste the incredible flavor combination of potatoes, caramelized onions, and good chicken stock, you'll see why I'm such a fan. I do recommend making your own chicken stock for this dish because a really rich broth is what makes the potatoes positively heavenly.

10 tablespoons unsalted butter

4 cups thinly sliced onions

2½ teaspoons salt

1¼ teaspoons freshly ground black pepper

5 pounds red bliss potatoes, peeled and sliced into ⅛-inch rounds

1 tablespoon finely chopped fresh thyme

1½ cups Chicken Stock (page 4), or canned low-sodium chicken broth

1. Preheat the oven to 400°F.

2. Melt 2 tablespoons of butter in a large skillet over medium heat. Add the onions and cook, stirring often, until caramelized, about 30 minutes. Season the onions with ½ teaspoon salt and ¼ teaspoon black pepper. Set the onions aside to cool.

3.    Using the same skillet, melt another 2 tablespoons of butter over medium-high heat, and cook about one-fourth of the potatoes until lightly caramelized, about 5 minutes. Season the potatoes with ½ teaspoon salt and ¼ teaspoon black pepper. Set the potatoes aside to cool. Repeat this process with the remaining butter, potatoes, salt, and pepper. Arrange one-fourth of the cooled potatoes in a slightly overlapping single layer in a 9 × 13-inch casserole. Scatter a third of the caramelized onions over the potatoes and sprinkle with 1 teaspoon thyme. Place another fourth of the potatoes on top of the onions, another third of the onions, and another teaspoon thyme. Repeat this process with half of the remaining potatoes and the remaining onions and thyme, finishing with a layer of potatoes.

4.    Pour the Chicken Stock over the potatoes and place the casserole in the oven. Bake the casserole for 25 minutes, reduce the temperature to 350°F, and continue to bake until the potatoes are golden brown, about 30 minutes more.

5.    Remove the casserole from the oven, and allow to cool for 10 minutes before serving.

# TWICE-BAKED
# POTATO CASSEROLE

• MAKES 12 SERVINGS •

If you love to doctor up your baked potatoes as much as I do, then this super-rich potato casserole will make you and your guests happy, happy. It's like a cross between stuffed baked potatoes and potato skins. Kick yours up with other ingredients, if desired—crumbled cooked sausage, chopped broccoli, chopped smoked salmon, you name it. Just about anything you like in or on a baked potato would be a welcome addition to this casserole. Any leftovers reheat well and are just as delicious.

10 large russet baking potatoes (about 7 pounds total)

8 tablespoons (1 stick) plus 1 tablespoon unsalted butter, at room temperature

1 cup sour cream

½ cup heavy cream

2 teaspoons salt

1½ teaspoons freshly ground black pepper

¾ pound bacon, cooked until crisp and crumbled

½ pound sharp white Cheddar cheese, cut into ½-inch cubes

¾ pound mild Cheddar cheese, grated (3 cups)

½ cup finely chopped green onions

3 eggs, lightly beaten

1. Preheat the oven to 400°F.

2. Scrub the potatoes well and rinse under cool running water. Pat dry with paper towels and prick the potatoes in several places with a fork. Place the potatoes in the oven and bake for 1 hour to 1 hour and 15 minutes, or until tender. Remove from the oven and set aside on a wire rack until cool enough to handle.

3.   When the potatoes have cooled, cut each potato in half and, using a spoon or a melon baller, scoop the flesh out of the skins, leaving as little flesh as possible. Place the potato flesh in a large bowl and add 1 stick of the butter, the sour cream, heavy cream, salt, and pepper and mash until chunky-smooth. Add the bacon, cubed white Cheddar, half of the grated Cheddar, the green onions, and eggs and mix thoroughly.

4.   Butter a 9 × 13-inch casserole with the remaining tablespoon of butter and reduce the oven temperature to 375°F.

5.   Place the seasoned potato mixture in the prepared casserole and top with the remaining grated Cheddar. Bake for 35 to 40 minutes, or until bubbly around the edges and heated through and the cheese on top is melted and lightly golden. Serve hot.

# Summer Squash and Zucchini Casserole

Here's a fancier version of the squash casserole that shows up every holiday season. But I figured, why not live on the edge and add some zucchini, fresh thyme, and now we're talking seriously good. I topped it with some Parmesan instead of standby Cheddar, but go with your own favorite. I do suggest that you start a new tradition of serving this dish in the summer, when all these vegetables are at their prime, for some out-of-this-world flavor!

1½ tablespoons unsalted butter

2 tablespoons olive oil

1 cup chopped onions

1½ teaspoons salt

1 teaspoon freshly ground black pepper

1 teaspoon minced garlic

2 pounds summer squash (about 6 medium), sliced into thin rounds

2 pounds zucchini (about 6 medium), sliced into thin rounds

1 teaspoon finely chopped fresh thyme

3 large eggs

¼ cup heavy cream

1 cup crushed butter crackers

½ cup grated Parmesan cheese (optional)

1. Preheat the oven to 350°F. Grease a 9 × 13-inch baking dish with ½ tablespoon butter.

2. Heat the olive oil and the remaining 1 tablespoon butter in a medium pot over medium-high heat. Add the onions, salt, and black pepper and cook until the onions are soft, about 5 minutes. Add the garlic and cook until fragrant, about 30 seconds. Add the squash and zucchini and cook until tender, stirring occasionally, about 20 minutes. Stir in the thyme and remove from the heat. Using a slotted spoon, transfer the vegetables to the prepared baking dish, reserving the cooking liquid.

3. Combine the eggs and cream in a medium bowl and whisk to blend. Gradually whisk the reserved cooking liquid into the egg mixture. When all the cooking liquid is incorporated, pour the mixture over the vegetables in the baking dish. Using a spoon, gently shift the vegetables around so the egg mixture is evenly distributed. Bake until the mixture sets, about 30 minutes. Remove from oven and sprinkle first with the crackers and then with the Parmesan, if using, and return to the oven. Bake until golden brown, 10 to 15 minutes.

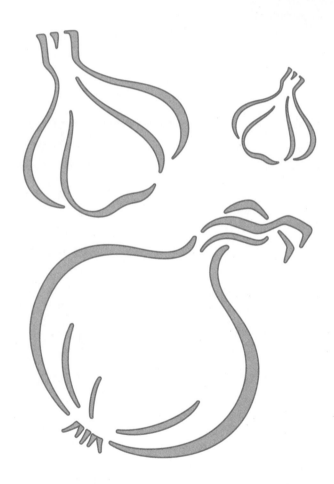

# EMERILIZED GREEN BEAN CASSEROLE

· MAKES 8 TO 10 SERVINGS ·

Don't turn the page! This recipe will make you think twice about green bean casseroles! When you start with fresh green beans, mix them with a homemade mushroom-béchamel sauce, gild the lily with some Fontina cheese, and then top the whole thing with some crispy fried onion rings like the ones we make at Emeril's Restaurant in New Orleans—you won't even recognize this as an updated version of that really tired old classic.

6 tablespoons plus 2 teaspoons unsalted butter

Vegetable oil, for deep-frying

2 medium yellow onions, thinly sliced into rings, and 2 cups chopped yellow onions

⅓ cup Crystal Hot Sauce

2¼ cups all-purpose flour

2 teaspoons Emeril's Original Essence

½ cup finely chopped celery

1 tablespoon minced garlic

1 pound white button mushrooms, wiped clean and ends trimmed, sliced

1½ teaspoons Emeril's Bayou Blast

¾ teaspoon salt

1½ cups Chicken Stock (page 4), or canned low-sodium chicken broth

½ cup heavy cream

2 pounds green beans, ends trimmed, blanched in salted water

¾ pound Fontina cheese, rind removed, cut into ½-inch cubes

1. Preheat the oven to 350°F. Lightly grease a 9 × 13-inch casserole with 2 teaspoons butter and set aside.

2. Heat at least 4 inches oil to 360°F in a large saucepan or deep fryer.

3. Separate the onion slices into individual rings. Combine the onion rings with the Crystal Hot Sauce in a mixing bowl and toss thoroughly. Place 2 cups of the flour in a large bowl and, working in batches, dredge the onion rings in the flour to coat. Transfer the coated onion rings to a colander or strainer and shake over the bowl containing the flour to release any loose flour. Fry the onion rings in batches until just lightly golden, about 1 minute per batch. As batches are completed, transfer the fried onion rings to a paper towel–lined baking dish to drain. Season the onion rings with the Essence and set aside. Note: It is important to allow the temperature to return to 360°F between batches.

4. Melt the remaining 6 tablespoons butter in a large saucepan over high heat and cook the chopped onions and celery until soft, about 6 minutes. Add the garlic and cook, stirring, for 1 minute. Add the mushrooms, Bayou Blast, and salt and cook, stirring frequently, until the mushrooms are soft and golden brown and have released their liquid, 4 to 6 minutes. Sprinkle with the remaining ¼ cup flour and stir to combine. Cook for 2 minutes, stirring constantly. Add the Chicken Stock and cream and continue to cook, stirring frequently, until the sauce is thick and creamy and any floury taste is gone, about 15 minutes. Remove from the heat.

5. In a large bowl, combine the green beans, mushroom sauce, and cubed Fontina cheese. Transfer to the prepared casserole dish and top with the fried onion rings. Bake for 20 to 25 minutes, or until hot and bubbly and the onion rings are golden brown. Serve immediately.

## — GREEN BEAN CASSEROLE —

You don't even need to bake this until you are ready to serve your guests. Just keep it covered and refrigerated until an hour before the festivities and then pop it in the oven. However, the onion rings remain crispiest if added to the casserole just before baking.

# Mexican Rice Casserole

This colorful rice dish is the perfect festive side dish for any south-of-the-border-inspired event. Try it with the Funky Southwest Pork Loin (page 202) or the Cheesy Chicken Tamales (page 175). It's equally delicious with or without the saffron, but you can also substitute a pinch of turmeric for a close approximation.

⅓ cup olive oil

3 cups chopped yellow onions

1 red bell pepper, chopped (1 cup)

1 green bell pepper, chopped (1 cup)

⅓ cup chopped seeded jalapeños (2 extra-large jalapeños)

1 tablespoon minced garlic

2½ cups long-grain white rice

2½ cups canned low-sodium chicken broth, or 2½ cups Chicken Stock (page 4)

2 cups peeled, seeded, and chopped ripe Roma tomatoes (1½ pounds)

2 teaspoons salt, or to taste, depending on the saltiness of the broth

2 teaspoons Emeril's Southwest Essence

2 pinches saffron (optional)

⅓ cup thinly sliced green onions (optional)

¼ cup chopped fresh cilantro (optional)

1. Preheat the oven to 350°F.

2. Heat the olive oil in a large saucepan or Dutch oven over medium-high heat. Add the onions, bell peppers, and jalapeños and cook, stirring, until soft, about 4 minutes. Add the garlic and cook for 1 minute. Add the rice and cook, stirring, until opaque and nutty in aroma, 2 to 3 minutes. Add the chicken broth, tomatoes, salt, Southwest Essence, and saffron, if using. Stir well and bring to a boil. Cover with a tight-fitting lid and transfer to the oven. Bake until the rice is tender and the liquid is absorbed, 25 to 30 minutes.

3. Remove from the oven and let sit, undisturbed, for 5 to 10 minutes. Fluff the rice with a fork and stir in the green onions and cilantro, if desired. Serve hot.

# RICE PILAF

This is my favorite and the easiest way to cook "plain" rice. I start the rice off on top of the stove and then finish it in the oven. Not only is it nice to have that cooktop burner available for something else, but once you've popped this baby into the oven and turned on the timer, there's no guess work as to when the rice is done, and no standing around to keep watch.

4 tablespoons unsalted butter

1½ cups chopped yellow onions

2 cups long-grain white rice

3½ cups canned low-sodium chicken broth, or 3½ cups Chicken Stock (page 4)

1 teaspoon salt, to taste

¼ cup thinly sliced green onions (optional)

1. Preheat the oven to 350°F.

2. Melt the butter in a large ovenproof saucepan or Dutch oven over medium-high heat. Add the onions and cook, stirring, until soft, 3 to 4 minutes. Add the rice and cook, stirring, until opaque and nutty in aroma, 2 to 3 minutes. Add the chicken broth and salt, stir well, and bring to a boil. Cover with a tight-fitting lid and transfer to the oven. Bake until the rice is tender and the liquid is absorbed, 25 to 30 minutes.

3. Remove the rice from the oven and let stand, undisturbed, for 5 to 10 minutes. Fluff the rice with a fork and stir in the green onions, if desired. Serve hot.

# — RICE PILAF —

One commonality of all pilafs is that the rice is browned in butter or oil before being cooked in stock. From that basic recipe you can venture in many directions—adding fresh vegetables, dried fruit, and your favorite seasoning. You can even add meat, poultry, or seafood and make the pilaf a main course.

# CHEESY GRITS

· MAKES 6 SERVINGS ·

It wasn't until I made New Orleans my home that I became a grits lover. Many of us who have been raised north of the Mason-Dixon line have no idea how satisfying grits can be. Hey, add a little cream and cheese to them and, well, what can I say? Now, although this makes a welcome addition to any breakfast or brunch menu, at my restaurants we often serve grits for dinner, too, as a side in place of mashed potatoes or rice. This should make a grits lover out of you!

¼ cup plus 2 tablespoons unsalted butter

4 cups water

1 teaspoon salt

1 cup quick grits (not instant)

1 large egg

⅓ cup heavy cream

1 teaspoon freshly ground black pepper

1 cup grated Gruyère cheese

⅓ cup freshly grated Parmesan cheese

1. Preheat the oven to 350°F. Grease a 2-quart casserole with 2 tablespoons butter.

2. Combine the remaining ¼ cup butter, water, and salt in a heavy medium saucepan over medium heat. When the mixture comes to a simmer, add the grits, stirring, until thoroughly combined. Continue to cook the grits at a simmer, stirring frequently, until thickened, about 15 minutes.

3. Meanwhile, whisk together the egg, cream, and black pepper. Stir into the cooked grits along with the cheeses. Pour the mixture into the prepared casserole and smooth the top. Bake until set, about 45 minutes. Remove from the oven and let stand for about 5 minutes before serving.

EMERIL'S POTLUCK

234

# — SAVE THOSE LEFTOVERS! —

The day after you make this dish, you can cut the cooled grits into slices or wedges and fry them in a hot skillet until they are crispy on both sides. Serve these grit "cakes" with eggs, sautéed shrimp—you name it!

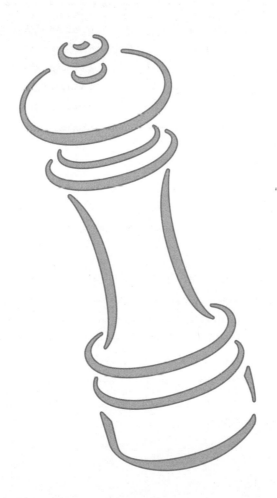

# MACARONI WITH FOUR CHEESES

• MAKES 6 TO 8 SERVINGS •

Hey, you know how much I love cheese. When trying to decide just which type I would include in this dish, I was stumped. So I did what any logically minded, cheese-loving chef would do: I included them all! Why not? All you mac 'n' cheese lovers out there, you're going to love this one!

7 tablespoons unsalted butter

4 tablespoons all-purpose flour

2 cups half-and-half

¾ teaspoon salt, plus salt for pasta water

¼ teaspoon freshly ground white pepper

¼ teaspoon Emeril's Red Hot Sauce

8½ ounces grated Parmigiano-Reggiano or other good-quality Parmesan cheese (about 2 cups)

1 pound elbow macaroni

½ teaspoon minced garlic

4 ounces grated Cheddar cheese

4 ounces grated Fontina cheese

4 ounces grated Gruyère cheese

¼ cup fresh bread crumbs

½ teaspoon Emeril's Original Essence or Creole Seasoning

1. Melt 4 tablespoons butter over low heat in a heavy medium saucepan. Add the flour and stir to combine. Cook, stirring constantly, for 3 minutes. Increase the heat to medium and whisk in the half-and-half, little by little. Cook until thickened, 4 to 5 minutes, stirring frequently. Remove from the heat, season with the ¾ teaspoon salt, white pepper, hot sauce, and 4 ounces Parmigiano-Reggiano. Stir until the cheese is melted and the sauce is smooth. Cover and set aside.

2. Preheat the oven to 350°F.

3.　Fill a large pot with water and bring to a boil over high heat. Add salt to taste and, while stirring, add the macaroni. Return to a boil, reduce the heat to a low boil, and cook for about 5 minutes, or until the macaroni is al dente (slightly undercooked). Drain in a colander and return the macaroni to the pot. Add 2 tablespoons butter and the garlic and stir to combine. Add the reserved sauce and stir until well combined. Set aside.

4.　Grease a 3-quart baking dish or casserole with the remaining tablespoon of butter and set aside.

5.　In a large bowl, combine 4 ounces Parmigiano-Reggiano with the Cheddar, Fontina, and Gruyère cheeses. Toss to combine. Place one-third of the macaroni in the bottom of the prepared baking dish. Top with one-third of the mixed cheeses. Top with another third of the macaroni and another third of the cheese mixture. Repeat with the remaining macaroni and cheese mixture. In a small bowl combine the bread crumbs, remaining ½ ounce Parmigiano-Reggiano, and the Essence and toss to combine. Sprinkle this over the top of the macaroni and cheese. Bake for 40 to 45 minutes, or until the macaroni and cheese is bubbly and hot and the top is golden brown. Remove from the oven and allow to sit for 5 minutes before serving.

# MISS HILDA'S BAKED BEANS

This is the recipe for my mother's famous baked beans. Well, they should be famous because these are the best baked beans I have ever eaten. See, these are not your average baked beans—my mother uses lots of mustard for a great tangy flavor. She cooks the beans so they still have some bite to them and aren't mushy. They bear no resemblance to the canned variety. Make some for your next cookout and see what I mean.

1 pound dried navy beans, picked over and soaked overnight in water to cover

1¼ teaspoons cayenne pepper

1 teaspoon salt

2 bay leaves

2 tablespoons olive oil

½ pound salt pork, trimmed and cut into cubes

4 ounces chopped bacon

1½ cups ketchup

1 cup chopped onions

½ cup chopped celery

½ cup firmly packed dark brown sugar

1 tablespoon powdered mustard

1 tablespoon chopped garlic

1 teaspoon freshly ground black pepper

1. Preheat the oven to 300°F.

2. Drain the beans and put them in a pot with ¼ teaspoon cayenne, the salt, and bay leaves. Add 8 cups water and bring to a boil. Reduce the heat to medium-low and simmer until the beans are just tender, 45 minutes to 1 hour. Remove from the heat and let sit for 5 minutes. Drain the beans and reserve 1½ cups of the cooking liquid.

3. Heat the oil in a large ovenproof pot or Dutch oven over high heat. Add the salt pork and bacon and cook, stirring, for 4 minutes. Add the ketchup, reserved cooking liquid, onions, celery, brown sugar, mustard, garlic, black pepper, and remaining 1 teaspoon cayenne. Cook, stirring, for 4 minutes. Reduce the heat to medium-low. Add the beans and stir gently to mix. Simmer for 5 minutes.

4. Transfer the beans to the oven and bake for 2 hours. Remove from the oven and serve hot. Remove the bay leaves before serving.

# Cajun Maque Choux

Maque choux is a stewed vegetable side dish, traditionally made with corn, tomatoes, and other vegetables. Here we've added okra, a mainstay on the Southern summer table when vegetables are at their peak, for a wonderful combination of textures, colors, and flavors. For you vegetarians out there, simply omit the bacon and use some oil as your fat, and substitute water or vegetable stock for the Chicken Stock.

6 ounces bacon, chopped

2 tablespoons unsalted butter

2 cups chopped yellow onions

2 teaspoons Emeril's Original Essence

1 tablespoon minced garlic

2 pounds okra, trimmed and cut crosswise into ½-inch slices

1 bay leaf

½ teaspoon chopped fresh thyme

½ teaspoon freshly ground black pepper

⅛ to ¼ teaspoon cayenne pepper, to taste

2 cups corn kernels (from 3 to 4 ears fresh corn)

1 cup Chicken Stock (page 4), vegetable stock, or water

2 cups chopped ripe tomatoes (2 large tomatoes, 1½ pounds total)

1 teaspoon salt

1.  Heat a Dutch oven over medium heat. Add the bacon and cook until well browned and crispy, about 8 minutes. Using a slotted spoon, transfer the bacon to a paper towel–lined plate to drain and set aside.

2.  Add the butter and onions to the Dutch oven and cook until soft, about 5 minutes. Add the Essence and garlic and cook until fragrant, about 30 seconds. Increase the heat to medium-high and add the okra, bay leaf, thyme, black pepper, and cayenne and stir to combine. Cook, stirring often, until the okra is crisp-tender, about 5 minutes. Add the corn and cook, stirring frequently, for 2 minutes. Add the Chicken Stock and cook for 7 to 8 minutes, stirring occasionally. Add the tomatoes and cook for 2 minutes. Add the salt and the reserved bacon, stir to combine, and serve immediately.

# EMERIL'S FAVORITE CABBAGE

● MAKES 2 QUARTS, 8 TO 10 SERVINGS ●

This is truly my favorite way to cook cabbage. You start with some bacon, and that sweet, smoky flavor marries perfectly with the onions and cabbage. Trust me—this is nothing like that bland cafeteria vegetable that you ate as a kid. And best of all, it's easy to make on the run. Make some up in a hurry for a perfect winter side dish!

½ pound bacon, coarsely chopped
4 cups thinly sliced onions
1¼ teaspoons salt
¼ teaspoon cayenne pepper
¾ teaspoon freshly ground black
   pepper

½ teaspoon sugar
3 bay leaves
1 head green or white cabbage
   (about 3½ pounds), cored and
   thinly sliced
One 12-ounce bottle of beer

1. Cook the bacon in a large heavy pot or Dutch oven over medium-high heat, until browned and slightly crispy, about 5 minutes. Add the onions, salt, cayenne, black pepper, sugar, and bay leaves. Cook, stirring, until the onions are soft, about 5 minutes. Add the cabbage and stir to mix well. Cook, stirring, until the cabbage just begins to wilt or soften, 3 to 4 minutes. Reduce the heat to medium-low, and add the beer. Stir to mix.

2. Cover and simmer, stirring occasionally, for 1 hour. Remove the bay leaves. Remove from the heat and serve warm.

# Carrot Soufflé

• MAKES 10 TO 12 SERVINGS •

Here is a casserole that will become a standard at your holiday table. Since carrots are always available, you can serve this year-round with roasted chicken or turkey, roasted pork or beef, and even grilled meats.

½ tablespoon vegetable oil

3 pounds carrots, chopped

6 large eggs

2 cups packed light brown sugar

½ pound (2 sticks) unsalted butter, at room temperature

½ cup all-purpose flour

½ cup milk

¼ cup fresh orange juice

1 tablespoon orange zest

1½ teaspoons baking powder

¾ teaspoon ground cinnamon

½ teaspoon freshly grated nutmeg

Pinch of salt

### FOR THE TOPPING

1 cup packed light brown sugar

1 cup chopped pecans

½ cup all-purpose flour

4 tablespoons (½ stick) unsalted butter, melted

1. Preheat the oven to 350°F. Grease a 9 × 13-inch casserole with the oil and set aside.

2. Bring a large pot of water to a boil, add the carrots, and cook until tender, about 15 minutes; drain. Combine the carrots with the remaining ingredients in a food processor and process until smooth, scraping down the sides of the bowl as necessary.

3. Spoon the mixture into the prepared casserole.

4. Combine the brown sugar, pecans, flour, and butter in a medium bowl. Stir to blend. Scatter the mixture over the top of the casserole and bake until the topping is lightly browned, 55 minutes to 1 hour.

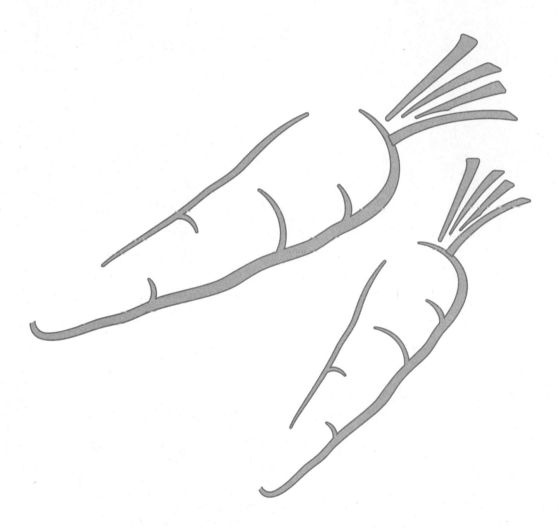

# BREADS

Baking bread gives me great satisfaction—like the fragrance while it cooks—wow! The Beer Bread smells so good I usually break off a piece straight from the oven. And the Kicked-Up Dinner Rolls can be served on a buffet table for holidays or at an elegant dinner party. The Cranberry Pecan Bread can go from breakfast to dinner, and the Buttermilk Biscuits are good at any hour.

# BASIC CORNBREAD

• MAKES 16 TO 20 SERVINGS •

This recipe is exactly what the name implies—basic cornbread. I created this simple Southern-style cornbread for the Creole Cornbread Stuffing (page 216). It is delicious (I could eat it for breakfast), but it's nothing fancy. If you want over-the-top cornbread, then try my Serious Southern Cornbread (page 247).

½ tablespoon unsalted butter,
   or bacon fat, softened, plus
   8 tablespoons, melted
4 large eggs
3 cups buttermilk
3 cups yellow cornmeal

1 cup all-purpose flour
1 tablespoon plus 1 teaspoon baking
   powder
1 tablespoon sugar
2 teaspoons salt
1 teaspoon baking soda

1. Preheat the oven to 375°F. Grease a 9 × 13-inch baking dish with the ½ tablespoon softened butter.

2. Combine the eggs, buttermilk, and 8 tablespoons melted butter in a large mixing bowl; whisk to combine. In a large bowl, add the cornmeal, flour, baking powder, sugar, salt, and baking soda; whisk to combine. Add the wet ingredients to the dry ingredients and stir until just combined. Pour the batter into the prepared baking dish. Bake until the top is golden brown and the edges have pulled away from the sides of the pan, 30 to 40 minutes. Remove the bread from the oven and allow it to rest for 5 minutes before cutting into squares and serving.

# SERIOUS SOUTHERN CORNBREAD

• MAKES 10 TO 12 SERVINGS •

This cornbread is not for wimps! It is made with buttermilk and without sugar, in keeping with the Southern cornbread tradition, and a bit of flour, which a lot of Southern cooks would frown upon, to create a more balanced cornbread. And, of course, I kicked it way up with sausage, cheese, and green onions. So watch out—this cornbread is rockin'!

¼ cup plus 2 tablespoons vegetable oil

½ pound smoked pork sausage, cut into small dice

1¼ cups all purpose flour

¾ cup yellow cornmeal

2 teaspoons baking powder

1 teaspoon salt

1 cup grated Cheddar cheese

⅓ cup chopped green onions

1½ cups buttermilk

2 large eggs, beaten

1. Preheat the oven to 400°F.

2. Heat 2 tablespoons oil in a large 9- or 10-inch cast-iron skillet over medium heat. Once the oil is hot, add the sausage and cook, stirring often, until most of the fat has been released and the meat is crisp, 7 to 8 minutes. Remove the sausage from the skillet and set aside on a plate. Place the skillet with the sausage fat in the oven. In a large bowl, combine the flour, cornmeal, baking powder, and salt and whisk to combine. Stir in the Cheddar cheese and green onions. Combine the buttermilk, the remaining ¼ cup oil, and the eggs in a medium bowl and whisk to combine. Add this buttermilk mixture to the dry ingredients and stir, mixing just until the dry ingredients are moistened. Fold the sausage into the cornbread batter. Remove the skillet from the oven and add the cornbread batter. Bake for 25 to 30 minutes, or until light golden brown and a wooden toothpick inserted in the center comes out clean. Allow the cornbread to sit for 5 minutes and then cut into wedges.

# BEER BREAD

Now, this is my kind of bread—made with beer! Seriously, beer makes a good, yeasty-tasting bread without the hassle of a traditional yeast bread. The result is a very rustic loaf that would be the perfect gift for a housewarming party or great to eat with a hearty stew.

- 4 tablespoons (½ stick) salted butter, melted, plus 1 teaspoon, softened
- 1½ cups plus 1 tablespoon whole wheat flour
- 1½ cups all-purpose flour
- 3 tablespoons dark brown sugar
- 1 teaspoon salt
- 1 teaspoon baking powder
- ½ teaspoon baking soda
- 2 large eggs, beaten
- One 12-ounce bottle of beer, preferably amber

1. Preheat the oven to 350°F. Grease and flour a 9 × 5 × 3-inch loaf pan with the 1 teaspoon softened butter and 1 tablespoon whole wheat flour.

2. Combine the remaining 1½ cups whole wheat flour, the all-purpose flour, sugar, salt, baking powder, and baking soda in a large bowl. Whisk to blend. Mix the eggs and beer in a medium bowl and whisk to combine. Stir the beer mixture into the dry mixture until just combined. Pour into the prepared loaf pan. Drizzle the remaining 4 tablespoons melted butter over the top. Bake the bread in the middle of the oven for about 40 minutes, or until a tester comes out clean. Let cool for 5 to 10 minutes in the pan and then turn out onto a rack to cool completely.

# BUTTERMILK BISCUITS

• MAKES EIGHT 3-INCH BISCUITS •

Biscuit making is considered a daunting task because it is easy to end up with biscuits that are hard as rocks. But I swear that this recipe takes the guesswork out of great biscuits. Don't overwork the dough—this is the secret to biscuits that are light and fluffy.

---

1¼ cups self-rising flour
¾ cup cake flour
¾ teaspoon baking powder
⅛ teaspoon baking soda
1 tablespoon sugar

½ teaspoon salt
4 tablespoons cold unsalted butter,
   plus 2 tablespoons, melted
1¼ cups buttermilk
¼ cup all-purpose flour

---

1. Preheat the oven to 475°F.

2. Sift the self-rising flour, cake flour, baking powder, baking soda, sugar, and salt into a large bowl. Using your fingers or a pastry cutter, work the 4 tablespoons cold butter into the flour until the pieces are pea size. Add the buttermilk to the flour mixture and, with your hands or a rubber spatula, stir just until the milk and flour come together to form a dough. Sprinkle some of the all-purpose flour on a work surface and place the dough on top of the flour. Using your hands, press the dough into a ½-inch-thick disk about 8 inches in diameter. Using a 3-inch round cutter dusted with flour, cut out dough rounds. Be sure to press straight down when cutting the dough—a twisting motion will prevent the dough from rising. You will need to re-form the scraps of dough to make 8 biscuits. Do this by pushing the scrap pieces together and pressing them into a ½-inch-thick disk.

3. Place the biscuits on a small sheet pan and brush the tops with the 2 tablespoons melted butter. Bake in the oven for 10 to 12 minutes, or until golden brown. Allow to cool briefly.

# CRANBERRY PECAN BREAD

. MAKES ONE 9-INCH LOAF, 8 SERVINGS .

**S**erve this quick bread alongside your holiday meal or toast some for breakfast! The secret ingredient is Grand Marnier, but if you want to go the nonalcoholic route, then substitute fresh orange juice.

8 tablespoons (1 stick) unsalted
    butter, plus 1 teaspoon, softened

½ cup Grand Marnier or other
    orange-flavored liqueur

¼ cup sugar

¼ cup water

¼ teaspoon ground cloves

1 cinnamon stick

1½ cups dried cranberries

1 teaspoon orange zest

¾ cup packed dark brown sugar

2 large eggs

2 cups all-purpose flour

1 teaspoon baking soda

½ teaspoon baking powder

½ teaspoon ground cinnamon

¼ teaspoon salt

¾ cup buttermilk

¼ cup fresh orange juice

1 teaspoon pure vanilla extract

1 cup chopped toasted pecans

1.    Preheat the oven to 350°F. Grease a 9 × 5 × 3-inch loaf pan with the 1 teaspoon softened butter.

2.    In a medium saucepan, combine the Grand Marnier, sugar, water, cloves, and cinnamon stick and bring to a boil. Stir to dissolve the sugar and add the cranberries. Reduce the heat to a simmer and cook until the berries have absorbed most of the liquid, about 5 minutes. Remove from the heat and allow the berries to cool in their liquid. Once cool, stir in the orange zest and remove the cinnamon stick.

3.    Combine the brown sugar, remaining 8 tablespoons butter, and the eggs in the bowl of an electric mixer and beat until light and fluffy. Sift together the flour, baking soda, baking powder, cinnamon, and salt. Combine the buttermilk, orange juice, and vanilla in a small bowl. Alternatively, add the dry ingredients and the buttermilk mixture to the creamed butter, beating after each addition. Fold in the reserved cranberry mixture and the pecans. Pour the batter into the greased loaf pan. Bake for 55 to 60 minutes, or until a tester inserted in the center comes out clean. Allow the bread to cool in the pan for 15 minutes and then turn out onto a wire rack to cool. Serve warm or at room temperature. (This recipe can be made ahead. Wrap tightly and store at room temperature for 1 day or freeze for up to 2 weeks.)

# KICKED-UP DINNER ROLLS

The dinner roll is an art form. And at their best dinner rolls are worth their weight in gold. Seriously, I would fight over the last really good dinner roll left in a bread basket. Now, I know this is a lot of buildup, but trust me—these dinner rolls deliver. They are absolutely outstanding!

1¼ cups whole milk

½ cup plus 2 teaspoons unsalted butter

¼ cup plus 1 teaspoon sugar

1 teaspoon salt

One ¼-ounce package active dry yeast

2 large eggs, lightly beaten

2 cups bread flour

2½ cups all-purpose flour

3 tablespoons nonfat dry milk

1. Preheat the oven to 350°F.

2. Combine the milk, ¼ cup of the butter, ¼ cup of the sugar, and the salt in a small saucepan over medium heat. Cook, stirring frequently, until the butter is melted and the sugar has dissolved, 2 to 3 minutes. Remove from the heat and set aside to cool to lukewarm before proceeding.

3. Combine the yeast and the remaining 1 teaspoon of sugar in ¼ cup of warm water (110°F). Set aside until foamy, about 10 minutes. Add the milk mixture to the yeast mixture and stir to combine. Add the eggs and stir to combine. Using a wooden spoon, stir the flour and dry milk, 1 cup at a time, into the dough. The dough will be quite stiff and somewhat sticky. If the dough gets too stiff to stir with a spoon, use your hands to mix.

4.    Lightly grease the inside of a large bowl with 1 teaspoon butter. Transfer the dough to the bowl and turn to coat. Lightly grease a piece of wax paper or plastic wrap with 1 teaspoon of butter and use it to cover the bowl. Set aside in a warm place until the dough is doubled in size, at least 3 hours. Melt the remaining ¼ cup of butter and set aside.

5.    After the dough has doubled, turn it out onto a lightly floured surface and knead until smooth and elastic, 2 to 3 minutes. Using a lightly floured rolling pin, roll to a ½-inch thickness. Using a sharp knife or dough cutter, cut the dough into 12 equal pieces. Arrange the dough in a metal 9 × 13-inch pan. Brush the tops of the rolls with the melted butter. Cover the rolls with plastic wrap and set aside in a warm draft-free area until doubled in size, about 1 hour.

6.    Bake the dinner rolls on the center rack of the oven until golden brown and puffed, about 18 to 20 minutes.

# PROSCIUTTO BREADSTICKS

• MAKES 24 BREADSTICKS •

I was inspired to make these breadsticks after tasting some similarly delicious ones in New York City that were made from leftover pizza dough. So I used my favorite pizza dough recipe, filled it with prosciutto, and shaped some breadsticks.

One ¼-ounce package active dry yeast

1 cup warm water (110°F)

3 cups all-purpose flour, plus more for kneading

8 tablespoons extra virgin olive oil

1½ teaspoons salt

8 ounces prosciutto, finely chopped (about 1½ cups)

Freshly cracked black pepper

1. Place the yeast in a large mixing bowl. Add the water and stir with a wooden spoon until the yeast is dissolved. (After a few minutes you should see bubbles appear on the surface of the yeast mixture; this will let you know that the yeast is working). Add 3 cups flour, 1 tablespoon of the olive oil, and the salt, and stir well to combine. Continue stirring until the dough pulls away from the sides of the bowl and comes together.

2. Place the dough on a lightly floured surface. Knead until it forms a smooth, elastic ball, 3 to 5 minutes.

3. Grease a large bowl with 1 tablespoon of the olive oil. Place the dough in the bowl, turning to coat with oil. Cover with a damp kitchen towel or plastic wrap. Place in a warm draft-free place and let rise until doubled in size, 1 to 2 hours.

4. Preheat the oven to 400°F.

5. When the dough has doubled, remove the towel and divide the dough in half. Keep a damp towel on the dough half that you are not working with and divide the

portion of dough on your work surface into 12 pieces. Cover the dough pieces with a damp towel.

6. Line an 11½ × 16-inch sheet pan with parchment paper. Working with 1 piece of dough at a time, roll the dough into a long thin rope by rocking your open palms over the dough in a back-and-forth motion. The dough rope should be 6 to 8 inches long. Use a lightly floured rolling pin to flatten and stretch the dough to about 12 inches long. Place 1 tablespoon of the chopped prosciutto along the center of the flattened dough, bring the edges of the dough up over the prosciutto, and pinch to seal. Using your fingertips and palms, gently roll the dough to make a log 13 to 14 inches long. Be careful—the seam where the dough was pinched may come undone. Simply pinch the dough again and gently roll it until it reaches the desired length.

7. Lay the breadstick on the parchment-lined sheet pan, and continue the process with the remaining 11 pieces of dough. Once you have all the breadsticks rolled and stuffed, use a pastry brush to brush 3 tablespoons olive oil over them. Season the breadsticks with cracked black pepper, and place the sheet pan in the oven. Continue making breadsticks with the remaining dough and prosciutto. Bake the breadsticks until light golden brown, about 20 minutes. Remove from the oven and serve hot or at room temperature.

— A KEEPER —

If you store these breadsticks in an airtight plastic container at room temperature, they will keep for a couple of days. These are great for parties!

# DESSERTS

Dessert is an absolute necessity, because a little something sweet is the perfect ending to a great meal. And at potluck get-togethers, there are usually lots to choose from—so here I've tried to come up with a dessert for every occasion. You have Flourless Chocolate Cake for the grown-up birthday party, Summer Fruit Salad for the ladies' brunch, Super Lemony Lemon Squares for a family barbecue, and My Very Own Tiramisu for the Italian feast. You get the picture—dessert is important. It's the final touch.

# Devil's Food Cake with Vanilla Buttercream Icing

• MAKES ONE 9-INCH 3-LAYER CAKE, 16 SERVINGS •

This cake lives up to its name with sinful goodness. Three layers of intensely chocolate cake with buttery vanilla frosting will make everyone happy, happy, and there's plenty of cake here to feed a crowd.

¾ pound (3 sticks) plus 1 tablespoon unsalted butter, softened

¾ cup unsweetened cocoa powder

2 ounces unsweetened chocolate, chopped

1½ cups boiling water

2¼ cups cake flour

1¼ cups all-purpose flour

1 teaspoon baking soda

1 teaspoon salt

1½ cups packed dark brown sugar

¾ cup granulated sugar

4 large eggs

½ cup sour cream

1 tablespoon pure vanilla extract

Vanilla Buttercream Icing (recipe follows)

1. Preheat the oven to 350°F. Use 1 tablespoon butter to grease three 9-inch cake pans. Line the bottom of each pan with a parchment paper round.

2. Combine the cocoa and chocolate in a medium bowl. Pour the boiling water over the chocolate mixture and whisk until smooth; reserve. Sift together the flours, baking soda, and salt into a medium bowl; reserve.

3. Place the ¾ pound butter in a large bowl and beat with an electric mixer on medium-high speed until creamy, about 1 minute. Add the dark brown and granulated

sugars and beat on high until light and fluffy, about 3 minutes. Stop the mixer and scrape down the bowl with a rubber spatula. Add the eggs, one at a time, beating 30 seconds on medium-high after each addition. Reduce the speed to medium and add the sour cream and vanilla. Beat until combined. Stop the mixer and scrape down the bowl. With the mixer on low, add about one-third of the flour mixture, followed by about one-half of the chocolate mixture. Repeat, ending with the flour mixture and beating until just combined. Stop the mixer and scrape down the sides of the bowl. Stir the batter gently to thoroughly combine. Divide the batter evenly among the cake pans and smooth with a spatula. Bake until a skewer inserted in the center of each cake layer comes out clean, about 25 minutes. Cool the cakes in their pans on a wire rack for about 15 minutes. Invert the cakes, one at a time, onto a large plate, peel off the parchment, and invert onto the rack.

4.    Cool completely before icing between layers, on sides, and on top with Vanilla Buttercream Icing. Serve at room temperature. (Any buttercream will not fare well in too warm conditions.)

## Vanilla Buttercream Icing

MAKES ABOUT 6 CUPS

9 large egg yolks
1 cup sugar
½ cup plus 2 tablespoons light corn syrup
1¼ pounds (5 sticks) unsalted butter, softened
2 teaspoons pure vanilla extract

1. In a large bowl, beat the yolks with an electric mixer until light in color; reserve.

2. Combine the sugar and corn syrup in a small saucepan (preferably nonstick) over medium heat, stirring constantly, until the sugar dissolves and the syrup comes to a rolling boil. Transfer the syrup to a heatproof bowl to stop cooking. Pour a small amount of the syrup into the yolks and begin beating with the electric mixer. Pour the remaining corn syrup into the mixture in a steady stream. Continue beating until completely cool and fluffy, about 5 minutes. Gradually beat in the butter and vanilla until the icing is light and fluffy, about 3 minutes. Use immediately. (Or cover and refrigerate for up to 5 days.)

## — DEVIL'S PLAYGROUND —

Don't leave this cake in the sun or any other warm place or you will wind up with a pool of melted butter in place of the icing. The icing's high butter content means that this cake likes moderate temperatures.

# FLOURLESS CHOCOLATE CAKE

• MAKES ONE 9-INCH CAKE, ABOUT 16 SERVINGS •

This one is a chocolate lover's dream come true because the sensation is chocolate, chocolate, chocolate! You could go into a chocolate coma after just a few bites. A little bit goes a long way, so this one-layer cake serves a crowd. It's perfect for a celebratory night—like, say, a New Year's Eve dinner party.

½ pound (2 sticks) unsalted butter, cut into ½-inch cubes, plus ½ tablespoon, softened

1 pound semisweet chocolate, coarsely chopped

¼ cup Kahlúa

8 large eggs

¼ cup sugar

1 teaspoon pure vanilla extract

½ teaspoon salt

Confectioners' sugar or cocoa powder, for decoration

1. Preheat the oven to 325°F. Using the ½ tablespoon butter, grease a 9-inch springform pan. Line the bottom of the pan with a parchment round. Tightly cover the pan underneath and along the outer sides with foil and set in a roasting pan. Bring a medium saucepan of water to boil.

2. Combine the chocolate, butter, and Kahlúa in a metal bowl set over simmering water or in the top of a double boiler. Melt the chocolate, stirring constantly, until smooth and creamy, about 5 minutes; reserve.

3. Meanwhile, combine the eggs, sugar, vanilla, and salt in a large bowl and beat with an electric mixer until frothy and almost doubled in volume, about 5 minutes. Fold one-third of the egg mixture into the chocolate mixture with a rubber spatula. Repeat this process two more times—until all of the egg mixture has been folded into the chocolate.

4. Pour the batter into the prepared springform pan and add enough boiling water to the roasting pan to come halfway up the side of the springform. Bake until the cake has risen slightly and the edges are just beginning to set, about 25 minutes. Remove the cake from the roasting pan and cool on a wire rack to room temperature. Remove the foil, cover, and refrigerate overnight.

5. Remove the cake from the refrigerator about 30 minutes before serving. Remove the springform side, invert the cake onto a large plate, and peel away the parchment paper from the bottom. Invert the cake onto another large plate or serving platter and garnish with confectioners' sugar or cocoa powder immediately before serving.

# GIGI'S CARROT CAKE

Gigi's Carrot Cake is legendary among our friends. But, hey, you know how I like to kick things up a bit. For you purists, all of my additions are optional, but why not try them? Oh, and though this cake makes a beautiful presentation when baked in three cake pans as described here, for convenience and transportability, feel free to bake this in one 9 × 13-inch baking pan. Just keep in mind that you will need to adjust the baking time accordingly—40 to 45 minutes should do the trick.

¾ pound (3 sticks) plus 1 tablespoon unsalted butter

½ cup dried currants (optional)

¼ cup brandy (optional)

3 cups grated carrots

2 cups all-purpose flour

2 cups sugar

2 teaspoons baking soda

2 teaspoons ground cinnamon

1 teaspoon salt

⅛ teaspoon freshly grated nutmeg

4 large eggs

1 teaspoon pure vanilla extract

1 cup chopped toasted pecans (optional)

¼ cup finely chopped crystallized ginger (optional)

PECAN-CREAM CHEESE ICING

12 ounces cream cheese, at room temperature

10 tablespoons unsalted butter, at room temperature

1½ pounds confectioners' sugar, sifted

1½ teaspoons pure vanilla extract

1½ cups toasted pecans

1. Preheat the oven to 350°F. Butter three 9-inch cake pans with 1 tablespoon butter. Set aside.

2. In a small saucepan, combine the currants and brandy, if using, and heat until the brandy comes to a boil. Cover, remove from the heat, and allow the currants to "plump" until they've absorbed the brandy, 15 to 20 minutes.

3.     Put the grated carrots in a medium bowl. Melt the remaining ¾ pound butter in a small saucepan and pour over the grated carrots. Stir to combine well and set aside.

4.     Sift the flour, sugar, baking soda, cinnamon, salt, and nutmeg into a large mixing bowl. Add the eggs, one at a time, beating thoroughly after each addition. Add the vanilla, plumped currants, and the carrot-butter mixture and beat until thoroughly combined. Add the chopped nuts and crystallized ginger, if using, and stir to combine. Divide the batter evenly among the three prepared pans, and bake until a cake tester inserted in the center of each cake layer comes out clean, 22 to 25 minutes. Remove the cakes from the oven and allow to cool in the pans on a wire rack for 5 to 10 minutes before turning out onto a rack to cool. When the cakes have cooled completely, frost as directed below.

5.     Meanwhile, make the icing by creaming the cream cheese and butter until smooth and fluffy, 2 to 3 minutes. Add the sugar and vanilla and mix on low speed until combined. Beat on high speed until the icing is smooth and creamy. Fold in the pecans.

6.     When the cakes have cooled completely, place 1 layer on a cake plate and top with one-third of the frosting. Smooth the frosting to the edges of the top of the cake layer and then top with another layer. Repeat with another third of the frosting and smooth to the edges as before. Top with the remaining layer and finish frosting the top of the cake with the remaining frosting.

7.     Serve immediately or refrigerate, wrapped in plastic wrap, until ready to serve, up to 2 days ahead.

# — GINGER —

Ginger is actually the root of a tropical plant found in Africa, the Caribbean, and Southeast Asia. Here, we use ginger in its candied form, meaning it has been preserved in sugar. Candied ginger is a great addition to all sorts of baked items from oatmeal cookies to gingerbread.

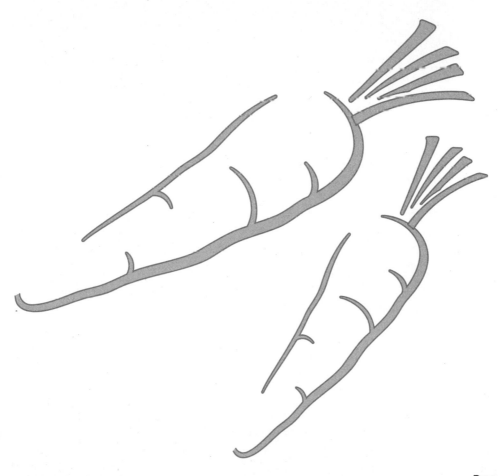

# HONEY SPICE CAKE

An ideal cake for a brunch, this is not quite a coffee cake, but the flavors are similar and the technique is easier. You could also serve this at any meal during the holidays because the spices give it a festive feeling. Use a good-quality honey, since that's what makes it special.

---

2⅓ cups sifted cake flour

1½ teaspoons baking powder

½ teaspoon baking soda

1 teaspoon ground ginger

1 teaspoon ground cinnamon

½ teaspoon ground cloves

½ teaspoon salt

1½ sticks unsalted butter

⅔ cup clover honey

½ cup sugar

3 large egg yolks

¾ cup plus 2 tablespoons plain yogurt

4 large egg whites

---

1. Preheat the oven to 350°F. Grease and flour one 9-inch tube pan or one 8- to 10-cup fluted tube or Bundt pan. Sift the cake flour, baking powder, baking soda, ginger, cinnamon, cloves, and salt together, then sift again into a large bowl. In another large bowl, beat the butter with an electric mixer on high speed until creamy. Gradually add the honey and ¼ cup of the sugar to the butter and beat on high speed until well mixed, 2 to 4 minutes. Beat in the egg yolks, one at a time. Beat on low and add the flour mixture in three parts, alternating with the yogurt in two parts. Beat until smooth, scraping down the sides of the bowl as necessary. In another large bowl, beat the egg whites until soft peaks form. Gradually add the remaining ¼ cup sugar, beating on high speed, until stiff. Fold the egg whites into the batter.

2. Pour the batter into the prepared pan and bake until a tester comes out clean, 45 to 55 minutes. Let the cake cool in the pan on a wire rack for 10 minutes and then invert the cake onto the rack and allow to cool completely.

# GLAZED LEMON POUND CAKE

. MAKES ONE 9-INCH LOAF CAKE, 8 TO 10 SERVINGS .

Lemon pound cake is the perfect, versatile dessert to keep on hand for unexpected guests at impromptu get-togethers. Keep one on your countertop for several days, or freeze for up to 2 months for a quick and easy dessert. You can toast a slice in the morning for breakfast, top it with ice cream or macerated berries for an elegant dessert, or enjoy it as a midnight snack!

½ pound (2 sticks) unsalted butter plus 1 tablespoon, at room temperature
1½ cups plus 1 tablespoon cake flour
2 tablespoons lemon zest
1¼ cups sugar

4 large eggs
2 tablespoons fresh lemon juice
1 teaspoon baking powder
¼ teaspoon salt
½ cup sour cream
Lemon Glaze (recipe follows)

1. Adjust the oven rack to the center position, and preheat the oven to 350°F.

2. Grease a 9 × 5-inch loaf pan with 1 tablespoon butter, and dust with 1 tablespoon cake flour, tapping out the excess.

3. Place the ½ pound butter and the lemon zest in a small saucepan set over low heat. Gently melt the butter, whisking constantly. Set aside. Combine the sugar, eggs, and lemon juice in the bowl of a standing mixer. Use the whip attachment to beat the mixture on medium speed for about 30 seconds. Reduce the speed to low, and in a slow and steady stream, pour the melted butter and lemon zest into the bowl. Sift the remaining 1½ cups cake flour, the baking powder, and salt into a medium bowl. Add the sifted flour mixture in 3 parts to the wet ingredients in the bowl of the stand mixer. Be sure to scrape down the sides of the bowl to ensure an evenly blended batter. Mix the batter just until blended, add the sour cream, and mix to blend.

4. Pour the batter into the prepared loaf pan and bake for 15 minutes. Reduce the oven temperature to 325°F, and continue to bake the cake until the top is a deep golden brown and a toothpick inserted in the center comes out clean, 40 to 45 minutes, rotating the pan after 20 minutes of baking. Remove the cake from the oven and place on a wire rack to cool in the pan for 10 minutes. Remove the cake from the pan and continue to cool on the rack until just warm. Pour the glaze over the cake while just warm.

## LEMON GLAZE

> 2 cups confectioners' sugar
> ¼ cup fresh lemon juice
> 1 tablespoon lemon zest

Sift the confectioners' sugar into a medium bowl. Stir in the lemon juice and lemon zest and use immediately.

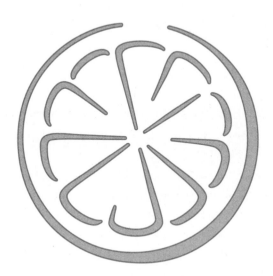

# Mr. Lou's Key Lime Pie

What would life be like without Key lime pie? I don't want to know! I have served many versions at my restaurants since Day One, and they are always popular. This one was created by my dear friend Lou Lynch, who was the first pastry chef at Emeril's Restaurant in New Orleans. Everything Mr. Lou, a very talented chef with a big heart, created was knock-your-socks-off good. Try his version here for sure-to-please goodness. It sticks to the classic formula, except that it has a sour cream topping instead of whipped cream or meringue.

1½ cups graham cracker crumbs

½ cup granulated sugar

4 tablespoons (½ stick) unsalted butter, melted

Two 14-ounce cans condensed milk

1 cup fresh Key lime or regular lime juice

2 large eggs

1 cup sour cream

2 tablespoons confectioners' sugar

1 tablespoon lime zest, for garnish

1. Preheat the oven to 375°F.

2. Combine the graham cracker crumbs, sugar, and butter in a medium bowl. Press together with your hands. Press the mixture firmly onto the bottom and up the sides of a 9-inch pie pan, and bake until brown, about 15 minutes. Remove the crust from the oven and allow to cool completely before filling.

3. Preheat the oven to 325°F. Combine the condensed milk, lime juice, and eggs in a large bowl. Whisk until well blended, then pour the filling into the cooled pie shell. Bake for 15 minutes; allow to cool in the refrigerator for at least 2 hours.

4. Once chilled, combine the sour cream and confectioners' sugar and spread over the top of the pie with a spatula. Sprinkle the lime zest on top as a garnish and serve chilled.

# STRAWBERRY SHORTCAKE

• MAKES 12 TO 16 SERVINGS •

This version of the classic American dessert uses sponge cake instead of biscuits. So, once you pour the strawberries with their juices all over the cake, it just soaks up all that goodness, and oh, baby, don't make me talk about it! It's easy to transport this to summer barbecue or beach party. Make the cake a day in advance and cover it with plastic wrap at room temperature until you're ready to serve the dessert. Macerate the strawberries for an hour or so. Whip the cream just before serving, and you're good to go!

½ pound (2 sticks) unsalted butter, melted and slightly cooled, and 2 teaspoons, at room temperature

6 large eggs, at room temperature

2 tablespoons milk, at room temperature

3⅓ cups granulated sugar

2 cups all-purpose flour

2 teaspoons baking powder

¼ teaspoon salt

3 pounds strawberries, rinsed, hulled, and sliced

½ cup Grand Marnier or other orange-flavored liqueur

1½ teaspoons orange zest

2½ cups heavy cream

5 tablespoons confectioners' sugar

1½ teaspoons pure vanilla extract

1.  Preheat the oven to 375°F. Grease a 9 × 13-inch glass baking dish with 2 teaspoons butter and set aside.

2.  Combine the eggs and milk in a large bowl and beat with an electric mixer on low speed until frothy. Add 1⅓ cups of the sugar and beat on high speed until the mixture is quite thick and pale yellow, 7 to 10 minutes.

3. Sift the flour, baking powder, and salt together into a medium bowl. Fold this mixture gently into the egg mixture. Gently stir in the melted butter and then transfer the batter to the prepared dish and bake in the center of the oven until risen and golden brown, about 30 minutes. Remove from the oven and let cool on a wire rack before proceeding.

4. Meanwhile, combine the strawberries, the remaining 2 cups sugar, Grand Marnier, and orange zest in a large bowl and toss to combine. Let stand at room temperature for 15 minutes, stirring occasionally, until the sugar is dissolved. Refrigerate, covered, until ready to assemble the dessert.

5. Combine the heavy cream with the confectioners' sugar in a large bowl and beat with an electric mixer or whisk until slightly thickened. Add the vanilla and continue to beat until the mixture nearly forms stiff peaks.

6. When ready to assemble the dessert, poke holes all over the cake with a cake tester or toothpick. Pour the strawberry mixture over the top of the cake, juices and all, spreading it evenly with a spatula and allowing the cake to absorb the juices. Top with the whipped cream and serve immediately, or refrigerate for up to an hour before serving.

## — SHORTCAKE IN A BOWL —

Kick the dessert up by cutting the cake into cubes and layering them with the macerated strawberries in a deep-sided glass bowl. Then top the whole thing with whipped cream for an impressive presentation!

# SIMPLY DELICIOUS
# CHEESECAKE

T his cheesecake is a close approximation to one I had at an Italian restaurant in
New York City. While similar to New York–style cheesecake and Italian-style
cheesecake, this one combines the best of both kinds. With its light lemony
flavor and sour cream topping, this dessert is a good way to end an Italian meal and also
makes a crowd-pleasing addition to any dessert buffet.

1 tablespoon unsalted butter, at
    room temperature
¼ cup bread crumbs
15 ounces ricotta cheese, at room
    temperature
1 pound cream cheese, at room
    temperature

6 large eggs
1½ cups sugar
2 cups sour cream
2 teaspoons pure vanilla extract
1½ teaspoons lemon zest

1. Preheat the oven to 350°F. Grease a 9-inch springform pan with the butter and
coat it with the bread crumbs, shaking out any excess.

2. Press the ricotta through a fine sieve and combine it with the cream cheese in the
bowl of an electric mixer. Beat on medium speed until very smooth, about 5 minutes.
Add the eggs, one at a time, beating until well incorporated. Add 1¼ cups sugar, ½ cup
sour cream, 1½ teaspoons vanilla, and the lemon zest and beat until very smooth and
light, 2 to 3 minutes.

3. Pour the batter into the prepared springform pan. Bake for 45 minutes, then
reduce the heat to 300°F and continue baking until the cake is set in the center, about
30 minutes longer. Remove the cake from the oven and reduce the heat to 250°F.

4.    In a small bowl, combine the remaining 1½ cups of sour cream, remaining ¼ cup sugar, and remaining ½ teaspoon vanilla. Stir until the sugar is dissolved. Pour this mixture over the top of the cheesecake and smooth with the back of a spoon or a spatula so that the sour cream mixture evenly covers the top of the cake. Return to the oven and bake for 10 minutes.

5.    Remove the cheesecake from the oven and cool on a wire rack. When the cake has cooled to room temperature, refrigerate, covered, until ready to serve.

6.    When ready to serve, run a sharp knife under warm water and wipe dry. Run the warmed knife around the edges of the springform pan to release the sides. Remove the springform, slice the cheesecake, and serve.

# New Orleans-Style Bread Pudding with Whiskey Sauce

While there are many recipes for bread pudding—both savory and sweet—you can't beat the classic version. This dessert is a mainstay at New Orleans family gatherings. I serve this repeatedly when entertaining during the holidays, and folks always come back for more.

12 to 14 cups 1-inch cubes day-old white bread, such as French or Italian

7 tablespoons unsalted butter

2 cups heavy cream

4 cups whole milk

6 large eggs

1¾ cups plus 2 tablespoons light brown sugar

4½ teaspoons pure vanilla extract

1½ teaspoons ground cinnamon

½ teaspoon freshly grated nutmeg

¼ teaspoon salt

½ cup raisins

Confectioners' sugar, for garnish

Whiskey Sauce (recipe follows)

1. Preheat the oven to 350°F.

2. Place the bread in a large bowl. In a small saucepan, melt 6 tablespoons butter and pour over the bread cubes. Use a rubber spatula to toss the bread and evenly distribute the butter. Grease a 9 × 13-inch casserole dish with the remaining tablespoon of butter and set aside.

3. Combine the heavy cream, milk, eggs, brown sugar, vanilla, cinnamon, nutmeg, salt, and raisins in a large bowl. Whisk to mix. Pour the cream mixture over the bread, and stir to combine. Allow the mixture to sit at room temperature for 30 to 45 minutes.

4.  Transfer the bread mixture to the casserole dish and bake until the center of the bread pudding is set, 50 to 60 minutes.

5.  Garnish the bread pudding with confectioners' sugar and serve warm with warm Whiskey Sauce.

• • • • • • • • • • • • • • • • • • • • • • • • • • • • • • • • • • • • • • • •

## WHISKEY SAUCE

MAKES ABOUT 3½ CUPS

2 cups heavy cream
½ cup whole milk
½ cup granulated white sugar
2 tablespoons cornstarch
¾ cup bourbon or other whiskey
Pinch of salt
2 tablespoons unsalted butter

In a 1-quart saucepan set over medium heat, combine the cream, milk, and sugar. Place the cornstarch and ¼ cup of the bourbon in a small mixing bowl and whisk to blend and make a slurry. Pour the slurry into the cream mixture and bring to a boil. Once the sauce begins to boil, reduce the heat to a gentle simmer and cook, stirring occasionally, for 5 minutes. Remove the sauce from the heat, add the salt, and stir in the butter and the remaining ½ cup of bourbon. Serve warm.

• • • • • • • • • • • • • • • • • • • • • • • • • • • • • • • • • • • • • • • •

# MY VERY OWN TIRAMISU

● MAKES 12 TO 14 SERVINGS ●

Tiramisu is one of those desserts that people often order when dining out, but rarely make at home. Here's a version that's easy for the home cook to put together. I use store-bought sponge or pound cake, eliminating the need to bake a cake. And I cook the eggs so the egg police won't be banging down my door. Use sweet Marsala wine because that flavor is key. And make it one day in advance because it's better after some downtime in the refrigerator.

12 large egg yolks

1 cup sugar

¼ cup light rum

4 cups chilled heavy cream

Four 8-ounce containers mascarpone cheese, softened

6 cups very strong brewed coffee or brewed espresso, cooled to room temperature

½ cup sweet Marsala wine

12 ounces sponge or pound cake, cut into 2-inch cubes

2 tablespoons unsweetened cocoa powder

1.   Combine the egg yolks, sugar, and rum in a medium bowl and beat with an electric mixer until thick and pale, about 2 minutes. Set the bowl over simmering water (or pour the mixture into the top of a double boiler) and beat with an electric mixer until the mixture has thickened, about 15 minutes. Remove from heat, continue to beat until cool to the touch, and then set aside.

2.   Whip the cream until stiff peaks form and reserve.

3.   Place the mascarpone in a large bowl and stir gently. Gradually stir the egg mixture into the mascarpone. Fold in the whipped cream.

4. Combine the coffee and Marsala in a shallow bowl. Dip 1 piece of cake at a time in the coffee mixture and then transfer to a large glass bowl, lining the entire bottom and arranging the pieces slightly up the sides. Spread half of the mascarpone mixture evenly over the cake. Sift 1 tablespoon cocoa powder over the mascarpone. Make another layer in the same manner with the remaining cake, mascarpone mixture, and cocoa. Chill the tiramisu, covered, for at least 6 hours, or preferably overnight.

## — MASCARPONE —

Mascarpone is an Italian cheese with a rich, buttery texture. Often referred to as Italian cream cheese, this double-cream to triple-cream cheese is made from cow's milk and has a delicate flavor that is equally at home in sweet and savory dishes.

# Emeril's Chocolate Pudding Extravaganza

• MAKES 10 TO 12 SERVINGS •

All right, this is completely over the top. The intensely chocolaty homemade pudding is sandwiched between a nutty shortbread crust and a tangy cream cheese filling, then it's all topped with whipped cream. Make this recipe at least two hours ahead (or the day before) and top with the whipped cream just before serving.

8 ounces bittersweet chocolate, chopped

8 ounces unsweetened chocolate, chopped

8 large egg yolks

2 cups sugar

½ cup cornstarch

1 teaspoon salt

7 cups milk

4 tablespoons unsalted butter, cut into small pieces, at room temperature

3½ teaspoons pure vanilla extract

2 cups all-purpose flour

1 cup salted butter, melted

1 cup finely chopped walnuts

4 cups heavy cream

½ cup confectioners' sugar plus 3 cups sifted

16 ounces cream cheese, at room temperature

1.  Preheat the oven to 350°F.

2.  Melt the bittersweet and unsweetened chocolates in the top of a double boiler, or in a metal bowl set over a pot of barely simmering water, stirring, until smooth. Remove from the heat.

3.    Lightly beat the egg yolks in a small bowl. Combine the sugar, cornstarch, and salt in a medium saucepan over medium heat. Add the milk in a stream, whisking constantly. Bring the mixture to a boil, whisking constantly to keep lumps from forming. Remove from the heat.

4.    Add 1 cup of the hot milk mixture to the yolks and whisk until smooth. Add the yolk mixture to the saucepan with the hot milk and bring to a simmer over medium-low heat. Simmer, whisking constantly, until thick and smooth, about 3 minutes. Remove from the heat and whisk in the melted chocolate, unsalted butter, and 2 teaspoons of the vanilla. Transfer to a large bowl. Cover with plastic wrap, pressing the wrap down onto the surface to prevent a skin from forming, and refrigerate until cool.

5.    Meanwhile, combine the flour, salted butter, and walnuts in a medium bowl and stir. Using your fingers, press this crust into a 9 × 13-inch baking dish, covering the bottom and coming a little bit up the sides. Bake the crust until golden brown, about 45 minutes. Let cool.

6.    Next, combine 2 cups cream, ¼ cup confectioners' sugar, and ¾ teaspoon vanilla in a large bowl. Whisk until stiff peaks form. Combine the cream cheese and the 3 cups sifted confectioners' sugar in a large bowl and cream them together using an electric mixer. Fold the whipped cream into the cream cheese mixture until just combined.

7.    Spoon the chocolate pudding into the prepared dish over the walnut crust. Top with the cream cheese filling, cover, and refrigerate for at least 2 hours or overnight.

8.    Just before serving, combine the remaining 2 cups cream, remaining ¼ cup confectioners' sugar, and remaining ¾ teaspoon vanilla in a large bowl. Whisk until soft peaks form. Garnish with the whipped cream before serving.

## — MORE CHOCOLATE —

To kick up this chocolate pudding, garnish it with chocolate shavings. Actually, chocolate shavings are an attractive garnish for many desserts. Just run a block of chocolate along a box grater and refrigerate the shavings until ready to use.

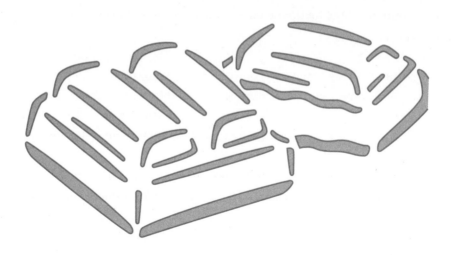

# Deep-Dish Banana Pudding with Chocolate Sauce

● MAKES 8 TO 10 SERVINGS ●

People go bonkers over this dessert. They fondly remember their mother's homemade version as well as the awful school cafeteria kind. Here's an updated banana pudding. The only change I made was to add a few kicked-up garnishes—some homemade chocolate sauce, toasted walnuts, and rum-spiked whipped cream, but it's just as good without these. If you are in a rush, then simply give them what they want—a bowl of banana pudding.

About 9 ounces vanilla wafers (from a 12-ounce package)

1 cup plus 2 tablespoons packed light brown sugar

¼ cup plus 2 tablespoons all-purpose flour

3 cups whole milk

3 large eggs

3 tablespoons unsalted butter

1 teaspoon pure vanilla extract

1 cup heavy cream

2 tablespoons confectioners' sugar

4 teaspoons dark rum

3 ripe bananas, sliced crosswise

Chocolate Sauce (recipe follows)

½ cup toasted chopped walnuts

1. Line the bottom and sides of a 9-inch-square baking dish with the vanilla wafers. Set aside.

2. Combine the brown sugar and flour in a medium saucepan set over medium heat; stir to combine. Add the milk, whisk, and bring to a boil over medium-high heat. Lower the heat to medium-low and simmer, whisking constantly, until thick, 3 to 4 minutes. Remove from the heat.

3. Whisk the eggs in a medium bowl. Gradually whisk about ¾ cup of the hot milk mixture into the eggs. Return the egg mixture to the saucepan with the remaining hot milk mixture and bring to a boil. Lower the heat and simmer, whisking constantly, until smooth and thick, about 2 minutes. Remove from the heat and add the butter and vanilla. Whisk until the butter is melted and the mixture is smooth. Transfer to a clean bowl and cool to room temperature.

4. In a medium bowl, whip the cream until soft peaks begin to form. Add the confectioners' sugar and whip until stiff peaks start to form. Add the rum and whip to incorporate. Set aside in the refrigerator.

5. Pour half of the pudding over the vanilla wafers, then top with the banana slices. Add the remaining pudding, smoothing it over the bananas. Cover tightly and chill at least 2 hours before serving.

6. When ready to serve, top with the whipped cream, and smooth with the back of a spoon. Drizzle Chocolate Sauce over the cream and top with the walnuts.

## CHOCOLATE SAUCE

MAKES 1½ CUPS

1 cup heavy cream
8 ounces semisweet chocolate, chopped
2 teaspoons pure vanilla extract

1. In a small heavy saucepan, bring the cream to a bare simmer over low heat.

2. Place the chocolate pieces in a medium heatproof bowl. Pour the cream over the chocolate and let sit for 1 minute, undisturbed. Add the vanilla and whisk until the chocolate melts and the sauce is smooth and thick.

3. Let the sauce cool slightly before using.

# — WHIPPED CREAM —

This dessert and several other recipes call for homemade whipped cream. One suggestion—do not make your whipped cream too far in advance. Homemade whipped cream only keeps its good looks for a few hours at most, then it starts to break down. It doesn't take long to make, so do it at the last moment whenever possible.

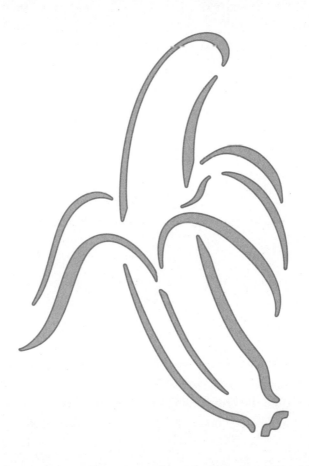

# Nuevo Cubano
# Bread Pudding

● MAKES 10 TO 12 SERVINGS ●

The idea for this bread pudding came to me when I was daydreaming about what we would be serving at our Miami restaurant. The recipe is based on a Cuban one that used canned fruit cocktail—once considered a luxury item. I substituted fresh fruit, and what a difference!

3½ tablespoons unsalted butter plus 2 tablespoons melted

1 cup ½-inch cubes fresh pineapple

1 cup ½-inch cubes bananas

1¼ cups plus 1 teaspoon packed light brown sugar

1¼ teaspoons ground cinnamon

¾ teaspoon ground allspice

½ teaspoon freshly grated nutmeg

6 large eggs

4 cups heavy cream

1 cup unsweetened coconut milk

1 teaspoon pure vanilla extract

12 cups ½-inch cubes day-old Cuban or French bread

Coconut Rum Sauce (recipe follows)

1 cup sweetened shredded coconut, toasted

1. Preheat the oven to 350°F. Grease a 9 × 13-inch baking dish with ½ tablespoon butter.

2. Melt 3 tablespoons butter in a skillet. Add the pineapple, bananas, 1 teaspoon brown sugar, ¼ teaspoon cinnamon, ¼ teaspoon allspice, and ¼ teaspoon nutmeg and cook until the fruit begins to soften, about 5 minutes.

3. Whisk the eggs in a large bowl. Whisk in the cream, coconut milk, remaining 1¼ cups brown sugar, vanilla, remaining 1 teaspoon cinnamon, ½ teaspoon allspice, and ¼ teaspoon nutmeg. Add the bread and the fruit and stir well, then mix in the remaining 2 tablespoons melted butter. Pour into the prepared dish.

4.    Bake until firm when pressed in the center, about 1 hour. Cool on a wire rack until just warm, about 20 minutes. Serve with warm Coconut Rum Sauce and garnish with the toasted coconut.

. . . . . . . . . . . . . . . . . . . . . . . . . . . . . . . . . . . . . . . . . . . . . . . .

## Coconut Rum Sauce

MAKES ABOUT 2 CUPS

½ pound (2 sticks) unsalted butter, melted
⅔ cup heavy cream
⅔ cup unsweetened coconut milk
1 cup granulated sugar
⅓ cup packed light brown sugar
1 large egg yolk, beaten
1 cup dark rum

Combine all the ingredients except the rum in a small saucepan and cook over medium-low heat, whisking constantly, until the sauce has thickened and coats the back of a spoon, about 10 minutes. Do not allow the sauce to boil or the egg will curdle and the sauce will not be smooth. (If this does happen, then simply strain through a fine-mesh sieve.) Remove from the heat, stir in the rum, and set aside to cool slightly.

## — TOASTED COCONUT —

To toast coconut, evenly distribute coconut flakes on a dry sheet pan and bake in a 350°F oven for 5 to 10 minutes, until light brown. Keep a close eye on the coconut because it can go from toasted to burned in a flash.

# CHOCOLATE PEANUT BUTTER PIE

• MAKES ONE 9-INCH PIE, 8 SERVINGS •

**M**any people I know have a fondness for a certain chocolate and peanut butter candy that's shaped like a cup. Well, here it is in pie form. A version of this is served at Emeril's restaurant in New Orleans to great acclaim.

1½ cups finely ground graham cracker crumbs

1 cup finely ground Oreo cookies (cream filling removed)

4 tablespoons (½ stick) unsalted butter, melted

6 tablespoons granulated sugar

4 ounces cream cheese, at room temperature

¼ cup confectioners' sugar

2 tablespoons milk

4 ounces melted semisweet chocolate

⅔ cup smooth peanut butter

1 cup heavy cream

¼ cup toasted chopped peanuts

Rich Chocolate Sauce (recipe follows)

1.  Preheat the oven to 375°F.

2.  Combine the graham cracker crumbs, Oreo cookie crumbs, butter, and 4 tablespoons of the granulated sugar in a medium bowl. Stir to throughly combine. Press the mixture firmly into a 9-inch pie pan and bake for 15 minutes. Remove the pan from the oven, let the crust cool completely, then wrap it with plastic wrap and place the pan in the freezer for at least 1 hour and for up to 2 weeks. Allow the crust to come to room temperature before filling.

3.  Combine the cream cheese, confectioners' sugar, and milk in a large bowl. Beat with an electric mixer until well blended and smooth, about 1 minute on medium speed. Add the melted chocolate and the peanut butter and continue to blend for another

minute on medium speed. Combine the cream with the remaining 2 tablespoons granulated sugar in another medium bowl. Beat with a whisk or electric mixer until stiff peaks form. Gently fold the whipped cream into the chocolate and peanut butter mixture until thoroughly incorporated and smooth. Pour the filling into the piecrust. Smooth the top of the pie with a spatula, cover, and refrigerate for at least 4 hours before serving.

4.   To serve, use a hot wet knife to slice the pie into 8 portions. Garnish with the peanuts and drizzle with the Rich Chocolate Sauce.

## RICH CHOCOLATE SAUCE

MAKES 1½ CUPS

¾ cup half-and-half
8 ounces semisweet chocolate chips
¼ teaspoon pure vanilla extract
1 tablespoon unsalted butter

1. In a small heavy saucepan, bring the half-and-half to a bare simmer over medium-low heat. Remove from the heat.

2. Place the chocolate in a medium heatproof bowl. Whisk the half-and-half slowly into the chocolate. Add the vanilla and butter to the sauce and whisk until the butter is completely incorporated. The sauce can be kept refrigerated in an airtight container for several days, but it must be returned to room temperature before serving.

# SUPER LEMONY LEMON SQUARES

• MAKES 2 DOZEN SQUARES •

Thlese rich bar cookies get a triple dose of lemon from lemon zest, lemon juice, and lemon-flavored liqueur. Wrap any leftover squares in plastic wrap and store them in the refrigerator for up to two days.

- 1½ sticks plus 1 tablespoon cold unsalted butter
- 1¾ cups plus 3 tablespoons all-purpose flour
- ⅔ cup confectioners' sugar, plus more for garnish
- ¼ cup cornstarch
- ¾ teaspoon plus a pinch of salt

- 4 large eggs, lightly beaten
- 1⅓ cups granulated sugar
- 1½ teaspoons lemon zest
- ⅔ cup strained fresh lemon juice
- ¼ cup whole milk
- 2 tablespoons Limoncello or other lemon-flavored liqueur (optional)

1.  Lightly butter a 9 × 13-inch baking dish with 2 teaspoons butter and line with 1 sheet of parchment or wax paper. Butter the paper with 1 teaspoon of the remaining butter and then lay a second sheet of parchment or wax paper crosswise over the first sheet. This parchment sheet should be large enough for the ends to be even with the tops of the long sides of the baking dish—this extra paper will function as handles to help you remove the lemon squares from the pan later. Set the dish aside.

2.  In a large bowl, combine 1¾ cups flour, the confectioners' sugar, the cornstarch, and ¾ teaspoon salt and mix thoroughly. Cut the remaining 1½ sticks butter into small pieces and add to the flour mixture. Using your hands, two forks, or a pastry blender, work the butter into the flour mixture until the mixture resembles coarse meal. Transfer the butter-flour mixture to the prepared baking dish and press into an even ¼-inch layer along the bottom and partly up the sides of the dish. Refrigerate for 30 minutes. While the crust is chilling, preheat the oven to 350°F.

3.	Bake the crust until golden brown, 20 to 25 minutes.

4.	Meanwhile, combine the eggs, granulated sugar, the remaining 3 tablespoons flour, and lemon zest in a medium bowl and whisk until smooth. Stir in the lemon juice, milk, Limoncello, and remaining pinch salt and mix well.

5.	When the crust is golden brown, remove it from the oven and reduce the temperature to 325°F. Stir the lemon mixture again, then pour over the warm crust. Bake until the filling is set, about 20 minutes. Transfer to a wire rack to cool completely. Grasp the extra paper that lines the two longest sides of the baking dish and remove the bars from the pan by pulling up gently. The entire dessert should easily dislodge and come away from the pan. Transfer to a cutting board and, using a clean knife, cut into squares, wiping the knife after each cut. Place a small amount of confectioners' sugar in a small sieve, and sprinkle the bars with the sugar. Serve immediately, or refrigerate, wrapped with plastic wrap, for up to two days, or until ready to serve.

## — LEMON SQUARES TO GO —

These babies are made to travel! Pack them in a covered container between layers of wax paper for a picnic or bake sale.

# AUNT EVE'S PEANUT BUTTER FUDGE

• MAKES 4 DOZEN 1½-INCH PIECES •

My friend Charlotte says that her Aunt Eve's peanut butter fudge is the best she's ever tasted. I was lucky enough to taste it and even luckier that Aunt Eve was willing to share her recipe. It's easy, too, but you do need a candy thermometer, and watch it closely so that you can remove the mixture when it reaches the right temperature. Then all it takes is a little elbow grease to beat the fudge mixture once it's been removed from the heat. This fudge makes a thoughtful gift at holiday time.

4 cups sugar
½ cup light corn syrup
½ pound (2 sticks) unsalted butter
1 cup evaporated milk
1 tablespoon pure vanilla extract

9 ounces (1 cup) smooth peanut butter
2 heaping tablespoons marshmallow cream

1. Lightly grease a 9 × 13-inch baking pan and set aside.

2. Combine the sugar, corn syrup, butter, and evaporated milk in a large saucepan. Cook over medium heat, stirring occasionally, until the mixture reaches 242.5°F on a candy thermometer, between the soft- and hard-ball stages.

3. Remove from the heat and stir in the remaining ingredients. Beat the mixture with a large wooden spoon until it gets very stiff. Pour into the prepared pan and let harden.

4. To serve, cut into pieces about 1½ inches square.

# Summer Fruit Salad

The fruit in desserts is often buried beneath some heavy, creamy sauce. So to make one where the fruit shines, I prefer a light champagne–vanilla syrup that complements the berries. Such a light, summery berry salad can be topped with a dollop of crème fraîche, a scoop of vanilla ice cream, or served on top of a slice of Glazed Lemon Pound Cake (page 267).

2 quarts (3 pounds) fresh strawberries, hulled and sliced

4 cups (1½ pounds) fresh blueberries

2 cups (¾ pound) fresh raspberries

2 cups (¾ pound) fresh blackberries

1 tablespoon finely chopped fresh mint

2 cups Champagne or sparkling wine

1 cup sugar

Pinch of salt

1 vanilla bean, scraped

2 tablespoons fresh lemon juice

1 tablespoon lemon zest

1. Combine the berries and mint in a large bowl.

2. Combine the Champagne, sugar, salt, and vanilla bean in a medium saucepan over medium-high heat. Simmer until the sugar dissolves and the mixture is syrupy, about 15 minutes. Remove from the heat and allow to cool until just warm. Remove the vanilla bean. Add the lemon juice and zest and stir to combine. Pour the syrup over the berries and toss to combine. Cover and refrigerate for at least 1 hour before serving.

# COURTNEY'S "KICKED-UP" FIESTA LOAF

• MAKES 6 SERVINGS •

Wow! You wouldn't believe the amazing entries people sent in for our "From Emeril's Kitchens" recipe contest that ran when the cookbook was released in 2003. We narrowed down the field from more than two-thousand entries and cooked ten finalist recipes in the Homebase test kitchen to determine the winner. And here it is—"Kicked Up" Fiesta Loaf by Courtney Klatt of Bexley, Ohio. It's meatloaf gone south o' the border . . . and Courtney suggests serving this with salsa to kick it up another notch!

---

½ pound ground sirloin

1 pound mild ground Italian sausage, casings removed

One 10-ounce can diced tomatoes and green chiles (do not drain)

¼ cup (2 to 3) finely diced jalapeños

½ cup diced red bell peppers

½ cup diced yellow bell peppers

1 large egg

½ teaspoon salt

½ teaspoon freshly ground black pepper

2 teaspoons Emeril's Southwest Essence

1 cup finely crushed tortilla chips

Salsa, for serving (optional), (page 8), or use your favorite brand

---

1. Preheat the oven to 400° F.

2. In a large bowl, combine the sirloin, sausage, diced tomatoes and green chiles, jalapeños, red and yellow peppers, and egg. Using clean hands, mix the ingredients together well.

3. Add the salt, pepper, and Emeril's Southwest Essence and mix well.

4. Add the crushed tortilla chips and mix until thoroughly combined.

5. Form the mixture into one large loaf and place in a nonstick loaf pan. Bake for 50 to 55 minutes, until the top of the loaf is nicely browned and the juices run clear.

6. Remove the loaf from the oven and serve warm. Top with salsa, if desired.

Emeril's
RECIPE
CONTEST
WINNER!

# WEB SITES

### CHEF EMERIL LAGASSE

www.emerils.com
Official Web site for everything
Emeril. You will find listings for all
his restaurants, shows, merchandise,
and in-depth background into Emeril's
culinary world, as well as a monthly
on-line magazine and recipes. Bam!

### FETZER VINEYARDS

www.fetzer.com
An environmentally and socially
conscious grower, Fetzer Vineyards
produces Emeril's Classics Wines for
the home chef.

### WATERFORD/WEDGWOOD

www.wwusa.com
The world's leading luxury lifestyle
group produces Emeril At Home,
ageless additions to the home kitchen.

### ALL-CLAD COOKWARE

www.emerilware.com
The cookware that Chef Emeril
believes in. Here you will find the
entire range of Emerilware by All-
Clad, from skillets to sauté pans.

### B&G FOODS

www.bgfoods.com
If you want to kick up your kitchen a
notch, look for Emeril's original spice
blends, salad dressings, marinades, hot
sauces, and pasta sauces distributed by
B&G Foods and available at
supermarkets nationwide.

### GOOD MORNING AMERICA

http://abcnews.go.com
Wake up to Chef Emeril on Friday
mornings on ABC, when he shares his
culinary creations with America.

### FOOD NETWORK

www.foodtv.com
Log onto the Food Network's site for
recipes and scheduling information for
*Emeril Live* and *The Essence of Emeril*
shows, and ticket information for
*Emeril Live*.

### HARPERCOLLINS PUBLISHERS

www.harpercollins.com
This informative site offers
background on and chapter excerpts
from all of Chef Emeril's best-selling
cookbooks.

### WÜSTHOF KNIVES

www.wusthof.com
Emerilware Knives gift and block sets,
made to Emeril's specifications by one
of the world's leading manufacturers
of quality cutlery.

### PRIDE OF SAN JUAN

www.prideofsanjuan.com
Emeril's gourmet produce brings
innovative salad blends and herbs to
the home kitchen.

### SANITA

www.sanitaclogs.com
Cook in style with Emeril's chef clogs.
Comfort for the busy chef.

# EMERIL'S RESTAURANTS

### EMERIL'S NEW ORLEANS
800 Tchoupitoulas Street
New Orleans, LA 70130
504-528-9393

### NOLA
534 Rue St. Louis
New Orleans, LA 70130
504-522-6652

### EMERIL'S DELMONICO
1300 St. Charles Avenue
New Orleans, LA 70130
504-525-4937

### EMERIL'S NEW ORLEANS FISH HOUSE
at the MGM Grand Hotel and
Casino
3799 Las Vegas Boulevard South
Las Vegas, NV 89109
702-891-7374

### DELMONICO STEAKHOUSE
at the Venetian Resort and
Casino
3355 Las Vegas Boulevard South
Las Vegas, NV 89109
702-414-3737

### EMERIL'S ORLANDO
6000 Universal Boulevard
at Universal Studios City Walk
Orlando, FL 32819
407-224-2424

### EMERIL'S TCHOUP CHOP
at Universal Orlando's
Royal Pacific Resort
6300 Hollywood Way
Orlando, FL 32819
407-503-2467

### EMERIL'S ATLANTA
One Alliance Center
3500 Lenox Road
Atlanta, GA 30326
404-564-5600

### EMERIL'S MIAMI BEACH
at Loews Miami Beach Hotel
1601 Collins Avenue
Miami Beach, FL 33139
305-695-4550

# INDEX

in creamy ham and potato pies, 125–26
in macaroni with four cheeses, 236
gumbo:
    Emeril's classic seafood, 108–9
    shrimp, okra, and tomato, 106–7

ham:
    hocks, in Emeril's favorite choucroute casserole,
        129–31
    in potato and leek soup, 110
    and potato pies, creamy, 125–26
herb-wrapped beef tenderloin, Creole mustard
    and, 188–89
homemade ranch dressing, 86
honey:
    in orange Emeril, 22
    spice cake, 266
horseradish coleslaw, 84

ice cream, in milk shakes for grown-ups, 14–15
icing:
    pecan–cream cheese, 263–65
    vanilla buttercream, 260

jambalaya, classic chicken, 168–69

key lime pie, Mr. Lou's, 269
kicked-up:
    cabbage rolls, 197–98
    dinner rolls, 252–53
    fiesta loaf, Courtney's, 292–93
    spinach and artichoke dip, 33–34
kickin' chili, 193–94
kielbasa, in Emeril's favorite choucroute casserole,
    129–31
knockwurst, in Emeril's favorite choucroute
    casserole, 129–31

lamb:
    olive-stuffed leg of, 210–11
    and white bean casserole, 123–24
lasagna:
    Bolognese, Charlotte's, 121–22
    grilled vegetable, with puttanesca sauce and
        pesto oil, 157–59
lassi, mango, 23

leek and potato soup, 110
lemon:
    glaze, 268
    pound cake, glazed, 267–28
    in sangria, 24
    squares, super lemony, 288–89
    squares to go, 289
lima beans, in Peggy's chicken potpies, 140–42
lime, key, pie, Mr. Lou's, 269
linguiça, in Portuguese tomato and sausage soup,
    95–96
loaf, Courtney's "kicked-up" fiesta, 292
lobster meat, in shellfish-stuffed cannelloni, 160–61
loin, pork, funky Southwest, 202–3

macaroni with four cheeses, 236–37
Manhattan clam chowder, 101–2
maque choux, Cajun, 240
margaritas, Emeril's fresh and fierce, 17
marinated:
    mushrooms, 40–41
    olives, 39
masa harina, in cheesy chicken tamales, 175–77
mascarpone, in my very own tiramisu, 176–77
mashed potatoes, 192
meat:
    and potato casserole, Alden's grandmother's,
        116–17
    see also specific meats
meatballs, sausage, with red gravy, Paul's "make
    the whole crew happy," 199–200
Mexican:
    breakfast casserole, 134–35
    rice casserole, 231
milk shakes for grown-ups, 14–15
mint juleps, frozen, 20
mirliton and shrimp casserole, 149–50
mushroom(s):
    in cowboy chicken casserole, 145–46
    in Emeril's beef Stroganoff, 186–87
    in Emerilized green bean casserole, 229–30
    marinated, 404–1
    in Peggy's chicken potpies, 140–42
    sausage-stuffed, 51–52
    in tuna tetrazzini, 155–56
    wild, and risotto casserole, 151–52

mustard, Creole, and herb-wrapped beef
    tenderloin, 188–89

New Orleans–style bread pudding with whiskey
    sauce, 274–75
niçoise salad, layered tuna, 69–70
nuevo Cubano bread pudding, 284–85
nuts:
    spiced, 37–38
    *see also specific nuts*

okra:
    in Cajun maque choux, 240
    shrimp, and tomato gumbo, 106–7
olive(s):
    and chicken pasta casserole, 143–44
    marinated, 39
    -stuffed leg of lamb, 210–11
orange:
    Emeril, 22
    in hot apple cider, 27
    in retro ambrosia, 89
    in sangria, 24
    spinach, and almond salad, 67–68
orzo risotto, Emeril's oven-braised osso buco with,
    208–9
osso buco, Emeril's oven-braised, with orzo risotto,
    208–9
oven-braised osso buco with orzo risotto, Emeril's,
    208–9
oven-poached salmon with pink grapefruit and
    tarragon sauce, 180–81
oysters:
    in Emeril's classic seafood gumbo, 108–9
    Rockefeller soup, 104–5

Passover brisket, 184–85
pasta:
    antipasto salad, 73–74
    casserole, chicken and olive, 143–44
    grilled vegetable lasagna with puttanesca sauce
      and pesto oil, 157–59
    macaroni with four cheeses, 236–37
    orzo risotto, Emeril's oven-braised osso buco
      with, 208–9
    penne à la vodka casserole, 132–33

rotini, in antipasto pasta salad, 73–74
    sheets, for Charlotte's lasagna Bolognese, 121–22
    ziti, eggplant, and sausage casserole, 138–39
paste, mojo, 203
Paul's "make the whole crew happy" sausage
    meatballs with red gravy, 199–200
pea, black-eyed, salad, 77–78
peanut butter:
    chocolate pie, 286–87
    fudge, Aunt Eve's, 290
pear, endive, and gorgonzola salad, 65–66
pecan(s):
    cranberry bread, 250–51
    -cream cheese icing, 263–65
    in Gigi's carrot cake, 263–65
    in retro ambrosia, 89
    topping, for carrot soufflé, 242–43
peppers:
    in grilled vegetables, 158–59
    stuffed, Rhena's, 195–96
penne à la vodka casserole, 132–33
pesto:
    cilantro, 61
    oil, 157–58
pies:
    chocolate peanut butter, 286–87
    creamy ham and potato, 125–26
    key lime, Mr. Lou's, 269
    Puerto Rican–style beef and plantain, 118–20
pilaf, rice, 232–33
pita chips, for baba ghanoush, 32
plantain and beef pie, Puerto Rican–style, 118–20
poached, oven-, salmon with pink grapefruit and
    tarragon sauce, 180–81
polenta:
    casserole, Chef Dave's, 127–28
    creamy, 128
poor man's beef Wellington, 190–92
popcorn, cheesy, 94
pork:
    in Charlotte's lasagna Bolognese, 121–22
    chops, smothered, 206–7
    loin, funky Southwest, 202–3
    roast with barbecue sauce, slow-cooked, 204–5
    salt, in Miss Hilda's baked beans, 238–39
    tenderloins, Asian, 201

Portuguese:
     dressing, Miss Hilda's, 218–19
     tomato and sausage soup, 95–96
potato(es):
     à la boulangère, 223–24
     chips, in tuna tetrazzini, 155–56
     and ham pies, creamy, 125–26
     and leek soup, 110
     in Manhattan clam chowder, 101–2
     mashed, for poor man's beef Wellington, 192
     and meat casserole, Alden's grandmother's,
          116–17
     in New England clam chowder, 99–100
     roasted, and garlic salad, 87–88
     salad, Emeril's favorite, 85–86
     and salmon casserole, Swedish, 147–48
potpies, chicken, Peggy's, 140–42
pot roast, Emeril's, 182–83
prosciutto:
     in antipasto pasta salad, 73–74
     breadsticks, 254–55
provolone cheese, in antipasto pasta salad, 73–74
pudding:
     bread, Creole breakfast, 136–37
     corn, 222
     deep-dish banana, with chocolate sauce, 281–83
     Emeril's chocolate, extravaganza, 278–80
     see also bread pudding
Puerto Rican–style beef and plantain pie, 118–20
punch, champagne, 25
puttanesca sauce and pesto oil, grilled vegetable
          lasagna with, 157–59

queso fresco cheese, in spinach enchiladas, 153–54
quiche, Cajun, 162–63

radishes, in endive, pear, and gorgonzola salad,
          65–66
raspberries, in summer fruit salad, 291
red gravy, 199–200
red kidney beans, in kickin' chili, 193–94
Rhena's stuffed peppers, 195–96
rice:
     Arborio, in risotto and wild mushroom
          casserole, 151–52
     casserole, Mexican, 231

in classic chicken jambalaya, 168–69
     in country captain, 170–71
     in kicked-up cabbage rolls, 197–98
     pilaf, 232–33
     for shrimp étouffée, 178–79
     in smothered pork chops, 206–7
ricotta cheese:
     in grilled vegetable lasagna with puttanesca
          sauce and pesto oil, 157–59
     in penne à la vodka casserole, 132–33
     in simply delicious cheesecake, 272–73
risotto:
     orzo, Emeril's oven-roasted osso buco with,
          208–9
     and wild mushroom casserole, 151–52
roast(ed):
     garlic soup, 97
     pot, Emeril's, 182–83
     potato and garlic salad, 87–88
     slow-cooked pork, with barbecue sauce, 204–5
     vegetable and goat cheese terrine, 57–59
rolls:
     cabbage, kicked-up, 197–98
     dinner, kicked-up, 252–53
rum:
     coconut sauce, 285
     in dark and stormy, 21
     in hot apple cider, 27
     light, in watermelon daiquiris, 18

salads:
     Asian broccoli, 75–76
     black-eyed pea, 77–78
     Charlotte's green bean, 79
     couscous, 80–81
     curried chicken, 71–72
     Emeril's eggplant, 82–83
     endive, pear, and gorgonzola, 65–66
     fruit, summer, 291
     horseradish coleslaw, 84
     layered tuna niçoise, 69–70
     potato, Emeril's favorite, 85–86
     retro ambrosia, 89
     roasted potato and garlic, 87–88
     spinach, orange, and almond, 67–68
     tomato, my big fat Greek, 64

salami, in antipasto pasta salad, 73–74

salmon:

-dill eggs, 44

oven-poached, with pink grapefruit and tarragon sauce, 180–81

and potato casserole, Swedish, 147–48

salsa:

for black bean soup, 8

in Courtney's "kicked-up" fiesta loaf, 292–93

simply, 8

sandwiches, brisket, 185

sangria, 24

sauces:

barbecue, 205

béchamel, for Charlotte's lasagna Bolognese, 121–22

chocolate, 282

coconut rum, 285

mayonnaise, 6–7

puttanesca, 157–59

rich chocolate, 287

sun-dried tomato, 58–59

tarragon, 181

whiskey, 275

*see also* salsa

sauerkraut, in Emeril's favorite choucroute casserole, 129–31

sausage:

eggplant, and ziti casserole, 138–39

meatballs with red gravy, Paul's "make the whole crew happy," 199–200

and tomato soup, Portuguese, 95–96

sausage-stuffed:

French bread, Helen's, 55–56

mushrooms, 51–52

savory:

piecrust, 9

spinach and artichoke bread pudding, 220–21

seafood gumbo, Emeril's classic, 108–9

shellfish-stuffed cannelloni, 160–61

shortcake, 270–71

in a bowl, 271

strawberry, 270–71

shrimp:

Asian boiled, 47–48

in Emeril's classic seafood gumbo, 108–9

étouffée, 178–79

and mirliton casserole, 149–50

okra, and tomato gumbo, 106–7

in shellfish-stuffed cannelloni, 160–61

stew, golden, 103

stock, 10

sirloin:

in Courtney's "kicked-up" fiesta loaf, 292–93

in Emeril's beef Stroganoff, 186–87

slow-cooked pork roast with barbecue sauce, 204–5

smothered:

pork chops, 206–7

*see also étouffée*

snapper, in Emeril's classic seafood gumbo, 108–9

sole, in Emeril's classic seafood gumbo, 108–9

soufflé, carrot, 242–43

soup, cold:

cucumber, 11

gazpacho, 112–13

soup, hot:

black bean, 92

cheese and beer, 93–94

oysters Rockefeller, 104–5

potato and leek, 110

roasted garlic, 97

tomato and Portuguese sausage, 95–96

Southern:

cornbread, serious, 247

-style corn chowder, 98

Southwest pork loin, funky, 202–3

spaghetti, in Paul's "make the whole crew happy" sausage meatballs with red gravy, 199–200

spice(d), spicy:

Alain's Asian wings, sweet and, 45–46

honey cake, 266

nuts, 37–38

spinach:

and artichoke bread pudding, savory, 220–21

and artichoke dip, kicked-up, 33–34

baby, in endive, pear, and gorgonzola salad, 65–66

enchiladas, 153–54

orange and almond salad, 67–68

in oysters Rockefeller soup, 104–5

vegetable(s):
    fresh, for classic blue cheese dip, 30
    grilled, 158–59
    grilled, lasagna with puttanesca sauce and pesto
       oil, 157–59
    roasted, and goat cheese terrine, 57–59
V8 juice, in gazpacho, 112–13
vinaigrette, French, 70
vodka:
    casserole, penne à la, 132–33
    green, coolers, 16

watermelon daiquiris, 18–19
Wellington, beef, poor man's, 190–92
whiskey sauce, 275
white bean and lamb casserole, 123–24

wine:
    marsala, in my very own tiramisu, 276–77
    red, in sangria, 24
    white, in golden shrimp stew, 103
wings, Alain's sweet and spicy Asian, 45–46

yogurt:
    in cold cucumber soup, 111
    in mango lassi, 23
    in marinade for olive-stuffed leg of lamb,
       210–11

ziti, eggplant, and sausage casserole, 138–39
zucchini:
    in grilled vegetables, 158–59
    and summer squash casserole, 227–28